THE
IRS
PROBLEM SOLVER

Also by Daniel J. Pilla

How to Double Your Tax Refund

How to Get Tax Amnesty

IRS, Taxes and the Beast

41 Ways to Lick the IRS with a Postage Stamp

Taxpayer's Ultimate Defense Manual

THE

IRS

PROBLEM

SOLVER

**From Audits to Assessments—
How to Solve Your Tax Problems and
Keep the IRS Off Your Back**

DANIEL J. PILLA

HARPER

BUSINESS

NEW YORK ∙ LONDON ∙ TORONTO ∙ SYDNEY

HarperCollins books may be purchased for educational, business, or sales promotional use. For information please write: Special Markets Department, Harper-Collins Publishers Inc., 10 East 53rd Street, New York, NY 10022.

Designed by Nancy Singer Olaguera

Library of Congress Cataloging-in-Publication Data

Pilla, Daniel J.
   The IRS problem solver: from audits to assessments—how to solve your tax problems and keep the IRS off your back / Daniel J. Pilla.
      p. cm.
   ISBN 0-06-053345-5
   1. Tax administration and procedure—United States—Popular works.
   2. United States. Internal Revenue Service—Popular works. I. Title.

KF6320.Z9.P555   2004
343.7304—dc21
                                                        2003047204

14 15 ❖/RRD 20 19 18 17 16 15 14 13

notice from the author and publisher

The author and the publisher disclaim all liability for any damages resulting from the application of the information given in this book. This book is designed to present the author's findings and opinions based on research, analysis, and experience with the subject matter covered. This information is not provided for purposes of rendering legal, accounting, or other professional advice. It is intended purely for educational purposes. In publishing this book, neither the author nor the publisher is engaged in rendering legal, accounting, or other professional service. If legal advice or other professional assistance is required, the services of a competent professional should be sought.

Because the United States currently functions under an evolutionary legal system, the reader bears the burden of assuring that the principles of law stated in this work are current and binding at the time of any intended use or application. Caution: The law in this country is subject to change arbitrarily and without notice.

To Jeannie

Who can find a virtuous woman? For her price is far above rubies.

The heart of her husband doth safely trust in her,

so that he shall have no need of spoil.

She will do him good and not evil all the days of her life.

Proverbs 31:10–12

contents

introduction

Do you remember when the IRS was in the hot seat? It was during the fall and winter of 1997 when angry members of the Senate Finance Committee grilled high-ranking IRS officials on wide-ranging allegations of official misconduct, disregard of its own rules and procedures, even maleficence toward citizens—especially middle-income taxpayers. Americans across the nation watched with a great sense of satisfaction as the tables were finally turned. Rather than the IRS causing fear and consternation in the lives of honest citizens, the agency found itself choking down the bitter taste of its own medicine.

The hearings into IRS abuse were the culmination of a decade of congressional action purportedly intended to curb what former Senate Finance Committee chairman William Roth referred to as "extraordinary powers." In his opening remarks, given September 23, 1997, on the threshold of what would become three days of explosive testimony, Senator Roth predicted,

> Over the course of the next 3 days we are going to see a picture of a troubled agency, one that is losing the confidence of the American people, and one that all too frequently acts as if it were above the law. This is unacceptable.[1]

The hearings that followed featured testimony from citizens whose lives were upset and businesses devastated by IRS actions. The hearings culminated in passage of the Internal Revenue Restructuring and Reform Act of 1998. Perhaps the single aspect of the hearings that most clearly communicated the culture of the IRS and the manner in which the IRS operates was the portion that featured testimony from current IRS employees. And it is not the fact that current IRS employees testified against their own agency. Rather, it is *how* they testified that was so remarkable. You see, due to fear of retaliation from their colleagues, all but one of the IRS employees testified to the committee while physically hidden from public view and with their voices electronically altered so as to be unrecognizable.

The testimony of these witnesses buttressed the claims of IRS abuse that I have made for years. In a general sense, I have accused the IRS of using tactics of bluff and intimidation, misinformation and disinformation, and in many cases simply outright lying to citizens concerning their rights and the IRS's powers. The result of this is that millions of citizens pay taxes they do not owe or are otherwise subjected to treatment that other more savvy or informed citizens do not experience.

This is where my expertise comes into play. As a tax litigation consultant with more than twenty-five years of experience dealing with the agency, I have helped tens of thousands of people from all walks of life deal with IRS problems of every description. And just like those citizens who testified at the abuse hearings, the vast majority of citizens I deal with are honest taxpayers doing their level best to comply with an increasingly complicated and convoluted tax code. The uncertainty that flows from such complexity creates a level of anxiety that most citizens never experience in any other area of their lives.

This uncertainty naturally leads to fear whenever the initials *IRS* are mentioned. Most people would rather undergo a root canal than suffer through a tax audit. The idea of finding an IRS letter in the mailbox terrifies folks because, frankly, they are sure the news must be bad. This fear and uncertainty creates a second problem. That is, people generally tend to roll over when it comes to the agency's demands.

Citizens do this believing either or a combination of two things: (1) if the IRS said it, it must be right, or (2) you can't fight the IRS anyway, so why bother?

These attitudes are responsible for countless millions of citizens paying taxes, interest, and penalties every year that they do not owe. Yet I have proved time and again that if you understand just a little about your rights and realize that the IRS's power is limited, you do not have to pay taxes you do not owe. That is the central premise of this book.

In the pages that follow, you will learn how to deal with:

- *IRS computer notices.* Each year the agency sends millions of "correction" notices that have been shown to be wrong about half the time. With the grand total investment of a postage stamp and about thirty minutes at the typewriter, you can defeat these notices and keep your money in your own pocket, where it belongs.

- *Penalty and interest assessments.* The typical tax bill nearly triples due to the addition of penalties and interest. But the IRS does not clearly explain that these additions can be canceled when you make the proper factual showing. The process is remarkably simple and highly effective when you have the right guidance in the first instance.

- *Tax audits.* The dreaded tax audit is probably responsible for more sleepless nights than any other area of law enforcement. But what the typical citizen does not know is that the tax auditor has no real power over you. The audit process is largely one of bluff and intimidation, cleverly designed to mask the fact that the IRS audit results are wrong between 60 and 90 percent of time. Moreover, the process of appealing an audit decision is simple, inexpensive, and very effective.

- *Delinquent tax collection.* The collection process is the most challenging of all IRS problems since it is in this area that the IRS uses its awesome tools of tax lien, wage and bank levy, and property seizure. But even when the IRS is threatening the worst, you have many important rights and the IRS's powers are limited in many important ways, allowing you to pay taxes on your terms, not theirs.

This book is not going to teach you to cheat on your taxes, evade the payment of taxes, or hinder the IRS in the administration of the tax laws. There are too many of those guides available, and sadly, they do nothing but sink people further into the quagmire of tax law enforcement. Instead, this book teaches the things that every American who earns income needs to know. At the core of this is the idea that your taxpayer's rights put you on such a footing that you cannot be abused by the agency if you understand how to use those rights. But the key is, you have to *know* the rights exist in order to use them.

In the aftermath of the congressional investigation into IRS abuse, citizens tend to argue that IRS abuse is no longer a problem. "The agency has been reined in," they say. This begs the question of whether the Restructuring Act was successful in trimming the claws of the IRS and improving taxpayers' rights to the point where rogue IRS actions are no longer a threat. A casual observer might think so after examining the question through a superficial lens. The superficial lens provides a glimpse at three factors that might lead the untrained eye to conclude that we no longer have to fear the agency. Those three factors are (1) a purported legal shift in the burden of proof to the IRS so that citizens no longer have to prove their innocence, (2) the creation of a new IRS Oversight Board to check the behavior of the IRS, and (3) a dramatic drop in IRS collection actions.

A closer examination of these three factors is necessary.

SHIFTING THE BURDEN OF PROOF

This element of the Restructuring Act received substantial media attention because it purported to shift the burden of proof to the IRS and off the shoulders of citizens. Such a move would be momentous since it would make it impossible for the agency to assert bogus claims. The reality, however, is that the law cannot possibly attain those goals.

The law added code section 7491, which states in part:

> If, in any court proceeding, a taxpayer introduces credible evidence with respect to any factual issue relevant to ascertaining the liability of the taxpayer for any tax imposed by subtitle A or B, the Secretary shall have the burden of proof with respect to such issue.

Please notice that the burden shifts only in "any court proceeding." The fact is, 97 percent of everything the IRS does is done out of court. As such, this law does not apply to a myriad of administrative actions, including tax audits, penalty assessments, and collection actions. Therefore, in the vast majority of cases, this burden of proof change means nothing.

But there is another serious limitation on the purported shift. That is, before there is a shift, the citizen must have "complied with the requirements under this title to substantiate any item."[2] Keep in mind that in countless provisions of the tax code, the law places the burden on the citizen to "substantiate" his claim. For example, he must substantiate his position regarding income, deductions, credits, payments, assessments, penalties, liabilities, property basis, exemptions, allowances, employees, return filings, filing status, elections, current address, marital status, and more.

The practical effect of this is that the IRS rests in essentially the same position now as it did before restructuring.[3]

THE IRS OVERSIGHT BOARD

The centerpiece of the restructuring legislation was the Internal Revenue Service Oversight Board (the Board). The nine-member Board is designed to function like a citizen review board. Board members are to be nongovernment employees and independent of the IRS. The Board was advertised as the main tool in the fight against IRS abuse. The law states that one of the Board's specific responsibilities is to "ensure the proper protection of taxpayers by the employees of the Internal Revenue Service."[4] But the reality is, the Board does not have the necessary power to accomplish that goal.

Consider this language from the statute, which delineates exceptions to the Board's powers:

> (2) The Oversight Board *shall have no responsibilities or authority* with respect to—
>   (A) the development and formulation of Federal tax policy relating to existing and proposed internal revenue laws, related statutes, and tax conventions,
>   (B) law enforcement activities of the Internal Revenue Service, including compliance activities such as examinations, collection activities, or criminal investigations,
>   (C) specific procurement activities of the Internal Revenue Service, or
>   (D) except as provided in subsection (d)(3), specific personnel actions.[5]

It is plain from this language that the substantive activities of the IRS do not fall within the sweep of the Board's oversight authority. In summary, the Board has no capacity to prevent the kind of abuses documented in the Senate Finance Committee hearings. In reality, the Board is a debating society with limited authority over a narrow band of administrative issues.

THE DROP IN COLLECTION ACTIONS

Surely if IRS collection actions have dropped substantially since restructuring, the beast must have been restrained, correct? Well, one thing is for sure, collection actions did in fact drop, but not for the reasons one might think.

According to the IRS, the number of tax lien filings dropped from 543,600 in 1997 to just 167,800 by 1999, a drop of about 70 percent. The number of wage and bank levies declined 86 percent, from 3,659,000 to 504,000, in the same period. But the most remarkable decline is in the area of property seizures, such as homes and businesses. Here, enforcement action went from 10,090 seizures in 1997 to just 161 in 1999, a reduction of 98.5 percent.[6] By narrowly focusing upon these numbers, it would seem that the IRS is out of business. That, however, is just not the case.

For starters, the agency's operating budget is now at an all-time high, this after three increases in the two budget cycles for 2001 and 2002. The IRS's 2003 budget is $10.4 billion, an increase of nearly 38 percent over its 1998 budget. The budget hikes were to increase staffing and collection action.

With respect to staffing, the IRS is spending $224.6 million to add nearly three thousand new full-time employees. The additional muscle is used to enhance the IRS's enforcement presence. And with respect to collection action, the numbers are moving north at alarming rates. Consider these increases in collection action between 2000 and 2001:

- Lien filings increased from 287,517 to 428,376, a growth of nearly 50 percent.

- Wage and bank levies went from 219,778 to 674,080, a growth of nearly 206 percent.

- Property seizures went from 74 to 234, a growth of more than 270 percent.[7]

In addition, the Commissioner reports that corporate audits and correspondence audits—audits conducted through the mail—are up 27 percent and 65 percent respectively.

While the IRS certainly is *not* out of business, it is likewise *not* the uncontrollable monster it once was. The fact is, the restructuring law added new taxpayers' rights and protections that are valuable tools in the fight against IRS abuse. But you have to know what those tools are and how to use them or they cannot help you.

At some point, virtually all Americans will have some kind of adversarial contact with the IRS. If you are reading this, you are probably facing such a contact now. It may take the form of a computer-generated notice, an audit, a penalty or interest assessment, or in the worse case, delinquent tax collection action. Regardless of the nature of your problem, you can avoid the frustration and the financial cost of managing it if you understand how the machine operates and how to make it work for you.

The solutions to most IRS problems are simple, painless, and fast acting—if the problems are confronted correctly and early in the process. It is only when simple problems are not handled quickly and properly that they become major threats to one's financial security and future. By following the actions I lay out in this book, you can be assured that what begins as a simple IRS problem never escalates to the kind of problem that finds its way onto the front page of your local paper. Of course, in this process, you also save money.

However, ignoring your IRS problems or failing to address them correctly and in a timely manner will not only cost you money, but increase the likelihood that the minor inconvenience and hassle will grow way out of proportion and out of control.

Daniel J. Pilla
White Bear Lake, Minnesota

If I have set it down it is because that which
is clearly known hath less terror than
that which is but hinted at and guessed.

–Sir Arthur Conan Doyle
The Hound of the Baskervilles

1

Basic Things You
Need to Know

Myths and Realities about the IRS

There are two great fears people share when it comes to dealing with the IRS. The first is a generalized fear of the unknown. Because the IRS is a huge agency powered by an incomprehensible code and funded with billions of dollars annually, people make the mistake of believing the agency can do "anything it wants" when it comes to tax law enforcement. This gives rise to the second fear, that you will "go to jail" if you run afoul of the agency. As a consequence, people tend to roll over to the agency rather than try to fight back, believing it will go better for them if they do not "make the IRS mad."

Because these attitudes are both false and responsible for millions of people paying untold billions in taxes they do not owe, it is meritorious to examine these notions in some detail, with an eye toward exposing the myths and realities about tax law enforcement. This way, you will better understand what to expect from the IRS in a given situation and in turn can intelligently determine the best course of action. Let us address the two common fears, beginning with the greatest fear.

WILL THE IRS PUT ME IN JAIL?

Whenever people think of IRS problems, names like Redd Foxx, Leona Helmsley, and Willie Nelson immediately come to mind. These of course are high-profile tax cases involving intensive enforcement action and, in the case of Leona Helmsley, an extended jail sentence. These high-profile cases are no accident. They are part of a long-standing IRS plan to utilize the media to publicize cases that promise to have a "positive impact" on "voluntary compliance."

This means very simply that people who are afraid of the IRS will "voluntarily" comply with its edicts, regardless of their legitimacy. Of course, the IRS defines the term *voluntary* in much the same way that gangsters do. The infamous line from the movie *The Godfather* comes to mind: "Either your brains or your signature will be on the contract."

Okay. Where do I sign?

This is "voluntary compliance." And by trumpeting the misfortunes of the poor slobs who do not comply, the IRS sends a clear message to the public: "If you don't toe the line, you can expect a similar fate."

This not only frightens people who *can* comply, but it terrorizes and drives underground those who, for whatever reason, *cannot*. This is one explanation of why there are between seven and ten million citizens who do not file their annual tax returns. These people are mostly in hiding and living in fear of going to jail for their tax transgressions.

You need to know, however, that with a universe of about 125 million individual tax returns filed every year and only about 2,500 criminal prosecutions, you have a better chance of being eaten by a shark than you do of going to jail for a tax crime.[1] What landed Leona Helmsley and others like her in jail were deliberately false statements in their tax documents and fabricating documents to support bogus deductions. Those convicted of tax-related criminal charges are guilty of deliberate, voluntary acts the purpose of which is to deceive and mislead the IRS, to unlawfully hide income, and to evade the payment of taxes.

This motivation is not shared by the vast majority of citizens. Instead, the majority of people in this country make every effort to comply with the law and pay what they owe. That they may make mistakes, miscalculations, and errors in judgment, obtain erroneous advice, or otherwise misinterpret the law does not make them criminals. Even the majority of those who owe taxes they cannot pay are not criminals. More often, they are victims of economic, medical, or other unforeseen circumstances beyond their control that leave them unable to pay on time.

The criminal sanctions in the tax code are reserved for premeditated tax cheats, not those who tripped over or fell into one of the innumerable pitfalls built into the code. The Supreme Court described it aptly when it said, "Even a dog distinguishes between being stumbled over and being kicked."[2]

This book is about empowering citizens to use their rights to fend off unjustified claims by the IRS and to manage and mitigate the legitimate ones. There is no way you can even begin to do that if you believe the IRS is going to kick your door in at three in the morning and haul you off to some rat-infested jail if you do anything other than turn out your pockets. You need to know that unless you undertake a deliberate plan to cheat, deceive, or mislead the IRS, you are not going to jail.

WHAT CAN I EXPECT FROM TAX LAW ENFORCEMENT?

If you are not going to jail, what is going to happen in a given scenario? The short answer is that the IRS will make contact with you at some level to address the dollars-and-cents aspect of your tax obligation. This is what we refer to as the *civil*, as opposed to *criminal*, elements of tax law enforcement and administration. The worst-case scenario in this theater is that you owe more money.

It is equally true, however, that before you can be made to pay more money, the IRS must follow certain prescribed procedures that limit its power, and you have clearly delineated rights that can be exercised to oppose the agency's demands. The limitations on the IRS and the rights you enjoy combine to assure that the IRS cannot do "anything it wants." In fact, as you will learn in the chapters to follow, when you exercise your rights, you will win your case the majority of the time.

The overwhelming majority of annual enforcement cases fall into one of three broad categories. They are (1) computer-generated contacts, (2) face-to-fact audits, and (3) civil collection of delinquent tax payments. As a subset of these categories, citizens face tax return filing issues, penalties and interest, and the need to appeal adverse IRS decisions. As this book unfolds, I examine each of these areas in great detail. For the time being, however, I paint with a broad brush to allow you to better comprehend how cases develop and where you stand with the IRS at any one time.

Computer-Generated Contacts

It should come as no surprise that over the past twenty years, the IRS has substantially increased its capability to do business with computers. Despite the agency's continuing complaints about outdated equipment, the fact is that massive changes have occurred in the IRS's computer arsenal. The agency uses its computers, among other things, to receive electronic filings of various tax forms, to credit and monitor payments of both current and delinquent taxes, and to make contacts with citizens regarding the status of their accounts. It is in the latter area that most people receive computer-generated letters as an initial IRS contact.

Computer-generated contacts enable the IRS to reach more people more "efficiently" than through the medium of face-to-face contacts. Using a number of programs I describe in detail in the opening pages of chapter 2, the IRS uses computer contacts to:

• Correct math errors in tax returns

• Correct clerical errors in returns

- Assess additional taxes attributable to unreported income

- Track down nonfilers.

These contacts are in the nature of an "examination," which is an inquiry into the correctness of your tax return. Through this process, the IRS reviews (or has reviewed) the return to determine its accuracy. Upon finding an error—real or imagined—the agency communicates that error through a computer notice. In broad terms, the notice states the error and sets forth the required remedial steps.

Computer notices of this nature generally come from the IRS service center where you filed (or were required to file) your return. The ten service centers throughout the nation receive returns and payments, process them, and issue general correspondence with respect to them. While service centers mail tens of millions of computer notices annually, a staggering percentage of them are not accurate.

Chapter 2 walks you through the process of responding to computer notices, challenging those that are not accurate, and mitigating those that are. The address of the IRS office that issued the letter is always featured prominently on the top of the letter and your response must be directed to that office.

Face-to-Face Audits

An audit, in its most basic sense, is an inquiry into the accuracy of your tax return. Audits have always been the cornerstone of the IRS civil enforcement machine. With the advent of computers, the agency is able to make its presence felt on a much broader scale than was possible through face-to-face audits. Still, the audit remains the IRS's chief means of maintaining a sense of presence in the lives of citizens and businesses.

The single largest myth associated with a tax audit is the notion that the IRS selects a return for audit *because* there is an error in the return. In fact, returns are selected to *determine* whether errors exist. Just because you are selected does not mean you did anything wrong. It does, however, mean that you must prove that your tax return is correct.

This is one concept that is both fundamentally important to effectively dealing with the IRS *and* antithetical to general U.S. law. We rightfully assume that we are "innocent until proven guilty." And while that certainly applies if you are accused of robbing a bank or selling drugs, it does *not* apply to the IRS. In virtually all your dealings with the IRS, you bear the burden of proving that your actions were correct; the IRS rarely has to prove you are wrong. When you grasp this concept and recognize what it takes to prove your case, there is little to be afraid of in connection with an audit.

Chapter 6 explains the audit process at length, walking you step-by-step through the elements of:

- The initial audit contact

- Face-to-face meetings with the examiner

- Preparing and presenting proof

- Challenging the decisions of tax auditors.

When you understand how to prove that your return is correct and how to challenge a tax auditor's determination, you will never pay taxes you do not owe.

Collecting Delinquent Taxes

If the chances of going to jail for a tax crime are literally one in fifty thousand, and the audit process holds no fear because of (1) the IRS's high error rate and (2) your right to appeal, what does that say about the collection process? Though the collection process is likewise riddled with errors and you enjoy important appeal rights, it is true that the agency's most fearsome powers rest in the hands of tax collectors. This is because tax collectors wield the power to file tax liens against property, issue wage and bank levies, and execute seizures of property, including homes and businesses.

There is no question that such powers pose an ominous risk to citizens, but in fact, these risks are relatively simple to mitigate. The reason is that important restrictions stand in the way of a given IRS employee's right to unilaterally execute a wage levy or property seizure. The IRS Restructuring Act, for all its faults, added important appeals rights for citizens involved in the collection function. These rights can stymie a rogue collection agent's effort to ruin your financial life. In short, the horror stories we have all heard about the IRS destroying a person's life or business would be the rare exception today, assuming you understand your rights, meet your minimum obligations, and stand prepared to execute your appeals options if necessary.

Chapters 9 and 10 discuss specific procedures you can follow to:

- Avoid or release wage and bank levies

- Prevent the filing of tax liens

- Stop property seizures

- Obtain the release of tax liens that wreck your credit

- Win freedom from the tax debt of a current or former spouse

- Appeal a proposed collection action that promises to destroy you financially.

When you understand the limitations to the IRS's right of collection, what happened to millions of citizens prior to the Restructuring Act never has to happen to you.

Penalties, Interest, and Other Issues

Sprinkled into the discussion of the major issues outlined above, I address critical points that wrap themselves inextricably around the key points. For example, it is impossible to discuss IRS problem resolution without addressing the question of interest and penalties. I have been told a thousand times, "I can pay my taxes. It's the penalties and interest I cannot pay." To illustrate how profound these additions are, consider that in 1996 the average amount owed by a delinquent citizen was $9,300. By 2001 that debt had risen to $34,000.[3]

Citizens who readily recognize their obligation to pay delinquent taxes cry out for relief from oppressive penalties and interest. And one of the greatest failings of the system is the lack of clear guidance on how to deal with penalties and interest. This is the one area where this book promises to help every American who earns a living in the United States. Because we all face the prospect of penalties and interest, we must all know how to handle them. If you learn nothing else from this book, the secrets to dealing with penalties and interest could make it the single best investment you ever make in your financial security.

This book is about much more than solving existing IRS problems. Just as important as solving problems is the need to *avoid* them in the first place. Both wage earners and self-employed small business owners face a myriad of potential IRS problems. These problems range in scope from simple computer contacts and audits to more complicated issues involving payroll taxes and business tax penalties. All these problems can be avoided with the execution of simple, inexpensive steps that insulate you from exposure to the agency's enforcement muscle.

Throughout the book, you will find clearly labeled discussions that delineate procedures for avoiding specific problems. It is vitally important to understand that these suggestions are not mere theoretical musings on my part. They are the result of intensive study, practice, and analysis of virtually every tax problem the typical citizen might encounter. It is impossible to spend twenty-five years *solving* tax problems without developing strategies to prevent them. In this sense, this book is a "two-for-one special."

WHERE DO I STAND WITH THE IRS?

The clarion call of Congress during the restructuring process was to remake the IRS into an agency more capable of understanding problems from the taxpayers' point of view and developing a management structure more responsive to citizens' needs. In response to this call, former Commissioner Rossotti peeled back vast layers of management and reorganized the agency into four "operating divisions."

Of the four operating divisions, you as the typical individual or small business owner care about only two of them, the Wage and Investment Income Division and the Small Business and Self-Employed Division. These are the only two divisions with which you are likely to interact. Each division is staffed with IRS personnel who are supposedly trained to understand the challenges faced by citizens within that division. In this way—theoretically—you deal only with IRS employees who understand what you are up against.

In an effort to minimize the undesirable effects of shuffling files from one function to another, the IRS's new model is designed to permit one operating division to control a file from the commencement of the case to its conclusion. While the jury is still out on whether this will make a remarkable difference in the quality of IRS's case handling, it is undeniable that it helps citizens better understand where they stand with the IRS at any given time. In fact, one of the key complaints I hear from citizens is that they never know where their case is. Let us clear that up right now.

The Wage and Investment Income Division deals exclusively with individuals whose sole source of income is wages or investment income such as stocks and bonds.

The Small Business and Self-Employed Division, as its name implies, deals with those whose income derives from self-employment, including businesses and corporations with gross revenue up to five million dollars.[4]

Within each operating division, the IRS maintains, among other things, operations dealing with taxpayer assistance and compliance enforcement. The latter function represents the business end of the IRS. Within the compliance element of each operating division are two key functions: Examination and Collection. The Examination function is staffed by revenue agents (RAs) whose job is to audit tax returns. The Collection function is staffed by revenue officers (ROs) whose job is to collect delinquent tax debts.

In addition to four operating divisions, the IRS has three key "functional units" with which you should be familiar. These units are organizationally distinct from the operating divisions and thus each is not answerable to the managers of any other unit or any division. This gives these units an important measure of independence from other IRS functions.

The first is the Appeals unit. Staffed by Appeals Officers (AOs), the job of Appeals is to review the decisions made by employees within the Examination and Collection functions. The Appeals process is designed to remove unilateral authority from the hands of lower-level IRS employees, thus restricting their ability to make assessments of taxes or execute enforced collection action.

The second is the Taxpayer Advocate Service (TAS). The Taxpayer Advocate functions as a liaison between you and the IRS. The TAS has the authority to stop the IRS from taking or continuing action that will cause a "hardship." The chief function of the TAS is to step in where normal channels failed to help you get your case heard by the proper personnel.

The third is the Criminal Investigation (CI) unit. Staffed by special agents (SAs), CI is charged with the duty of investigating tax crime allegations. When a case is turned over to CI for investigation, all other enforcement functions cease until the criminal elements of the case are disposed of. Potential ramifications of such cases include grand jury subpoenas and federal indictments—two processes I like to avoid whenever possible.

One key to knowing where you stand when dealing with the IRS is to understand the peculiar task of the IRS employee you are dealing with. For example, revenue officers are not auditors. ROs collect taxes—period. So if you are contacted by an RO, the IRS believes you owe money and wants to get paid. On the other hand, if you are contacted by a revenue agent, you are under audit, and at least until the audit is complete and your appeals rights are exhausted, you do not owe more money.

WHAT IF I DON'T KNOW WHO CONTACTED ME?

My first undertaking when dealing with a tax problem is to determine the posture of the case. This is easy to ascertain simply by reviewing the contact letters and determining the type of agent who made the contact. The formula is simple. Let us review. Revenue agents audit returns. Revenue officers collect taxes. Appeals officers review decisions. Special agents investigate tax crime allegations.

In many cases, a client cannot tell me the posture of the case, or he lost recent letters, or the case has been on hold for so long that the prior contacts are stale. In that situation, it is helpful to obtain internal IRS documents to figure out where you stand. The documents I speak of are known as Master Files. The IRS keeps Individual Master Files (IMF) for personal tax returns and Business Master Files (BMF) for business returns. These master file records constitute a transcript of your account with the IRS. They provide detailed historical information on every action executed in your case, including the date of each action.

To obtain your Master File records, make a written request to the Disclosure Office at the service center where you file your returns. The addresses of the ten IRS service centers are listed at the end of this chapter. Identify the letter as a request under the Freedom of Information Act. Ask for your Master File covering the years in question. Be sure to provide your social security number, sign the letter, and provide a copy of a photo ID showing your signature. Ask for an IMF to cover personal tax returns or a BMF to address business tax returns. In about six to eight weeks, the IRS will release the Master File.

Also ask for the current edition of IRS Document 10978. This publication lists the meaning of the various computer codes used to communicate the information in the Master File. The document is helpful to understanding the Master File.

WHAT IF I GET A KNOCK ON THE DOOR?

While it is true that most IRS problems can be solved on your own if you know what course to follow, some problems require the assistance of counsel. Because of their nature and complexity, these problems are beyond the scope of this book. However, I would be derelict if I failed to at least identify them.

There are three situations that might rightfully be referred to as "a knock on the door." Though they are not common, they do occur—and with growing regularity. In any of these cases, you should immediately consult experienced counsel to determine your best course of action.

1. *A civil lawsuit seeking a judgment.* In certain cases where there is prolonged tax delinquency, the IRS may begin a suit in federal court to obtain a judgment against you. Federal judgments are good for twenty years and the lawsuit carries with it the prospect of losing your home and other property. Do not fool with such an action. Get experienced counsel immediately to determine your defenses and remedies to the suit.

2. *The issuance of a summons or subpoena.* In the course of an intensive investigation, the IRS may resort to the issuance of a summons commanding you to give testimony or records to an IRS investigator, or worse, issue a subpoena requiring your appearance before a grand jury. Both situations portend serious consequences and you should immediately consult experienced counsel to ascertain your legal obligations and potential defenses.

3. *A visit from a special agent.* Special agents are the IRS's criminal investigators. If they pay you a visit in connection with your tax affairs, their questions are almost always preceded with a ritualistic reading of your Miranda rights. Anytime a criminal investigator advises that you have the right to remain silent, you are generally best served by *following that advice*—at least until you have the opportunity to discuss the matter with counsel. And you should waste no time in consulting experienced counsel *before* speaking with a special agent.

Address IMF/BMF requests to the Disclosure Office, Internal Revenue Service, at the service center's address as shown below:

Andover
310 Lowell Street
Andover, MA 01810

Fresno
PO Box 24014, MS 891
Fresno, CA 93747–8337

Atlanta
4800 Buford Highway, MS 93
Chamblee, GA 30341

Kansas City
PO Box 24551, MS 7000
Kansas City, MO 64131

Austin
PO Box 934, MS 7000
Austin, TX 78767

Memphis
5333 Getwell Road
Memphis, TN 38118

Brookhaven
1040 Waverly Avenue
Holtsville, NY 11742

Ogden
PO Box 9941
Ogden, UT 84409–9941

Cincinnati
200 W. Fourth Street
Covington, KY 41019

Philadelphia
11601 Roosevelt Boulevard
Philadelphia, PA 19154

2

End the Fear of Going to the Mailbox

Handling IRS Computer Notices

As much as it might like to, the IRS cannot audit every citizen in a face-to-face environment. True, the IRS collects substantially more tax dollars through face-to-face audits than it does in any other manner, but it's also true that the agency will most likely never have the resources to audit each of the more than 125 million individual tax returns. Consequently, the IRS relies heavily upon its computer systems to conduct electronic audits.

COMPUTER AUDITS TAKE UP THE SLACK

The IRS has substantially increased the use of its computers over the past fifteen years. Computers now perform a wide range of electronic audits using information available to the IRS from its own files and from third-party sources. When a computer audit finds an error in a return, the computer kicks out a notice explaining that the IRS reviewed the tax return, found an error, and corrected it. Usually additional tax is owed as a result of the correction. The notice includes a demand for payment of the tax, with interest and penalty.

This process is broadly referred to as the correction program. The correction program encompasses a wide range of procedures designed to "correct" improper or incomplete tax returns. Each year the IRS mails millions of these notices.

THE HISTORY OF THE CORRECTION PROGRAM

Under normal conditions, the IRS is not free to unilaterally assess taxes against you. You have important rights to challenge any proposed assessment. When you issue a proper challenge, the IRS cannot make the assessment or undertake collection until your appeals rights are exhausted. These procedures are known as the "deficiency procedures."[1] Because your right to appeal precedes the IRS's right of assessment, the deficiency procedures offer protection against arbitrary claims. The notice of deficiency is a detailed, written explanation of why you owe more money and offers you the opportunity for Tax Court review before you have to pay an increased tax.

The chief problem with correction notices is that Congress wrote exclusions into the deficiency procedures to cover "math errors." Originally the exclusions were very narrow and applied only in situations where a simple math error appeared in a tax return. In that case the IRS did not have to respect the deficiency procedures before making an assessment if it simply corrected the error. After all, what is there to appeal if one has merely added one's deductions incorrectly?

However reasonable this exclusion may have been in the beginning, over time it became fertile ground for abuse. And over time Congress added more exceptions to the deficiency procedures. There is now an impressive list of circumstances under which the IRS may assess additional taxes without regard to your appeals rights. These exceptions turned the correction program into a systematic mail-order campaign that the IRS uses to collect billions of dollars annually.

The sheer volume of correction notices portends not only huge revenue for the agency but huge problems for people. In its 2001 annual report to Congress, the IRS's National Taxpayer Advocate reported that an average of 25 percent of the individual tax returns filed contained errors. Based upon that, we know that about 31 million citizens received a correction notice in just one year.

And while this number is certainly staggering, this is not the worst part of the problem. More serious is the error rate in the correction notices. Stated another way, the errors the IRS purports to correct in its millions of notices are often nonexistent. Not only is this true today, but it has been true for well over a decade—and the IRS knows it.

As early as 1986, I made the claim on national radio that the IRS was mailing bills to the public that it either knew or should have known were not correct. My allegation may well have prompted a General Accounting Office (GAO) study of the situation. The study began in April 1987 and the findings were released in July 1988. The results of the analysis are shocking. Among other things, the GAO stated:

> Our review of correspondence and related cases at three service centers indicated that the IRS's letters, the adjustments discussed in the letters, and/or the action taken by the IRS in response to the taxpayers' inquiries was often incorrect, unresponsive, incomplete or unclear. Such notices sometimes resulted in the assessment of incorrect tax and penalties. Equally serious, however, are the potential for confusion and frustration on the part of taxpayers and the extra time and expense IRS and taxpayers incur in processing of additional correspondence needed to resolve the issue.[2]

More specifically, the GAO found that 48 *percent* of all IRS correspondence and actions regarding account adjustments were either "incorrect, unresponsive, unclear or incomplete." Further, in 68 *percent* of the cases studied, the IRS failed to comply with its own "procedures designed to foster good taxpayer relations."

In 1990 the GAO revisited the issue, asking this simple question, "What did the IRS do to correct the problems identified in the 1988 report?" The answer was equally simple: "Not much." The GAO's assessment was that it was "not likely" that any substantial improvements to the system would be made anytime soon.[3]

And while the IRS claims to have made strides in correcting the problem, the facts indicate a different story. In 1994 the GAO examined forty-seven of the most common notices the IRS uses to communicate with citizens. According to the GAO, thirty-one of those notices—66 percent of those examined—used unspecific language, unclear references, inconsistent terminology, illogical presentation of material, and provided insufficient information and guidance.[4]

Each year since 1996, the year of inception of the Taxpayer Advocate's annual published list of the top twenty problems with the IRS faced by citizens, erroneous notices have enjoyed prominent ranking on that list. In 1996 erroneous notices ranked as number four.[5] The 2002 Taxpayer Advocate's report shows that the problem is only getting worse, ranking erroneous notices as number three. Furthermore, the TA's analysis of the situation shows a continuing, systemic problem. The Taxpayer Advocate writes:

> However, we remain concerned that the IRS has not yet placed enough emphasis on the process and there are still major weaknesses in its improvement efforts. The current initiatives do not provide for specific information on notices related to a taxpayer's error.[6]

As if it were not bad enough to receive an errant notice from the IRS that is vague, misleading, poorly written, or just flat wrong, it gets even worse when people try to enlist the aid of IRS personnel to correct the problem. To do this, people naturally phone the IRS at its toll-free telephone assistance lines in an effort to better understand the agency's claim. In its 2001 Annual Report to Congress, the Taxpayer Advocate summarized this aspect of the problem by observing:

> Taxpayers who call the IRS to ask for a better explanation may receive incomplete or incorrect answers from the toll-free sites.

Filing season 2001 data indicates that IRS employees gave correct information about account-related issues 69 percent of the
time.[7]

19

End the Fear
of Going to
the Mailbox

That is to say, the IRS gave *incorrect* information *31 percent* of the
time. If we are talking about 31 million notices, we can conclude that
9.6 million people received incorrect information about a notice that
itself had a fifty-fifty chance of being wrong in the first place. It is no
wonder most people just throw up their hands and pay the stupid bill.

WHAT KIND OF CORRECTION NOTICES CAN I RECEIVE?

The IRS uses approximately *three hundred* form letters to communicate alleged errors. Clearly we cannot examine all of them. However, I discuss the most common ones below.

The IRS Claims You Didn't Report All Your Income

Through a process known as the Automated Underreporter
(AUR) Program, IRS computers search its files for all information
returns bearing your social security number. The most prominent
information returns are Forms 1099 and W-2. The computer then
compares those information returns with the income shown on your
income tax return. The process is intended to ensure that you report
all your income as required. When a failure to report is detected, the
IRS mails a notice. Assessments arising from the AUR Program are
among the top problems faced by citizens every year.

The IRS Claims You Made a Math or Clerical Error

The IRS computers analyze your return to ensure that all mathematical computations are accurate and to determine whether any
clerical or procedural failures exist. An example of a clerical error is
where a Schedule C, *Profit or Loss from Business*, is attached to the
return but you neglect to transfer the profit from Schedule C to Form

1040. This error prevents the correct computation of tax. When such a failure is detected, a notice is mailed out.

The IRS Claims You Failed to File Your Return

Using information returns, IRS computers determine whether a person required to file a return did in fact file that return. The IRS estimates that as many as seven to ten million people fail to file their tax returns when required by law. Many of those people, however, have information returns on file with the IRS reporting substantial income. The IRS compares these information returns with its tax return database to determine whether those required to file did so.

If it discovers that you failed to file, the IRS issues a notice asking that you either file the return or explain why you are not required to file. This process is known as a Tax Delinquency Inquiry (TDI). It kicks off the process of procuring a tax return and collecting delinquent taxes. The following chart illustrates how the TDI program has grown over the past few years.[8]

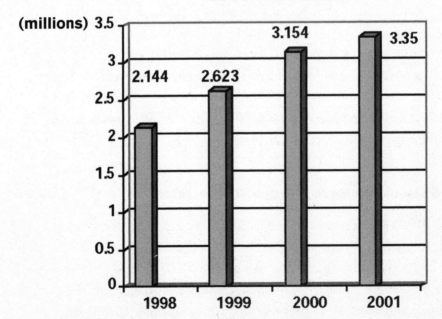

Correction Notices

THE CURE FOR ERRANT CORRECTION NOTICES

If you receive an incorrect bill from a phone company, a department store, or any other private business, you most likely refuse to pay it. Instead, you inform the company that its notice is in error, you politely but firmly demand that its records be corrected, and you ask that the dunning notices be terminated.

Your response should be no different when dealing with the IRS. You must write a letter informing the IRS, politely but firmly, that the correction notice is in error. You must demand that it be corrected immediately.

Most people quail at the thought of challenging the IRS in this fashion. People believe the IRS will begin immediate enforced collection action or even put them in jail if the bill is not paid. Not only is this not true, but this attitude is the principal reason that the mail-order tax collection campaign is so successful.

We need to understand that despite the unique procedures governing correction notices, the IRS nevertheless cannot arbitrarily assess taxes without your consent. You have the absolute right to challenge correction notices, but you must act properly to succeed.

IF IT'S SO EASY, WHY DO SO MANY PAY?

There are two primary reasons people opt to pay rather than fight back. First, and probably foremost, is the idea that if you run afoul of the IRS, it will grind you into financial powder. This notion was planted in the conscience of America long ago and was reinforced by the IRS during the 1980s and 1990s as the agency carried out one of its chief goals—making its presence felt throughout society. High-profile enforcement cases such as those of Willie Nelson and Leona Helmsley helped greatly to carry that banner.

The second and equally compelling reason so many pay is that the IRS is negligent when it comes to explaining your rights. It was for this very reason that in 1988 Congress compelled the IRS to produce a clear and understandable statement of taxpayers' rights. The product of that command is IRS Publication 1, *Your Rights as a Taxpayer*. However, the August 2000 edition of Publication 1 is just *two* pages long.

By contrast, this is my eleventh book on the subject of taxpayers' rights. Now, either I am incredibly long-winded, or the IRS left something out of its discussion. (In fairness, when Publication 1 was first released, it was *four* pages long. However, during the period of time when Congress added *more* rights to the tax code, the IRS actually *reduced* the scope of its explanation of those rights, a fact I have always found fascinating.)

Not surprisingly, Publication 1 says nothing about responding to correction notices. Instead, it refers you to another publication, IRS Publication 594, *The IRS Collection Process*. This publication is only slightly more helpful, but still does not reveal the secret to legally and effectively challenging correction notices. The January 2000 edition of Publication 594 provides the following:

What if you believe your bill is wrong?

If you believe your bill is wrong, let us know as soon as possible. Call the number on your bill, write to the IRS office that sent you the bill, call 1-800-829-1040, or visit your local IRS office, if you prefer.

To help us correct the problem, gather a copy of the bill along with copies of any records, tax returns, and canceled checks, etc., that will help us understand why you believe your bill is wrong.

If you write to us, tell us why you believe your bill is wrong. With your letter, include copies of all the documents you gathered to explain your case. Please do not send original documents. If we find you are correct, we will adjust your account and, if necessary, send you a corrected bill.

For the reasons I address below, this advice misses the mark laid out by Congress. This is why it comes as no surprise to me that, according to the Taxpayer Advocate, most citizens are unsure about how to challenge notices and do not understand their rights in connection with them. For example, following the advice of Publication 594 might well get you engrossed in a conversation with the IRS regarding its correction notice but is unlikely to lead to cancellation of the tax.

This is evidenced by the last sentence of the quoted statement, where the IRS says it will adjust the account "If we find you are correct." This language suggests that the burden of proof is on the citizen with regard to correction notices. As we shall see, that is simply not true.

HOW TO CHALLENGE CORRECTION NOTICES

The key to challenging correction notices is remarkably simple. You must write a letter declaring that you *disagree* with the IRS's calculation. The authority for your response is code section 6213(b)(2), which reads,

> a taxpayer may file with the Secretary within 60 days after notice is sent under paragraph (1) a request for an abatement of any assessment specified in such notice, and upon receipt of such request, the Secretary shall abate the assessment.

Very few tax laws are simpler than this. You have sixty days from the date of the notice to respond by "filing a request for abatement." If you do, the IRS has *no choice* but to "abate the assessment." The abatement is the process of canceling the debt as though it never existed. The specific language of your letter is outlined in detail later in this chapter.

Please note that the law affords the IRS *no latitude* in complying with your request. The IRS may not dispute or ignore your timely written request. What's more, you have no burden of proof on the issue. The statute does not say you must "prove the notice is wrong" in order to win the abatement. It merely states that the IRS "shall abate the assessment" upon demand.

Now, admittedly, if the IRS is so evidently incompetent or malfeasant in issuing correction notices in the first place, one has to wonder whether we can really expect satisfaction—even from a correct response. It probably comes as no surprise that historically the IRS has failed to respect proper responses. My repeated complaints about these failures eventually led IRS attorneys to issue procedural guidance to service center employees on the topic in 1998. You need to be aware of this guidance because it will help you should the agency fail to deal correctly with your proper response. The guidance also helps to better understand the process of making a correct response.

In particular, the guidance discusses what is to happen if a citizen disagrees with a correction notice. The guidance reads, in part:

> However, if the taxpayer still does not agree, it is not necessary for the taxpayer to offer a satisfactory justification. In fact, *no reason for an abatement request need be given at all.* This is because the right to abatement is absolute: Under section 6213(b)(2), abatement shall occur upon request, and a timely abatement request *must be honored.* Finally, doubt should be resolved in favor of abating the assessment and resolving the matter through normal deficiency procedures.[9]

Does the agency have recourse if it truly believes you owe the tax? Yes. In that case, the IRS may reassert the liability after the abatement. If it does, however, "any reassessment of the abated tax must occur through the deficiency procedures." This way, you are entitled to your full appeals rights before the assessment becomes final, *and* you do not have to part with one dime of your money before the issue is resolved.

The reality is that 50 percent of the time, the IRS makes no effort to reassess taxes abated through the process described here, because the notices are bogus to begin with.

Do not make the mistake of phoning the IRS's toll-free assistance phone numbers to *question* the notice. Many people make this mistake because of the guidance provided in Publication 594. Two things happen when following this process. First, citizens receive incorrect or incomplete information from IRS employees 31 percent of the time.

Second, rather than making the abatement, IRS personnel often advise citizens that they will "research" the matter and get back with an answer. This often takes several weeks. In the meantime, the sixty-day deadline ticks away and nothing can be done to extend it. Consequently, the time to respond with a written abatement request often expires before the IRS completes its research. The next thing the citizen receives is a more demanding collection notice.

The IRS's legal guidance speaks directly to this issue, saying,

> a taxpayer's decision not to request abatement of a math error assessment is a waiver of the taxpayer's procedural rights, including the statutory right to contest the adjustment in the Tax Court.

This is precisely why you must respond to correction notices *in writing*—not by phoning. And contrary to the suggestion in Publication 594, *do not* write with questions or inquiries. Rather, demand abatement in a polite and professional manner, but clearly and unequivocally. In the sections to follow, I give clear examples of how to do this.

Never forget that failure to exercise your rights within the time prescribed by law constitutes a *waiver* of those rights.

HOW TO NEUTRALIZE THE IRS COMPUTERS

The IRS may correct a tax return, make a summary assessment of additional tax, and issue a bill to collect the assessment when the return contains:

1. An error in addition, subtraction, multiplication, or division

2. An incorrect use of a table provided by the IRS if that is apparent from the existence of other information on the return

3. An entry of an item that is inconsistent with another related entry

4. An omission of information required to be supplied to substantiate an entry on the return

5. A deduction or credit exceeding a statutory limit

6. An omission of a correct taxpayer identification number when required by law

7. An entry claiming the credit with respect to net earnings from self-employment, to the extent the tax on such net earnings has not been paid

8. An omission of information required for the earned income credit.[10]

After making a correction, the IRS must issue a notice that "shall set forth the error alleged and an explanation thereof." Unfortunately, the notices fail to clearly state the alleged error and provide no explanation of your rights. The Taxpayer Advocate flatly declares, "Math error notices are vague and do not clearly explain changes in returns." Even worse, "Taxpayers who call the IRS to ask for a better explanation may receive incomplete or incorrect answers."[11]

This adds to the confusion and greatly contributes to the large rate at which errant notices are paid. In addition, the IRS often goes beyond the statute's authority, asserting corrections in cases other than those described above. In all events, a proper and timely response will solve the problem before it escalates into a serious collection matter.

Let us examine specific correction notices and their responses.

The Mathematical Correction

I use the phrase *mathematical correction* in a broad sense. For purposes of this discussion, assume that the mathematical correction is any correction made as a result of the IRS detecting one of the eight errors listed above (though I address the missing taxpayer identification number separately below). As you review that list, observe that in reality, errors in addition, subtraction, multiplication, or division are just one of eight errors or omissions the IRS is permitted to correct.

An example of a math error and the procedures to cancel it is afforded through the case of Dave, who operated his own small printing business. He attached Schedule C, *Profit or Loss from Business,* to his tax return as required. After filing his tax return, Dave received a notice clearly marked "Correction Notice—Amount Due IRS." It claimed that an additional $84.25 was owed.[12] To explain the correction, the IRS stated only that "an error was made in the income section of your return when the amount of your capital gain (or loss) was transferred from Schedule D."

After examining his return, Dave discovered that he had not filed Schedule D since he did not have any capital gains. On the other hand, his Schedule C income was correctly transferred to Form 1040, so the correct tax was computed. Dave quickly realized that the IRS correction notice was in error.

Dave wrote a simple letter demanding abatement and mailed it to the IRS within the sixty-day deadline. The critical attributes of the letter are that it must plainly state that:

- You are in disagreement with the IRS's determination

- The tax should be abated in full

- The IRS should mail a notice of deficiency ensuring your right to appeal if the agency believes the correction is justified.

Please review Exhibit 2–1. That sample letter can serve as a guide for challenging any correction notice.

EXHIBIT 2–1

Your Name
Address
City, State, Zip

Date:
SSN:

Internal Revenue Service

Dear IRS:

Reference is made to your letter (copy enclosed), stating that my return for [year] was changed due to an alleged error.

Be advised that I disagree with your statement that I owe additional taxes. This is notice under the provisions of code section 6213(b)(2)(A) that the IRS is to immediately abate this assessment. Please note that I make this demand within the sixty-day period prescribed by law. Therefore, the IRS *has no alternative* but to abate the assessment.

If the IRS insists that this assessment is legitimate, I demand that the IRS mail a notice of deficiency as required by code section 6213(b)(2)(A) so that I may exercise my right to petition the Tax Court.

I look forward to your notice that the tax has been abated.

Thank you very much,

Your Name

Failure to follow these simple procedures can sometimes turn a very small problem into a giant one. Let me illustrate. Some time ago, I spoke with a woman who informed me that she had received a correction notice. A single mother with three young children, she was living paycheck to paycheck. Any unanticipated expense often spelled trouble. Consequently, when the IRS demanded more than $350, she was stunned. The notice declared that an addition error had resulted in an underpayment.

She brought the notice to her tax preparer, who reviewed the return and declared that there was no error. Despite the preparer's commitment to stand behind the return, he had no clue about to how to rein in the collection machine. Rather than demand abatement in writing, he made phone calls to the IRS that naturally led nowhere and he wrote letters to the service center *questioning* the increase.

With the passage of time, the sixty days expired. No longer did the citizen enjoy the right to abatement. However, the IRS now gained the right to enforce collection through liens and levies. A long period of silence persuaded the preparer and his unfortunate client that the IRS was "researching" the matter and would soon respond.

Respond it did, but not in the manner hoped. The IRS levied the woman's checking account. The blow was devastating. Several checks bounced that she wrote for living expenses. She had to borrow money from friends and family to make the checks good.

Sadly, these events were entirely predictable and would have been completely avoidable, if she or her tax preparer understood and followed the simple abatement procedures explained here.

The Arbitrary Notice

The arbitrary notice is a mutated form of the mathematical correction. The important difference, however, is that the arbitrary notice fails to describe what "correction" was made. Because no reason is given, I refer to the notice as "arbitrary." If this notice is intended to constitute a mathematical correction, it fails to "set forth the error alleged and an explanation thereof" as required by law.

Moreover, as with most correction notices, it fails to clearly describe the right of abatement or the process of appeal.

If the notice is *not* intended to constitute a mathematical correction, it is illegal. This is because the statute permits the IRS to correct an account only if one of eight mathematical or clerical errors exists. The agency has no authority to assess and collect with a correction notice for other failures, such as the failure to report income or even the failure to file a return.

Because an arbitrary notice does not specify the nature of the account change, you cannot make an intelligent decision about whether the IRS is correct. For this reason, a letter demanding abatement accomplishes two important goals. First and most important, a timely response results in abatement. This is critical given that these notices routinely seek payment of hundreds, sometimes thousands of dollars. Secondly, abatement leads to the issuance of a notice of deficiency if the IRS is disposed to pursue the matter. Recall that a notice of deficiency is the document that clearly itemizes all changes and computations leading to a tax increase. You have the right to appeal the notice of deficiency before the tax is collectible.

With a notice of deficiency in hand, you can easily determine whether the calculations are accurate or merely an elaborate effort to separate you from your money. In the event of the former, you should pay the tax. In the event of the latter, you should exercise your right of appeal and challenge the IRS's allegations.

For example, Rodney once received an arbitrary notice seeking more than five thousand dollars. Because the IRS failed to describe the reasons for the change, Rodney could not determine whether the IRS (1) lost his return, (2) never received his return, (3) disallowed deductions on his return, or (4) simply took a wild stab at collecting another five grand.

Rodney filed a written demand for abatement of the assessment. In his demand he pointed out that the agency failed to explain the reasons for the increase, and he plainly demanded that a notice of deficiency be issued so that he could exercise his right of appeal. Please see Exhibit 2–2 for an example of this response.

EXHIBIT 2–2

Your Name
Address
City, State, Zip

Date:
SSN:

Internal Revenue Service

Dear Sir:

Reference is made to your letter of [date], concerning tax year ———. A copy of the notice is enclosed for your reference. The letter states that "We changed your tax return to correct your account information." The letter states that I owe $———.

The notice does not provide details of the reason why the IRS changed my account or why I am alleged to owe additional taxes.

Please be advised that I disagree with your statement of my account balance. This is notice under the provisions of IRS code section 6213(b) that you are to abate the tax liability shown in your notice immediately.

Under the terms of that statute, the IRS has *no alternative* but to abate the assessment. Before collection action is taken, I demand that a notice of deficiency be mailed in accordance with code section 6213(a) so that I may exercise my right of appeal.

Under the law, I have sixty days in which to protest this assessment. My protest is timely. Therefore, the tax must be abated immediately.

I look forward to your notice verifying the tax abatement.

Sincerely,

Your Name

As a result of Rodney's response to this arbitrary notice, the IRS stopped billing him for the alleged tax and never did mail a notice of deficiency, proving that the claim was bogus to begin with. Forcing the IRS to choose between abatement and a notice of deficiency forced it to abandon its claim.

The Missing Taxpayer Identification Number (TIN)

One area where Congress really turned up the heat is that of social security numbers. Changes in the law over the past ten years have brought us to the place where social security numbers of third parties are required to be reported on tax returns in a variety of situations. Chiefly, social security numbers are required for minor children claimed as dependents on tax returns. But even beyond that, social security numbers are required for purposes of claiming the child care credit, education credits, and a host of other tax advantages.

The IRS uses social security numbers to police these claims. For example, the social security numbers of minor children are used to cross-check other returns and ensure that no other citizen claims that particular exemption. The governing statutes usually allow the IRS to deny the claim if no number or an incorrect number is provided. In turn, code section 6213 allows that denial to be treated as a math error.

Since the inception of the rules requiring social security numbers for minor children, correction notices on this issue have been among those most commonly issued by the IRS. According to the "National Taxpayer Advocate's FY2001 Report to Congress," of the more than 7.5 million correction notices issued in 1999, more than 3.3 million were attributable to code sections providing benefits for children. Chief among them were (1) dependent exemptions, (2) the child tax credit, and (3) the Earned Income Tax Credit. At the core of these code sections is the requirement for a valid social security number for any child claimed in connection with that benefit.

Notices challenging a social security number also suffer from the IRS's accuracy plague. Therefore the best approach to this claim is to provide the number in the letter demanding abatement. The letter should be substantively the same as those outlined in Exhibits 2–1 and 2–2 save that the social security number in question should be provided with the letter. If you have access to the actual social security card bearing the number in question, provide a photocopy of the card. (*Never* send original documentation to the IRS.)

If the number belongs to a nonfamily member and you do not have access to the card, ask that person to complete IRS Form W-9, *Request for Taxpayer Identification Number and Certification*. This form declares the correct social security number and certifies that the information is accurate. Have the form signed by the person whose number is in question, such as a baby-sitter or child care provider. By submitting the completed Form W-9 together with an abatement request, you will defeat a math correction of this nature every time.

Notice of Unreported Income

The growing legion of information-reporting requirements puts the IRS in a position where about 80 percent of the information shown on tax returns can be verified from third-party information, and the IRS is increasing its use of other available information even as I write. The eventual goal is to have complete access to all possible financial data on every citizen and to use that data for tax enforcement purposes.

Earlier I explained the processes the IRS uses to cross-check information return data with tax returns. To review, the IRS checks returns to ensure that (1) tax returns are filed by those required to file and (2) all income is reported on the return. If computers detect either a missing tax return or unreported income, the computer generates a statement explaining the omission. The notice computes the additional taxes, with interest and penalties, and demands immediate payment. The notice resembles the correction notices outlined above. This process is the core of the IRS Automated Underreporter Program.

There is one small factor to consider when discussing an assessment growing from either a missing tax return or unreported income. It is the fact that such assessments are *illegal*. As you review the list of the eight authorized uses of a correction notice, you find that unfiled returns and unreported income are *not* among them. Still, the IRS makes assessments using correction notices in these cases all the time. And according to one Treasury Department study, 76 percent of all abatements made by the IRS are attributable to these erroneous assessments.[13]

I once worked with a man who received such a statement. The IRS alleged that it received a Form 1099 showing that the man received dividend income of about eight thousand dollars from a company in Vancouver, Washington. The notice alleged that the income was not reported on his return. It went on to compute the additional tax the man owed (including penalties and interest) and demanded payment of the liability.

The actual tax calculation based on the alleged dividend income was correct. The problem was that the man never received dividend income from the company in Vancouver and moreover had nothing whatsoever to do with that company.

In response to the demand, he sent a letter demanding abatement using the model shown in Exhibit 2–3. This letter expressly addresses the question of the alleged unreported income. The letter *specifically declares* that the alleged income was not received and that as a matter of fact, all income from all sources was accurately reported on his return. Lastly, it declares under penalty of perjury that the facts contained in the letter are true and correct. This statement provides verification that the facts presented in the letter are accurate and adds credibility to the claims. I discuss this process in more detail in chapter 3.

EXHIBIT 2-3

Your Name
Address
City, State, Zip

Date:
SSN:

Internal Revenue Service

Dear IRS:

Reference is made to your letter of ———— [date], concerning tax year ————. (Copy enclosed.) The notice states that I underreported my income by $————. The notice states that the IRS recomputed my tax liability based on consideration of the alleged unreported income.

PLEASE TAKE NOTICE that I object to the recalculation of my income tax liability. Please take notice that I did not receive the amount of $———— that you allege to be income from ————. I did not earn any money from the ———— company.

The tax return I filed for ———— [year] fully and accurately reported all my income from all sources. I did not omit any income and your claim that I underreported $———— income during that year is inaccurate. I did not receive any additional income during ——— [year].

This is notice to you under the provisions of code section 6213(b) that you are to immediately abate the tax liability shown in your notice. Under the terms of that statute, the IRS has no alternative but to abate this assessment. Before any collection action is taken, I demand that a notice of deficiency be mailed in accordance with code section 6213(a) in order that I may exercise my right of appeal. In any event, the tax *must be abated*.

Under the law, I have sixty days in which to protest this assessment. My protest is timely. Therefore, the tax must be abated immediately.

I look forward to your notice verifying the tax abatement.

Under penalty of perjury, I declare that the facts stated in this letter are true and correct in all respects.

Sincerely,

Your Name

USE A STANDARD COVER FORM

The IRS service centers process millions of pieces of mail each month. Even under the best of circumstances, mailing a letter to the Internal Revenue Service is much like placing a note in a bottle, then dropping it into the Atlantic. One of the biggest complaints I hear from people dealing with the IRS is the agency's lack of response to their letters or claims.

Even assuming that the IRS does not deliberately ignore requests for abatement and assuming further that all service center employees can in fact read, it is not uncommon for communications such as these to be misplaced or otherwise mishandled. To remedy this, I suggest you use a cover form to plainly and quickly communicate the fact that a *claim* is being made and that it requires attention and processing by the agency. The form most useful in this regard is IRS Form 843, *Claim for Refund and Request for Abatement*, Exhibit 2–4. Form 843 is typically used to make claims for refund, but some tax regulations also recommend its use when making requests for abatement.

When you attach Form 843 to your written demand for abatement, the form acts as a cover letter immediately communicating the fact that you are making a claim against the agency. The claim and its attached written demand are then forwarded to the appropriate office for processing. Without Form 843 as your cover form, you risk having your demand for abatement misrouted or not processed at all.

Completing Form 843 is simple. When dealing with abatement requests of this nature, add a line to the top margin of the form that reads, "Demand for Abatement of Tax Pursuant to Code Section 6213(b)." Next, provide the information sought in lines 1 through 3. Line 4 is irrelevant to this claim. Line 5 is the space where you provide an explanation justifying your requested action. Type the words *See Attached Letter*. Now attach your letter demanding abatement written in accordance with the samples provided. Finally, sign and date Form 843.

EXHIBIT 2–4

Form **843**
(Rev. November 2002)
Department of the Treasury
Internal Revenue Service

Claim for Refund and Request for Abatement

▶ **See separate instructions.**

OMB No. 1545-0024

Use Form 843 only if your claim involves (a) one of the taxes shown on line 3a or (b) a refund or abatement of interest, penalties, or additions to tax on line 4a.
Do not *use Form 843 if your claim is for —*
- *An overpayment of income taxes;*
- *A refund for nontaxable use (or sales) of fuel; or*
- *An overpayment of excise taxes reported on Form(s) 11-C, 720, 730, or 2290.*

Type or print		
Name of claimant		Your SSN or ITIN
Address (number, street, and room or suite no.)		Spouse's SSN or ITIN
City or town, state, and ZIP code		Employer identification number (EIN)
Name and address shown on return if different from above		Daytime telephone number

1 Period. Prepare a separate Form 843 for each tax period
From _____ to _____

2 Amount to be refunded or abated
$

3a Type of tax, penalty, or addition to tax:
☐ Employment ☐ Estate ☐ Gift ☐ Excise (see instructions)
☐ Penalty — IRC section ▶ _____

b Type of return filed (see instructions):
☐ 706 ☐ 709 ☐ 940 ☐ 941 ☐ 943 ☐ 945 ☐ 990-PF ☐ 4720 ☐ Other (specify)

4a Request for abatement or refund of:
☐ Interest as a result of IRS errors or delays.
☐ A penalty or addition to tax as a result of erroneous advice from the IRS.

b Dates of payment ▶

5 **Explanation and additional claims.** Explain why you believe this claim should be allowed, and show computation of tax refund or abatement of interest, penalty, or addition to tax. If you need more space, attach additional sheets.

Signature. If you are filing Form 843 to request a refund or abatement relating to a joint return, both you and your spouse must sign the claim. Claims filed by corporations must be signed by a corporate officer authorized to sign, and the signature must be accompanied by the officer's title.

Under penalties of perjury, I declare that I have examined this claim, including accompanying schedules and statements, and, to the best of my knowledge and belief, it is true, correct, and complete.

Signature (Title, if applicable. Claims by corporations must be signed by an officer.) _____ Date _____

Signature _____ Date _____

For Privacy Act and Paperwork Reduction Act Notice, see separate instructions.

Form **843** (Rev. 11-2002)

ISA

HOW TO MAIL THE DEMAND

Keep in mind that the IRS receives millions of pieces of mail each month. For this reason, simply mailing your letter using first class mail gives you no evidence that the IRS actually received your submission. This is especially important for tax return filing since both the IRS and the U.S. Postal Service (USPS) routinely lose mail.

The solution to the problem is to mail *every* letter to the IRS using certified mail with return receipt requested. This procedure is a service provided by the USPS. For a small fee, the USPS requires the recipient to *sign* for the letter, and a signature verification card is then returned to the sender. In cases where the receipt of your letter is in question, the dispute ends with the production of a signed USPS return receipt card.

Mail the claim form and your letter demanding abatement to the service center that issued the notice. Be careful to make a photocopy of your response before sending it, and be equally careful to mail your response within the applicable time frame using certified mail with return receipt requested. Attach your postal receipts, including the certification card, to your copy of the demand. This way you have an accurate record of the correspondence.

LITTLE PROBLEMS–LITTLE SOLUTIONS

The overarching message of this discourse is simple: You must be prepared to handle a computerized notice. With each passing day, the potential that you may be on the receiving end of such a notice grows. But when prepared, the problems created by IRS demands remain little problems. If you are unprepared and taken by surprise, the little problem can quickly become a very large, ugly, and costly problem. We take comfort in knowing that virtually every IRS problem begins with a notice. Those discussed in this chapter are easily managed when you understand your rights.

3

End the "My Word Against Yours" Stalemate

The Secret Weapon in IRS Dispute Resolution

I once spoke with a woman who was notified by the IRS that she had failed to file a form critical to her small business corporation. The woman questioned the attorney who created the corporation. He explained that because the matter involved taxes, her accountant was required to file the form. The accountant told her that he "might have filed it" but he could not recall.

Was the IRS correct and the form was not filed? Or was the form filed as required but the sleepy accountant merely neglected to keep a record? Even if the accountant did assure her that the form was filed, how would she persuade the IRS of this fact? Given that—at best—it would be her word against theirs, surely the IRS would reject her statement and conclude that the form was not filed.

This kind of problem presents itself regularly—but there is a very simple solution. This chapter lays out exactly how to employ that solution.

END THE DISPUTE NOW

Attorneys use a very simple document to clear up disputed facts in the "my word against yours" debate. That document is known as an affidavit. An affidavit is nothing more than a detailed, written statement setting forth claims of fact (historical events). The contents of the affidavit become testimony when verified by a notary public. Testimony is evidence given under oath by a witness in a legal proceeding. Affidavits are vitally important in the "my word against yours" contest with the IRS. This is because the IRS rarely, *if ever*, has any hard evidence to refute your sworn statement.

When an affidavit is written properly, signed, notarized, then presented to the IRS as proof of your actions, the affidavit must be treated as testimony, just as though offered to a judge in a courtroom. More important, that testimony must be *accepted* and *acted* upon by the IRS *as truth* in the absence of evidence to the contrary.

To put this into perspective, consider the woman whose accountant could not remember whether he filed a critical corporate tax form. The IRS claimed that the form was not filed and sought to deprive her of favorable tax treatment she would otherwise enjoy. In such a case, she could not suggest to the agency that the form *should* have been filed or that she *must* have submitted it. But she must submit an affidavit declaring that the form was *in fact* filed and offering a specific explanation of how she accomplished the filing. If she responded with an affidavit, the IRS would be forced to accept her pronouncement as gospel.

You might ask, "Why should the IRS accept her word for it if they know the form was not filed?" Please understand that the IRS does not "know" whether she filed the form or not. IRS employees merely review computer records and determine that the form does not "appear" to have been filed because it does not show up on the computer files. The difference is profound.

No IRS employee can claim that he shadowed you all year, watched your every move, and therefore has personal knowledge of the fact that you did not file a given form. IRS notices regarding alleged failures to act are not based upon the personal knowledge of any single person. The notices are based solely and exclusively upon computer searches. A document that was *mailed* to the IRS but never *arrived* at the service center, or one that arrived but was *lost* or somehow misprocessed, will *not* appear on the computer record. However, that does not mean you failed to file the form.

The next question is, "Why don't they just look for it?" Bear in mind again that the typical service center receives tens of millions of paper submissions annually. And while there are procedures in place to physically find a given document, finding it is possible only if it was entered into the system in the first place. This is why the IRS queries its computer systems to determine whether a document was entered into the system. If it does not show the document as entered into the system, it merely notes in computer-generated files that "no record of receiving the return exists."[1] Though this shows that the IRS does not have the document in its system, it *does not prove* you never mailed it.

Now you might say, "I file my tax returns and I pay my taxes. Why do I have to worry that the IRS might suggest I failed to do so?" Consider this: The 125 million or so individual tax returns filed in 2001 were mailed to just ten IRS service centers. While the IRS pushes to promote electronic filing, the vast majority of returns are still filed in paper form the old-fashioned way—through the mail. Service center employees perform the labor-intensive task of sorting returns and preparing them for data processing. While the IRS has made great strides in data processing, the mail must still be opened and handled before the computers take over. Within this aspect of the process, great potential for error exists.

Individual tax returns are only one aspect of the processing work done in the service centers. The IRS processes about a hundred million business tax returns annually as well as about 1.3 billion information returns (though most of those are filed electronically), tens of millions of letters and other correspondence, and a myriad of forms related to the administration of the tax laws. And, on average, the IRS processes more than sixty-two million separate payments each year. Suffice it to say that the IRS faces a blizzard of paper filings, electronic filings, and tax payments annually, the majority of which hit between January and April.

In addition to the various processing errors discussed more generally in chapter 2, the IRS accuses approximately two million people of failing to file tax returns in a given year. In many of these cases, the IRS prepares what it calls a substitute for return (SFR) if it receives no satisfactory response from the citizen. However, as we already know from our general discussion of IRS notices, these nonfiler claims are incorrect about half the time. Consequently, the IRS assessments under the SFR program are likewise incorrect. However, those details do not hinder the IRS when it comes to enforcing collection of their assessments.

In the area of tax collection, the IRS likewise makes mistakes in processing that lead to claims for taxes that have already been paid. For example, in its annual discussion of the IRS financial statements, the General Accounting Office routinely points to a "pervasive problem" that results in inaccurate account balances. The problem is caused by the IRS's failure to properly credit payments made by citizens to their accounts. In 1999 the GAO described this problem in detail, reporting that this condition led to a situation where the IRS pursued "collection efforts against taxpayers who had already paid their taxes in full."[2]

This is just one of the IRS's many accounting problems. The most recent GAO report on the issue shows that the IRS continues to be "hindered by significant errors and delays in recording taxpayer information and payments." The GAO concludes that these unresolved problems "erode the confidence of the nation's taxpayers in the integrity and fairness of the tax collection system."[3] This is a colossal understatement—to say the least.

The Taxpayer Advocate states that "lost or misapplied payments" are a very common problem in the TA's inventory of cases. In just the two filing seasons of 2000 and 2001, the IRS lost or misdated the payments of nearly two hundred thousand citizens, leading to the improper assessment of penalties and interest.[4] The TA describes these failures as "flagrant or egregious errors, which violate either statutes or the IRS's own established administrative procedures." The TA gives the following as just one example of how these errors cause "serious harm" to citizens:

> The IRS misapplied payments made by a taxpayer. The Service then defaulted her installment agreement and levied $25,000 from her IRA. Later, the IRS located her missing payments and applied them to her account. The IRS then reinstated her installment agreement and returned the levied funds to the taxpayer. However, current law prevented the taxpayer from restoring the proceeds to her IRA. She was also required to include the $25,000 distribution in her taxable income for the year in which the levy occurred.[5]

The 2002 Taxpayer Advocate's report makes the sobering declaration that "due to the large volume of payments we handle each year, it is virtually impossible to ensure that the process is error free."[6]

Not all problems are the fault of the IRS. Many tax payments are now funneled through the IRS's Lockbox Program. This is a network of financial institutions that process remittances of taxes by citizens on behalf of the IRS. Remittances through intermediaries supposedly reduce the IRS's workload, making it easier for the agency to manage the annual storm of payments. However, in 2001 it was discovered that more than seventy thousand checks valued at more than $1.2 billion were missing at the lockbox site operated by the Mellon Bank in Pittsburgh.[7] This touched off great concern over whether individuals would be double-billed for payments made but lost or stolen from the Mellon Bank office.

All of this evidence supports the clear finding that just because you pay your taxes and file your returns and other required documents on time, there's no guarantee that you will not be challenged by the

IRS. In fact, given the ever-increasing number of payments, tax return filings, and other documents processed, I submit that you have a greater, not lesser, chance of being challenged by the IRS as time goes on. But with the affidavit as part of your defense arsenal, you are virtually assured of winning the "my word against yours" contest.

PROVING YOU FILED A FORM–THE BASICS

With the IRS, an ounce of prevention is worth a thousand pounds of cure. By following certain steps prior to filing any tax form, you can avoid the "my word against yours" quagmire. These are the basics:

1. Never mail anything to the IRS, whether a tax return, a payment device, etc., without keeping an *exact* photocopy of the submission. Your claim that you filed a given document or paid a tax is more plausible when you can provide the IRS with a copy of the disputed document.

2. Never mail any letter to the IRS, *especially* your income tax return and related documents, without using certified mail, return receipt requested. This service, provided by the USPS for a modest fee, could be worth hundreds of times what you paid for it if you end up in a dispute with the IRS.

3. Carefully store both the return receipt card and the postage receipt (which bears a USPS postmark with the date of mailing) with your copy of the submission. Both postage receipts are critical because one shows the date of mailing and the other shows the signature of the recipient and the date the submission was received. In the case of the IRS, this card will bear a stamp from the service center that received your mailing. If you do not use certified mail, you have absolutely no record of the postmark date. That can be trouble.

4. Never send multiple documents in a single envelope. As you will see later in this chapter, the IRS regularly fails to process all docu-

ments mailed in a single envelope. Therefore, if you are filing three separate tax returns, send each one in a separate envelope. The additional mailing costs will more than pay for themselves in terms of hassle and expense you might avoid later.

USING AN AFFIDAVIT TO PROVE YOU FILED

Before we discuss the affidavit's specific uses, it is important to understand its various elements. This way, you can adapt my examples to your specific facts and circumstances, regardless of the nature of the IRS claim.

Please examine Exhibit 3–1. This is the skeleton of an affidavit. It shows nine separate areas into which you insert your specific facts. Let us address them in turn:

Area 1 is where you provide your name, address, social security number, and date of the affidavit.

Area 2 refers to the specific demand made by the IRS. Note the date of the demand and attach a copy to the affidavit, clearly marked as a copy.

Area 3 is the opening line of the affidavit, declaring that you have been sworn to tell the truth. What follows is therefore testimony, just as if given in a courtroom.

Area 4 is the body of the affidavit. This is where you set forth all relevant facts. To begin with, provide background information such as the year in question, the type of claim made by the IRS, and the date you received its notice. Give this information in simple, concise paragraphs.

Area 5 is where you set forth specific facts to contradict the IRS claim. Do this in short, concise paragraphs also. For example, if the claim is that you failed to file a tax return, declare with *specificity* the date the return was deposited with the USPS. Attach a copy of your return and copies of the postal receipts for certified mail. NOTE: *Never send your original documents to the IRS*. Provide clear photocopies only!

EXHIBIT 3–1. Affidavit Skeleton

1. Name
   Address
   City, State, Zip
   Date of Affidavit
   SSN

2. RE: IRS Notice Dated ——— (copy attached)

3. STATE OF ———
   COUNTY OF ———

   I, [your name], being first duly sworn on oath, depose and state:

4. Background facts regarding the IRS notice, including:
   a. Date of receipt
   b. Specific demand made
   c. Tax year at issue.

5. Specific claims and facts to the contrary, including:
   a. Date your form was mailed, manner in which mailed, and address to which mailed
   b. Copies of return receipt documents attached (if available)
   c. Copy of form in question attached, from your retained file copy (if available).

6. Specific investigative steps taken to prove filing, including:
   a. Conversations with IRS personnel
   b. IRS documents (attach copies if available).

7. Ultimate conclusion drawn from all facts:
   a. You did in fact file document or pay tax
   b. IRS's claim to the contrary to be canceled
   c. All penalties and interest to be canceled.

8. Your signature

9. Subscribed and Sworn to before me, a Notary Public, in and for the

County of ———, State of ———.

Notary Public _____

My Commission Expires: ———

Area 6 is used to provide information regarding the investigative steps taken. For example, it is common for people to phone the IRS upon receiving a curious notice. Sometimes conversations with IRS personnel can be telling in one way or another, as I explain in more detail later in this chapter. If so, describe the conversation in the affidavit, including the employee's name and ID number, which IRS personnel are obligated to provide. Also, if you obtained documents of any kind relative to your claim, submit copies if they offer any probative information. For example, a canceled check showing the IRS deposit stamp proves that the IRS in fact received the payment you made.

Area 7 must set forth the ultimate conclusion to be drawn from the facts set forth in the affidavit. In the case of a failure to file a claim, for example, declare that you *in fact* filed the return on time. Also declare that the IRS claims to the contrary should be canceled or abated, together with any alleged additional interest and penalties.

Area 8 is the space for your signature, which should be affixed to the affidavit in the *presence* of an authorized notary public in and for your county. Notaries are readily available at banks and insurance companies and charge a very small fee to notarize a document.

Area 9 is known as the "jurat." It is the official verification by the notary that the statements were made by you under oath. With a notary's signature and official stamp on the affidavit, your statements become sworn testimony entitled to the same respect as though made in a court of law.

SPECIFIC AFFIDAVITS THAT OVERTURN ERRONEOUS IRS ALLEGATIONS

Let us examine specific cases of how to use an affidavit to defeat IRS claims.

The IRS Claims You Did Not File Your Tax Return

You face two potential problems if you do not file your tax return using certified mail. The first is that the form may not arrive at the service center on time, or *at all*. The second is that after the form does arrive, it may be lost or somehow misprocessed.

We know that the IRS issues nearly two million notices each year claiming that citizens failed to file their tax returns, many of which are erroneous. Most situations involving lost returns start with a mere service center notice. In such a case, the IRS mails a letter claiming that it "has no record of receiving your return." The notice asks that you either prove you filed the return or cure the filing delinquency. This problem is easily corrected by using an affidavit such as that shown in Exhibit 3–2.

The nonfiling allegation also arises in cases where you already have a tax delinquency for prior years. In that situation you may be on an installment agreement to pay delinquent taxes when the IRS suddenly claims that you failed to file a current return. In this case, the IRS threatens to revoke your installment agreement if you do not file your return. This can be very serious since the absence of an installment agreement allows the agency to enforce collection through wage and bank levies.

Another common situation in which an affidavit is beneficial is when the IRS claims your return was filed late. A tax return is considered filed on the date it is mailed, if it is filed on time. Envelopes containing tax returns received by the IRS after the filing deadline are supposed to be examined to determine the postmark date. However, if returns are not processed properly, IRS personnel can record the received date as the filing date. In this manner, returns are mistakenly treated as though they were filed late. If this happens, a notice is mailed to the citizen demanding a late filing penalty.

Jack owed the IRS money for several years and he failed to file tax returns for three subsequent years. Before settlement negotiations could proceed, Jack had to cure his filing delinquency. I instructed him to prepare the delinquent returns and file them using certified mail with return receipt requested. Jack retained copies of his returns and carefully preserved the certified mail postal receipts for his files.

Several months after Jack filed the delinquent returns, the collection officer monitoring the case accused Jack of failing to file one of those returns. Settlement negotiations would stall and Jack's wages could be levied if the problem were not cured immediately. To counter the allegation, we drafted an affidavit to prove that the return was indeed filed.

The affidavit declared that Jack filed three returns at once by mailing them in a single envelope. The affidavit stated that the returns were mailed via certified mail, and he attached to the affidavit copies of both postal receipts and a copy of the tax return itself. Please see Exhibit 3–2, Affidavit of Jack, for an example of what Jack submitted to the IRS.

Other than the bald claim that Jack did not file the return in question, the IRS was unable to present any evidence to contradict Jack's affidavit. My speculation is that when his envelope containing the three separate tax returns was received, an IRS processor noticed two returns but overlooked the third. Consequently it was never processed and the IRS computer records indicated that it was not filed.

After reviewing our affidavit, the IRS conceded without further dispute that Jack's return was in fact filed as claimed. The affidavit's precise clarity and affirmative declarations disarmed the IRS's contrary assertion.

Obviously, when your facts and circumstances are different from those discussed in Jack's affidavit, you are responsible for adapting your statement to your own facts. For example, when responding to the claim that you filed your return late, you must be careful to note that timely filing means mailing prior to midnight on the due date of the return. Jack's affidavit is a good example of how to craft a response, but it cannot function as a form letter for every situation. Such may be said of every affidavit in this chapter.

This problem and others like it are avoidable when you follow the four basic steps set out above.

EXHIBIT 3–2. Affidavit of Jack

STATE OF ——
COUNTY OF ——

1. My name is Jack ——. My address is ——. My social security number is ——.

2. On —— [date], Revenue Officer —— made the claim that my income return for the year —— was not filed. This statement is in error.

3. The return was filed on —— [date]. The return was filed together with returns for the years —— and ——. An envelope containing the three returns was mailed via certified mail, return receipt requested, to the IRS Service Center in Kansas City, MO. Attached to this affidavit as Exhibit A is a true copy of the receipt for certified mail, Item No. ——, dated ——. Also in Exhibit A is the Post Office Domestic Return Receipt for Item No. ——, bearing the "received" stamp of the IRS at 2306 Bannister Road, Kansas City, MO.

4. All three returns were mailed to the IRS in the same envelope on —— [date], with first class and certified mail postage prepaid.

5. The IRS received my return for —— [year] on —— [date].

6. Attached to this affidavit is a true and correct copy of my retained copy of the original tax return filed on —— [date]. The original was mailed to the IRS as indicated above.

7. The claim that I failed to file a tax return for —— [year] is incorrect. The return was filed by mailing the same via certified mail to the IRS Service Center in Kansas City. Based upon these facts, the claim of failure to file for —— [year] should be set aside as invalid.

Subscribed and sworn to before me this —— [date].

Jack ——

Notary Public: _____

My Commission Expires: ——

The IRS Claims You Did Not Obtain a Filing Extension for Your Tax Return

For those of us who scramble for more time to file our returns every April, Form 4868, *Application for an Automatic Extension of Time to File US Individual Income Tax Return,* is a welcomed friend. With this form, you obtain an automatic four-month extension of time to file Form 1040, pushing the deadline from April 15 to August 15. The extension frees you of penalties for failure to file the return on time provided you pay your estimated taxes as required.

Please note that filing the extension form does not give you an extension of time to pay taxes. That is available under another procedure, discussed in the next section. The filing extension form contains a brief section that asks you to estimate your total income tax debt for the year in question. This can be done based upon your prior year's tax liability. The estimated tax debt must be paid through a combination of wage withholding (quarterly payments for self-employed people) and a final payment mailed with the filing extension, Form 4868. The estimate is reconciled with your actual tax debt when you file the return.

Because the filing extension does not give you more time to pay your taxes, use it only when you need more time to gather records essential to preparing your return. Maybe you are dealing with third parties such as corporations or partnerships and need records from those entities before you can finish your return. Also, people often lose records during the course of a year to fire, flood, residential or business moves, etc. These records have to be reconstructed in order to prepare an accurate return. Use the filing extension form to win more time to get the job done.

In any event, the IRS misprocesses these forms as well. For this reason, you must be prepared to handle the agency's claim that you filed your return late, even if you used the filing extension, Form 4868, properly.

Paul received a notice from the IRS assessing a late filing penalty for his alleged failure to file his tax return on time. We shot back an affidavit to counter the claim. Please see Exhibit 3–3.

Prior to April 15, Paul filed Form 4868, pushing his filing deadline to August 15. Paul's return was filed on August 9. Therefore the return was filed on time. Paul's affidavit carefully pointed out that he filed Form 4868 (a copy was attached) and also explained the reasons why he needed additional time to file. Unfortunately, postal receipts were unavailable because Paul did not use certified mail. Nevertheless, he firmly declared in his affidavit that the extension was filed *prior* to April 15 and his return was filed *prior* to August 15.

Shortly after Paul submitted the affidavit, the IRS notified him that the penalty was abated. Paul's one-page affidavit saved him $116.52. Not a bad return on investment, considering that the cost of mailing the letter was less than three dollars.

You can often avoid this problem by simply submitting a copy of your filing extension form with your tax return when you file it. This way, service center processors are alerted to the fact that you filed the extension. It is even more helpful if you provide copies of the USPS certified mail cards with your return at the time of filing.

The IRS Claims You Paid Your Taxes Late

Form 1127, *Application for Extension of Time for Payment of Tax*, has been a great mystery within the IRS. For years the agency has denied that the form even exists. I vividly recall a former IRS commissioner's appearance on a network TV morning talk show one April 15 several years ago. The host asked him what a person could do if he could not pay his taxes by midnight. The commissioner just shrugged, not even articulating any kind of answer. As a result of this kind of misinformation, few citizens understand that an extension of time to pay is available or how to obtain it.

Many people using the filing extension, Form 4868, do not actually need additional time to file their returns—they need time to pay their taxes. However, Form 4868 does not extend the time to *pay* the tax. Your taxes must be paid on or before April 15, or you face interest and the failure-to-pay penalty. That is where the payment extension, Form 1127, comes into play. If granted, it buys you up to six additional months to pay your taxes, without penalties (but interest accrues). Even if the IRS turns down your request, you can use Form 1127 as the basis for canceling penalties later on.

In chapter 9, under the heading *Avoiding Wage and Bank Levies*, I give you all the details on using the payment extension form to prevent enforced collection action. The key here is that you must use this form in connection with filing a tax return. Do not expect the IRS to grant a payment extension if you do not file your return on time.

But because of the processing errors at the IRS service centers, even using the payment extension form is no guarantee that the IRS will not bill you for failure to pay penalties. Therefore, if a bill for penalties arrives, fire off an affidavit substantially the same as that shown in Exhibit 3–3. The difference is that this affidavit must address the payment extension, Form 1127, rather than the filing extension, Form 4868. The text of your affidavit must also address the facts that (1) your return was filed on time, and (2) under the terms of Form 1127, the payment of your tax liability is *not* late.

EXHIBIT 3–3

Paul M. ———

Address

City, State, Zip

Date:

SSN:

Internal Revenue Service

Regional Service Center

Andover, MA 05501

STATE OF ———

COUNTY OF ———

AFFIDAVIT

Reference is made to your Request for Payment, dated ——— (copy attached to this affidavit). The notice demands payment of $116.52 in penalty and interest for "late filing" my federal income tax return.

For the reasons stated in this affidavit, the penalty is improper and should be abated. These are the facts:

On ——— [date] I filed with the IRS a properly signed and executed Form 4868, *Application for Automatic Extension of Time to File US Individual Income Tax Return.* A true and correct copy of the application is attached to this affidavit. The reason for filing the application was that certain records of my income were not available to me from which I could prepare and submit a correct tax return. Without the records, it would have been impossible for me to submit a truthful and accurate tax return.

By filing Form 4868, the IRS extended the period in which I could file a timely tax return to and including August 15. I submitted the return by mailing it on ——— [date]. Thus the return was filed *before the extended filing period expired.*

My reason for filing the application was to comply with my legal requirements to submit a tax return that is timely, truthful, and accurate in all respects. By filing the return prior to August 15, ———, which I did do, I complied with the timeliness aspects of my obligations.

Based upon these facts, it is clear that I did not file my return late as alleged by the IRS in the attached notice. Therefore the penalty is improper and should be abated.

Paul M. ———

Subscribed and sworn to before me this ——— [date].

Notary Public: _____

My Commission Expires: ———

The IRS Claims You Owe Penalties for Failure to Pay Estimated Income Taxes

If you do not make the required estimated income tax payments, the IRS penalizes you based upon a complicated formula. When you know you underpaid your estimated taxes, the law requires that you submit the underpayment penalty at the time of filing Form 1040. The form for calculating the underpayment is Form 2210, *Underpayment of Estimated Tax by Individuals*. The form is attached to Form 1040 and submitted at the time of filing the return.

The common thread running through this chapter is that the IRS fails to properly process forms, returns, and correspondence that people file. The underpayment penalty form is no exception. For this reason, even if you file the form properly and pay the penalty, do not make the mistake of believing that the IRS will not challenge you. If it does, stand ready with an affidavit.

For example, Doug filed his federal income tax return and paid his liability of $7,181.65 on April 15 but had neglected to make estimated tax payments during the course of the year. Consequently, he added the penalty for underpaying estimated taxes to his tax bill and filed the underpayment penalty form with his tax return. His submission was sent via certified mail with return receipt requested.

Shortly thereafter, Doug received a demand for payment of penalties, allegedly for underpaying his estimated taxes. Because he paid the penalty when the return was filed, the notice constituted a double charge.

Doug responded with an affidavit. Please see Exhibit 3–4. Doug's affidavit included copies of Form 1040, Form 2210, and the canceled check used to pay the tax and penalty in full. Doug also included copies of the postal receipts to prove that he had filed the return and that the IRS received it. Lastly, he articulated the ultimate declaration that the penalty was paid and that the additional assessment should be abated.

The IRS responded to Doug's affidavit with a notice saying that it canceled the additional penalty. This simple process saved Doug over four hundred dollars.

EXHIBIT 3–4

Doug ————

Address

City, State, Zip

Date:

SSN:

Internal Revenue Service Center
Kansas City, MO 64999

STATE OF ————

COUNTY OF ————

AFFIDAVIT OF DOUG ————

1. Reference is made to your Request for Payment, dated ———— (copy attached). The notice demands payment of $421.83 in penalty and interest for allegedly underpaying my estimated income tax liability. For the reasons stated in this affidavit, the penalty is improper and should be abated. The facts are:

2. I filed a timely tax return. A true and correct copy of my Form 1040 with all its accompanying schedules is attached to this affidavit. The tax liability shown on Form 1040 is $7,181.65. In addition to the sum of $7,181.65, I included in my payment to the IRS the amount of $390. As shown on page 2 of Form 1040, that amount was computed as the penalty for underpayment of estimated taxes. Form 2210, *Underpayment of Estimated Tax by Individuals*, was used to compute the $390. It was attached to Form 1040. See attached copy.

3. When the tax return was filed, I included full payment of the tax, plus the $390 penalty. The total remitted to the IRS was $7,571.65. Attached to this affidavit is a copy of the check (front and back) used to make the payment. Forms 1040, Form 2210, and the check for full payment were mailed to the IRS via certified mail. Attached to this affidavit are copies of the postal receipts showing that the IRS received these documents.

4. Based upon these facts, it is clear that I have already properly computed and paid the penalty for failure to make estimated tax payments. Therefore your notice and demand for payment are improper and must be abated.

Doug ————

Subscribed and sworn to before me this ———— [date].

Notary Public: _____

My Commission Expires: ————

The IRS Claims You Failed to Pay Your Taxes

Claims alleging that you failed to pay your taxes are treated in much the same manner as those regarding the failure to file returns. In this case, however, you have the advantage of being able to more definitively trace your payment. If you used a check, the actual canceled check is available, either through your own records or from bank records. Your bank statement shows whether the check was actually cashed. That is helpful in determining whether the payment was lost, as in the Mellon Bank cases, or somehow misapplied by the IRS. Payments through other means, such as money order, cashier's check, or credit card, are equally traceable.

In the vast majority of cases, a simple affidavit that makes reference to the date of payment and the payment device and that provides a copy (both front and back) of the canceled check or other payment evidence does the job. An example of such an affidavit is shown in Exhibit 3–5.

While the Taxpayer Advocate's annual report teaches that it is impossible to completely avoid the misapplication of payments to the IRS, I have five simple steps to follow that will minimize your risk. They are:

1. Use an easily traceable payment device to pay your taxes. For example, a check is easily traceable through your bank account. If you do not have a checking account, use a bank cashier's check rather than a money order. Cashier's checks are more easily traced than money orders.

2. Be sure to clearly write your entire name and social security number on the face of the payment device, along with the tax period for which the payment is made.

3. Include a cover letter explaining what the payment is for and include your full name and social security number in the cover letter. When paying taxes at the time of filing your tax return, use IRS Form 1040-V, *Payment Voucher*. This simple form helps to ensure that your payments are properly posted to your account.

4. Make separate payments on separate tax accounts using separate payment devices. Be sure to send each payment under separate cover rather than group them in a single submission. Likewise, do not commingle business and personal tax payments in a single submission.

5. Always send your correspondence via certified mail with return receipt requested.

EXHIBIT 3–5. Affidavit of [Your Name]

Name
Address
City, State, Zip

Date:
SSN:

STATE OF ———

COUNTY OF ———

1. By letter dated ———, the IRS notified me that my taxes for the year have not been paid. This statement is in error.

2. My taxes for the year in question were paid at the time of filing my tax return. The return was filed on ——— [date] by mailing it to the IRS service center at ——— [address]. The return and payment were mailed via certified mail. Attached to this affidavit are true and correct copies of the U.S. Postal Service receipts showing the date of mailing and showing that the IRS received my tax return and check on ——— [date].

3. My taxes in the amount of $——— were paid with my personal check, number ———. Attached to this affidavit is a copy of the face and reverse side of check number ———. The copy shows that the check was written on ——— [date] and was processed by the IRS through the ——— [name of bank as shown on back of canceled check]. The check then cleared my bank on ——— [date]. Also attached to this affidavit is a true copy of my bank statement for the month of ———, indicating that check number ——— was paid on ——— [date]. [If taxes were partially paid through wage withholding or with more than one check, include copies of Form W-2 and all other checks.]

4. Based upon these facts, it is clear that I have already paid my federal income taxes in full. Therefore your notice and demand for payment are improper and are due to be abated.

Your Name

Subscribed and sworn to before me ——— [date].

Notary Public: _____

My Commission Expires: ———

Using the IRS's Own Records Against It

Because of the scope and breadth of the IRS's systems, it is common for the left hand to miss what the right hand does. For example, because of the agency's somewhat disjointed computer systems, it is possible that a return or other document filing appears on the agency's service center computers but does not appear on field computers used by individual agents. When you know you filed a tax return with the service center but local IRS personnel question the filing, it is sometimes fruitful to use IRS Form 4506, *Request for Copy or Transcript of Tax Form,* to prove you filed the document.

Form 4506 is a simple form that asks the service center to provide either a photocopy of your tax return or a transcript showing the tax return information. If the service center has the form on file, it provides a copy of the document and a certification that it is a "true and correct" copy. The certification sports an impressive IRS seal and the signature of the service center official responsible for maintaining the records.

Don used this form to his benefit during his audit. In the course of the examination, the agent questioned Don regarding another return. Eventually the agent accused Don of not filing the return. Don could not understand the accusation since he certainly did file. He presented his retained copy to the agent but the agent was unimpressed. Since the document was not mailed via certified mail, the agent was disinclined to believe it was filed.

Rather than argue with the agent, Don simply made a request of the service center for a copy of the return he knew he filed. He used Form 4506 to make the request. A short time later, the service center mailed Don a copy of the tax return.

This was either a case of the left hand not knowing what the right hand was doing or the agent was simply harassing Don. In either event, the request for tax return, Form 4506, produced a signed and "sealed" copy of the return that unequivocally settled the claim in Don's favor.

THE MOST COMPLETE APPROACH TO THE
AFFIDAVIT PROCESS

In each of the above examples, I showed how one person solved his problem with a simple affidavit. In each situation, certain aspects of the case made success more probable. And while no person had everything going for him, each was successful. Often you have no control over the circumstances of the case, but there are almost always steps you can take to help ensure success.

Through my experiences, I developed a list of steps that constitute the most complete approach to resolving a given situation. I use these procedures as my model for the perfect approach even today. Here they are:

1. *Do not ignore the problem.* If the IRS is corresponding with you, there is something amiss—even if the agency's demand seems irrational or unreasonable. You cannot hope the problem will go away or fix itself once the IRS comes to its senses. Sometimes it is helpful to phone the IRS for clarification on issues, but recognize the high error rate of the agency's employees and always follow up your conversations with a letter of confirmation. Be sure to act within the time period for asserting your rights. Remember: If you do not assert your rights within the time allowed by law, you waive them—period.

2. *Keep careful notes of any conversations you have with IRS personnel.* Include the name of the person you spoke with, that person's employee ID number, and the date of your conversation. Record your conversation using an "I said/he said" format. Make the notes as complete and as accurate as possible. Sign them, date them, and place them in your personal file. Your notes can provide the basis for explaining your actions and establishing any admissions the IRS might make, and they serve as an excellent means to refresh your recollection of the conversation months, even years later.

3. *Submit information requests to the IRS to help gather documents to the extent possible.* The two key ways of doing this are (1) IRS Form 4506 and (2) the Freedom of Information Act (FOIA). As I outline in chapter 1, you can use the FOIA to obtain your Individual or Business Master File records. These are computerized logs of your account history. These files are very helpful for proving return filing dates, as well as showing IRS activity on the account.

4. *Most important, create an affidavit that is very specific as to the steps you followed to discharge your legal duties.* The affidavit should also describe the steps taken to resolve the problem. Attach copies of relevant documents and the notes of any conversations with IRS personnel. Finally, the affidavit must boldly and clearly declare that you discharged your duty (e.g., filed the return or paid the tax) and clearly ask the IRS for a ruling to that effect.

When you apply these lessons, expect to prevail in any dispute where the matter boils down to your word against theirs. The following case study illustrates this point.

In 1989, Dave formed a new corporation to operate his small business. To take advantage of small business corporation status (the so-called S corporation), Dave filed IRS Form 2553, *Election by Small Business Corporation*, within the time required. At the same time, Dave applied for an Employer's Identification Number (EIN). He mailed all the proper forms to the service center. Shortly thereafter, the IRS notified Dave in writing that it had assigned an EIN to his new business.

While preparing his business tax return, Dave's accountant noticed that the IRS had sent a forms kit for regular corporations, not S corporations. The accountant speculated that the IRS never received the S election. "What will happen if they didn't?" Dave asked. "They will treat you as a regular corporation, and that will cost you money," responded the accountant.

Concerned, Dave phoned the IRS to try to avert the problem. After he explained the situation, the IRS assister stated, "Because of

the volume of work at the service center, data entry operators sometimes neglect to process multiple forms submitted in a single filing.
They may have overlooked the 2553."

Dave questioned the IRS employee as to the procedures for solving the problem *before* the IRS assessed additional taxes or penalties.
The assister explained that there was nothing Dave could do but wait
for the storm. To make matters worse, she even explained that it was
highly unlikely the IRS would permit a retroactive S election. That
meant Dave would be stuck with increased taxes attributable to the
IRS's processing error.

Dave reported all his findings to the accountant, saying "We dis-
covered the problem before the IRS did. We must be able to fix it."
The accountant's response was simple: "I don't think even your friend
Dan Pilla can get you out of this one."

With that challenge, I went to work. I assigned Dave the task of
making a record of his conversation with the IRS assister. As closely
as possible, Dave wrote down his conversation using the "I said/she
said" format. The notes could be used later to establish Dave's good
faith effort to resolve the situation.

Next, I made an FOIA request for copies of the documents Dave
filed. Because the IRS had issued an EIN to his new corporation, it was
certain the agency had at least received that application. This fact
would help to prove that the small business election form was also filed.

With the return filing deadline approaching, we decided to file
the corporate tax return as though the S election were properly made
and waited for the IRS to react. As expected, just two months after
filing the return, Dave received a notice claiming that no S election
was on file and threatening to disregard his S status.

In response, Dave submitted a thorough affidavit carefully describing how the small business election form and the application for EIN
had been mailed. We provided copies of each form and the transmittal
cover letter. Since the IRS had issued an EIN, a copy of that letter was
attached to the affidavit.

The affidavit detailed both Dave's conversation with the accountant and his conversation with IRS personnel. We attached to the affi-

davit copies of Dave's notes of the latter conversation. Next, Dave explained that an FOIA request had been made for all documents. A copy of the IRS's acknowledgement of that request was also attached to the affidavit.

Finally, the affidavit declared that Dave had filed the small business election form in a timely fashion and that the failure to process it was the IRS's error. He concluded his affidavit by stating that the corporate tax return should be accepted as filed. The affidavit was signed and notarized and the original mailed to the IRS via certified mail.

Just a few weeks later, the IRS agreed in writing to accept the S election retroactive to the time it was filed.

USE A COVER LETTER

Affidavits should never be transmitted to the IRS without a cover letter. The substance of the cover letter is very simple. It should explain that the affidavit is submitted in response to the IRS claim and constitutes proof that you filed your form or paid your taxes, contrary to the agency's claim. The cover letter should also contain a demand that the IRS reverse its position.

Given the track record of affidavits in resolving disputes with the IRS, I can state unequivocally that they are truly the best defense for the innocent citizen. With the affidavit, you establish facts that the IRS must consider in making a decision in your case. In the absence of evidence to the contrary (which never exists when the IRS is mistaken), your affidavit will carry the day.

4

Coping with Tax Penalties

How to Keep Tax Bills from Exploding

Tax penalties are the IRS equivalent of being taken out to the woodshed. Quite literally, penalties impose punitive treatment for failure to comply with your legal obligations. In a broad sense, penalties are intended to:

- Make citizens understand that noncompliance carries a cost

- Deter noncompliance by imposing explicit pecuniary fines

- Create the perception of fairness of the tax system by penalizing those who do not comply.

Unfortunately for the average citizen, penalties have mutated into much more than a tool of effective tax administration. They have become big business for the IRS. The assessment of penalties and interest routinely doubles, even triples a tax bill. This often makes it extremely difficult—sometimes impossible—for honest citizens to pay delinquent taxes.

Even when the underlying tax can be paid, the addition of penalties, at the very least, adds insult to injury. To most people, the addition of penalties communicates the notion that they are tax cheaters, who deserve some kind of punishment for violating IRS regulations.

The reality is that the vast majority of people hit with penalties are not deliberate tax cheaters. They are honest citizens doing their best to comply with an increasingly complex tax code, and they are doing so against the backdrop of growing financial pressures. For example, the most common penalties are those for failure to file returns and failure to pay taxes. Yet, most citizens hit with these penalties are victims of unforeseen personal or economic circumstances over which they had no control. They are victims of circumstances that placed them in a position where they had to make the difficult choice between paying their taxes and feeding their families. When faced with such a choice, reasonable people almost always opt to feed the family. But choosing to feed your family does not make you a tax cheater. For these reasons, the vast majority of penalty assessments are improper and subject to cancellation.

This chapter unlocks the secrets to winning cancellation of tax penalties. For millions of citizens, these secrets will spell the difference between a final, reasonable solution to their tax problem and financial bondage to the IRS for years to come.

A BRIEF HISTORY OF TAX PENALTIES

To understand the problems penalties pose, let us take a quick look at their history. The number of penalties in the tax code and the number of assessments of those penalties have, in a word, exploded over the years. For example, there were just thirteen penalty provisions in the 1954 code. By 1988 the number had grown to about a hundred and fifty.

This increase led to a congressional inquiry into penalty administration in the late 1980s. The result was legislation intended to reduce the number of penalties. But while there was a slight reduction in the number of penalty provisions—from about 150 to about 140—there was no drop in penalty assessments. That is to say, the IRS continues to assess penalties against individuals and businesses in growing numbers.

In fact, total penalty assessments rose steadily during the 1990s. Whereas in 1990 the IRS assessed 29.677 million penalties against individuals and businesses for a total revenue of $11.84 billion, in 2001 the IRS assessed 32.49 million penalties for a total revenue of $19.132 billion.[1] That is an all-time high in terms of revenue from penalties and represents an increase of nearly 21 percent over the 2000 figure of $15.835 billion.

Even worse, the 1980s legislation did nothing to address the

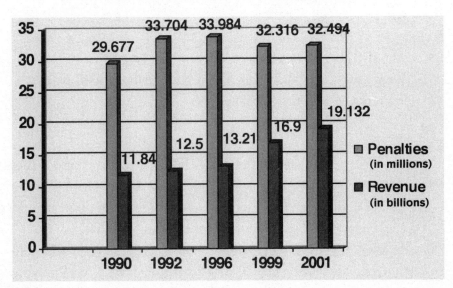

Penalty Assessments and Revenue

Even worse, the 1980s legislation did nothing to address the indiscriminate manner in which the IRS uses penalties. This is one key reason for the steady growth in penalty assessments. As in virtually every area of civil tax law, the burden of proof is on the citizen regarding the propriety of all but a precious few penalty provisions. This means that *you* must prove that a penalty assessment is improper. The IRS does not have to prove that its actions are proper.

Because of this, the IRS perceives that it is free to assess penalties against any person for any reason. Once assessed, the penalty is removed only after the citizen proves that the assessment is improper. Thus, in order to have any hope of canceling a penalty, you must understand your rights to challenge a penalty and how to do so. In the vast majority of cases, this is simple.

A chief reason the IRS is so successful collecting penalty assessments is that so few people understand their right of cancellation. The IRS addresses penalty cancellation in its Publication 1, *Your Rights as a Taxpayer,* but the discussion is hardly exhaustive. The sum and substance of the agency's treatment of the issue amounts to this sentence:

> The IRS will waive penalties when allowed by law if you can show you acted reasonably and in good faith or relied on the incorrect advice of an IRS employee.

This statement is accurate but by no means complete. The fact is, precious few people realize they have the right to abatement if they "acted reasonably" and even fewer understand how to prove it. Sadly, the IRS does not even begin to address the process. But I do, and my formula has twenty-five years of proven success behind it.

In fact, my experience shows that a properly crafted, well-documented abatement request meets with success up to 80 percent of the time. Given that we are usually dealing with thousands of dollars in penalties and interest on penalties in any given situation, it is well worth the effort to make such a presentation.

THE IRS PENALTY POLICY AND PHILOSOPHY

In 1992 the IRS adopted a comprehensive penalty policy and for the first time developed a Penalty Handbook designed to standardize penalty assessments and abatements.[2] The goal was to ensure that penalties are not used for improper purposes and that once a penalty is assessed, you have every opportunity to present a defense to an open-minded reviewer. Under the policy, a person is more likely now than ever to win abatement of penalties.

Examining the IRS Penalty Policy Statement and key aspects of the Penalty Handbook help us to better understand when penalties are intended to apply and how to get them canceled if they do not apply. The problem is that both the policy statement and the handbook are buried deep within the endless pages of the IRS Manual. Without the help of this book, the typical citizen is likely never to benefit from either tool.

IRS Penalty Policy Statement P-1-18 makes it clear that penalties are *not* to be used for the purposes of raising revenue. Rather, penalties are intended to punish noncompliance and deter potential noncompliance. The agency's penalty programs are to focus solely on the question of whether they do the best possible job of encouraging compliant conduct.

This means that the addition of penalties should not be "automatic" in the sense that a citizen must pay them regardless of the facts. The facts of the case dictate whether penalties apply. In cases where the facts show that your actions were not deliberately negligent or intentional, the penalties do not apply and *must be canceled*.

This is a marked departure from policies of the past, where penalties were used merely as a means to increase tax collection. Penalties were often added to the bill simply to up the ante for delinquent citizens. That, of course, made it even more difficult to clear the slate. As it stands now, penalties focus more upon one's good faith and reasonable cause than upon the IRS's lust for more revenue.

To this end, the current penalty system is designed to:

- Ensure consistency of results with penalty assessments and abatements

- Ensure accuracy of results in light of the facts and the law

- Provide methods for citizens to have their interests heard and considered when challenging a penalty

- Require impartiality in reviewing requests for abatement and a commitment to achieving the correct decision

- Allow for reversal of initial determinations when sufficient information is presented showing that the penalty is not proper

- Ensure that penalties are used for their proper purpose and not as bargaining points in the development or processing of cases.

The IRS Penalty Handbook echoes these statements and provides much additional insight into the purpose of penalties and the reasons the IRS will cancel penalties. I refer to the handbook throughout this chapter.

THE KEY TO CANCELING PENALTIES "GOOD FAITH AND REASONABLE CAUSE"

Virtually every one of the over 140 penalty provisions of the tax code contains a "good faith" or "reasonable cause" provision. This means that when you acted in good faith and based upon a reasonable cause for your actions and *not* out of a deliberate effort to cheat, deceive, or mislead the IRS, the penalty does not apply. Penalties are designed to achieve voluntary compliance by penalizing deliberate noncompliant behavior. They are *not* intended to make matters worse for delinquent citizens who are otherwise honest.

To win cancellation of a penalty, you must establish that you acted in "good faith" and based upon a "reasonable cause" for your actions. Let us examine both of these concepts in detail.

WHAT IS "GOOD FAITH"?

The idea of "good faith" speaks to a person's motive or intent in carrying out his actions or failures to act. You act in good faith when your actions, even if erroneous, were not intended to break the law and were based upon an underlying, sincere belief that you were behaving properly.

The following are a few specific examples of what constitutes good faith.

Ignorance of the Law

Citizens generally ignorant of the complicated tax laws and the myriad of regulations to implement them are not required to know the law in the same way that a lawyer is required to know the law. The maxim that "ignorance of the law is no excuse" generally does not apply to tax laws. Proving that you did not know your actions were incorrect can establish good faith and reasonable cause. The Penalty Handbook supports this conclusion, acknowledging that some citizens "may not be aware of specific" obligations under the tax code. It goes on to state that good faith and reasonable cause "may be established if the taxpayer shows ignorance of the law in conjunction with other facts and circumstances."[3]

To determine whether ignorance of the law is an appropriate defense, the IRS considers:

- Your education. If you are uneducated in matters of tax and finance generally, the IRS will hold you to a lower standard than it would a tax professional penalized for the same act.

- Whether you have been subject to the tax in the past. Those with personal experience in a given area of tax law are expected to know their duties under the law, whereas somebody with no experience would be cut some slack. For example, a person just starting a small business for the first time might not know about the requirement to make quarterly estimated payments.

- Whether you have been penalized for the same conduct in the past. Patterns of improper conduct are not looked upon favorably by the IRS.

- If there were recent changes in the tax forms or law that you could not reasonably be expected to know.

Reliance on Counsel

An extension of the above argument is the so-called reliance defense. This defense suggests that you relied in good faith upon the advice of a professional to guide your conduct. Because tax laws are so complex, you meet your general duty to ascertain your obligations if you seek the advice of qualified counsel and, based upon full and accurate disclosure of the facts, reasonably follow that advice. The handbook declares that "reliance on the advice of a tax advisor" is a defense. The handbook goes on to state, however, that the defense is "limited to issues generally considered technical or complicated."[4]

To prove this defense, you must show that you provided the adviser with all the relevant information needed to pass upon the question. You must then show that you followed counsel's advice and that the advice was "reasonable." It would not be reasonable for an adviser to suggest, for example, that a person earning wage income has the right to deduct all family vacation expenses as business expenses.

Counsel includes an income tax preparer, enrolled agent, attorney, accountant or other tax planner or expert upon whose advice you rely in good faith. Even if that advice later proved inaccurate, negligence is defeated when reasonable reliance is established.

Sometimes when this defense is asserted, the IRS asks if you sought a "second opinion" regarding your question. By this the agency suggests that you had a duty to question the advice or your adviser. In essence, the IRS tries to put you on trial for not knowing or learning that the advice you received was inaccurate.

You need to know that the law places no duty on you to obtain a second opinion unless the advice is so patently frivolous that a reasonable person would know it was inaccurate. On the other hand, where the advice involves technical, substantive or complicated issues of law, you have a right to rely upon that advice. As the Supreme Court has said:

> Most taxpayers are not competent to discern error in the substantive advice of an accountant or attorney. To require the taxpayer to challenge the attorney, to seek a "second opinion," or to try to monitor counsel on the provisions of the Code himself would nullify the very purpose of seeking the advice of a presumed expert in the first place.[5]

IRS Advice

Reliance upon the advice of the IRS is a defense against negligence if you can prove you received the advice from the IRS. Code section 6404(f) declares that a citizen is not subject to "any penalty" if it is attributable to "erroneous advice" provided "in writing" by an employee of IRS. The defense is available when each of the following applies:

- The written advice was reasonably relied upon.

- The written advice was in response to a specific written request.

- You provided adequate or accurate information upon which to base the advice.

Proving this defense is a simple matter. You need only present a copy of the IRS's letter containing the advice in question. You must also demonstrate that you provided all necessary and accurate information upon which to base the advice. This is proved by providing a copy of the letter you mailed seeking the advice.

Unfortunately, not all advice provided by the IRS is in writing. In fact, the IRS only provides advice in writing when the citizen submits his *request* in writing. The vast majority of citizens seek advice from the IRS via its toll-free telephone system. And as we discussed, the IRS's verbal advice is often inaccurate. Reliance upon the IRS continues to be a defense when the advice is verbal but is more difficult to prove.

According to section 6404(f), the IRS is required to abate penalties only when they are based upon erroneous "written" advice. However, the IRS declares that it has "extended this relief to include erroneous oral advice when appropriate."[6]

If you seek oral advice, you must document the date you phoned, the person you spoke with, including their employee ID number, the specific office you phoned, the questions asked, and as completely as possible, the answers received. This information is necessary to prove that a penalty is subject to abatement. Be sure to keep this information in your permanent tax file for the year in question. The better solution is simply to seek all advice in writing.

The "Notice" Requirement

Generally speaking, a citizen must be "on notice" that a given position taken in his return is erroneous before penalties can be assessed. I do not mean by this that the IRS is under an obligation to phone or write every citizen with an opinion of the adequacy of his return prior to filing it. This will not happen and is not required.

However, the IRS publishes regulations, statutes, court rulings, and other authority covering laws, rules of law, and operational guidelines in volumes of reference materials. When the IRS or the courts have not expressed an opinion as to the tax treatment of a particular item or transaction and it is shown by the citizen that no negative opinion existed at the time the treatment was elected, penalties cannot apply. When a published negative opinion as to the tax treatment of a particular item is on the books, you are considered "on notice" as to the IRS's official position, even though you may not have personally *read* that opinion or ruling. This is why it is so important to carefully research the legality of any particular structure or transaction, or engage a professional to do so, prior to assuming any potentially troublesome tax posture.

Good Faith Mistake

An extension of the above argument applies when a good faith mistake was made in your interpretation or application of the law, rulings, or regulations. Generally speaking, a mistake does not evidence good faith. However, when the surrounding facts and circumstances evidence that you acted reasonably and responsibly in determining your legal obligations, and nevertheless you made a mistake, that can be justification for abatement of a penalty, especially where complex issues are involved. The handbook states that "the reason for the mistake may be a supporting factor if additional facts and circumstances support the determination that the taxpayer exercised ordinary business care and prudence."[7]

WHAT IS "REASONABLE CAUSE"?

In the Penalty Handbook, the IRS provides detailed discussion of numerous reasonable cause grounds, many of which I discuss in the course of this chapter. Please note that those discussed here are not the *only* grounds that constitute reasonable cause. They are merely some common reasons. The reality is that *any* reason establishing that you did not deliberately intend to cheat, mislead, or deceive the IRS qualifies as reasonable cause if your explanation is adequately linked to the act that is penalized.

The idea of reasonable cause speaks to the surrounding facts and circumstances that helped to shape one's motive or intent. Reasonable cause is nothing more than a good reason, based upon common sense and existing circumstances, for acting or failing to act. Reasonable cause exists when you show a causal link between your actions or failures to act and the circumstances claimed as reasonable cause.

Let me give you an example. Bernard made a contribution of certain paintings to charity. He deducted the value of the paintings on his return and used that value as the basis of his charitable contribution. Before donating the paintings, he had them appraised by a member of a reputable appraisal association with expertise in the area. Copies of the appraisals were attached to Bernard's tax return to support his claim. Later it was shown that the appraisals in fact *overvalued* the paintings and a portion of Bernard's deduction was disallowed. The IRS asserted a penalty for making an inaccurate statement on his tax return (the so-called accuracy penalty is discussed more specifically later).

Bernard argued that he had "reasonable cause" for using the value shown on the return since that value was determined by a qualified appraiser. Bernard argued that he relied upon the appraisals in "good faith," believing them to be accurate. As it turned out, the appraisals were inaccurate, but that did not justify the IRS's demand for the negligence penalty. Bernard's reliance in good faith on the appraisals constituted a "reasonable cause" justifying his actions, thereby vitiating any penalties.

A critical aspect of this argument is that you must make full disclosure to the IRS of all applicable facts in the first instance. I refer to this process as audit-proofing and discuss it later in this book. Let me give you another example.

David lived abroad for several years during the 1980s. He was under the impression that his income was not taxable because he earned it through overseas sources. On his tax return, David showed the full amount of the income and its source and explained why he believed it was not taxable. He computed his tax liability without regard to his foreign income.

This he did two years running. After he filed the second return, the IRS challenged David's treatment and asserted a penalty. David argued that he made full disclosure of the facts in the tax return. He argued that full disclosure evidenced good faith and that the explanation in the return set forth "reasonable cause" for his treatment of the income as nontaxable. It was ruled that David's act of full disclosure did indeed show good faith and "reasonable cause" justifying abatement of the penalty.

Keep in mind that the facts you present as reasonable cause must bear a direct relationship to the issue challenged. It is inappropriate to suggest, for example, that a death in your family in 1999 constitutes "reasonable cause" for an error in your 1997 tax return. However, such an act may well constitute reasonable cause if the timing and impact of the death were such that you were unable to discharge your filing obligation for the 1999 return.

I once had a client whose wife fell ill in the fall of 1999 due to an allergic reaction to medication. She slipped into a coma, recovered for a brief period, then suddenly died in early April 2000. The combination of (1) her tragic illness, (2) my client's near full-time care of his wife and the household during her illness, and (3) her unexpected death at a young age devastated him. For nearly a year he was unable to attend to his affairs. He did not file his 1999 tax return on time. Under the circumstances, he had a reasonable cause for his actions.

Common reasonable cause grounds include:

- Medical problems, including death, injury, or prolonged illness

- Serious disruption of one's life as through a traumatic move, fire, flood, or other disaster

- Financial problems such as the loss of a job, a failed business, or general economic problems that spill over to you

- Personal problems such as a divorce, alcohol or drug abuse, or similar problems associated with a family member, if these problems led to general financial problems, not just IRS problems

- Lost or unavailable records for reasons attributable to good faith and not negligence.

As this discussion progresses, bear in mind that reasonable cause can be *any reason* that mitigates the assumption that you deliberately disregarded IRS rules or otherwise acted negligently.

WHAT ARE THE COMMON PENALTIES YOU FACE?

Let us turn our attention to the common penalties assessed and how to challenge them through the use of a simple letter. While the IRS has over 140 penalty provisions at its disposal, only a handful are used with regularity. Therefore I address the more common penalties and what is needed to win cancellation of those penalties.

What to Do If the IRS Assesses the Failure-to-File Penalty

Code section 6651 provides a penalty for both filing late and paying late. This is the so-called delinquency penalty. Delinquencies for failure to file and failure to pay make up the largest segment of penalty assessments each year. For example, total penalty assessments during 2000 and 2001 were 30.861 million and 32.494 million respectively. Of these, 13.217 million and 14.956 million were for failure to file and failure to pay on time. Let us address the late filing and failure-to-file penalties.

The maximum penalty for failure to file is 25 percent of the tax owed on a return. This is calculated at the rate of 5 percent per month for any part of a month that a return is late, up to five months, for a maximum of 25 percent.

The penalty for failure to file by the due date is not applicable when you show that the "failure is due to reasonable cause and not willful neglect."[8] IRS regulations provide that failure to file on time is due to reasonable cause if you show that you exercised "ordinary business care and prudence" and were nevertheless unable to file on time.[9] When the failure is due to no fault of your own or to circumstances beyond your control, the failure-to-file penalty must be abated when these facts are clearly documented.

In addition to the reasonable cause factors discussed earlier, the Penalty Handbook lists additional defenses establishing reasonable cause for a filing delinquency. Keep in mind, however, that the defenses discussed above and the following list are just a sample of qualifying reasons and should not be read as an exhaustive list of reasonable cause grounds.

- The return is mailed on time but not delivered by the post office in time.

- The return is filed on time but at the wrong IRS office, such as when a return required to be mailed to Ogden, Utah, is mailed to Kansas City.

- The delay is due to erroneous information provided by the IRS or to IRS failure to provide necessary requested forms and instructions within sufficient time to file on the due date.

- The delay is caused by the death or serious illness of yourself or an immediate family member.

- The delay is caused by your unavoidable absence, thereby preventing the completion and submission of the return.

- The delay is caused by fire, flood, civil disturbance, or other casualty to your home, business, or business records.

- You demonstrate that you personally visited an IRS office to obtain tax help, but through no fault of your own, you were unable to obtain help.

- You were unable, for reasons beyond your control, to secure all the records necessary to complete the return accurately prior to the due date.

- You received advice from a competent tax adviser, such as an attorney or accountant, to the effect that you were not required to file a return.

Keep in mind that the duty to file a tax return rests with the citizen. The fact that you might have delegated its preparation to a paid professional does not by itself relieve you of the failure-to-file penalty if the preparer does not complete the return on time.

An example of how to make a penalty abatement request in this situation is provided by the case of my client Ed, who filed his return nearly one year late. When the return hit the service center, the IRS immediately bounced a penalty letter back to Ed seeking more than six thousand dollars for failure to file on time.

Ed responded with a request for abatement demonstrating that his failure to file was based upon a reasonable cause and not willful neglect. More specifically, Ed showed that, despite his own best efforts to prepare and submit the return on time, he was unable to do so through no fault of his own. Exhibit 4–1 is an example of Ed's letter.

EXHIBIT 4–1

Edward ———
Address
City, State, Zip

Date:
SSN:

Dear IRS:

This letter is in response to your notice of [date], demanding payment of $6,687 for the year ———. The assessment is for late filing and late payment penalties, plus interest.

This letter is a protest to the assessment of the penalties and a request for abatement for reasonable cause as shown below. The facts below establish reasonable cause supporting my request for abatement.

For the year in question, I submitted a filing extension, IRS Form 4868. The extension pushed the filing deadline up to August 15, ——— [year]. I submitted the extension because records necessary for the accurate preparation of my tax return were not in my possession by the April 15 filing deadline. I needed more time to obtain the needed records.

The missing records included documents showing the receipt of income and payment of deductible expenses in connection with a limited partnership of which I am a limited partner. The transmittal of the necessary information from the partnership to me is perennially late. Ordinary business care and prudence dictate that before I can prepare my return accurately, I must have this information.

Next, in December ——— [year], I moved my residence. After the move, I was unable to locate many of the other personal records necessary to complete my return accurately. The records were misplaced through no fault of my own. After going through every box and searching in every possible location, I located the records and immediately brought them to my tax preparer. This was in ——— [date], several months after the filing extension was up. I did not realize that I had a right to seek a second request for extension. However, I was unable to file a correct return by August 15 due to the missing records. Once those records were found, I took immediate steps to prepare the return and pay the tax owed in a prudent business manner.

I did not act in a "willfully negligent" manner as that phrase is used in the tax code. My reason for not filing or paying on time was due to "reasonable cause" as set forth above. I delayed filing the return to be sure that the return was true and accurate in all respects, as required by law. It was impossible to file an accurate return without the information mentioned above.

My actions of filing late were a direct result of the legal requirement to file a truthful return. Ordinary business care required that I not file an incorrect tax return. For this reason, I acted in a reasonable manner and not due to willful neglect.

Based upon the facts and circumstances, I submit that the assessed penalties for failure to file and failure to pay in a timely manner are due to be abated. I hereby request that the penalties be abated.

Under penalty of perjury, I declare that all of the facts contained in this demand for abatement are true and correct in all respects.

Sincerely,

Edward ————

Please note from Exhibit 4–1 that Ed took great care to *fully explain* the circumstances behind his failure to file on time. He set forth facts and circumstances that allowed the IRS to draw the conclusion that his failure was not a deliberate act but rather was due to circumstances beyond his control. In your letter, avoid vague or generalized references to events or circumstances. A letter that is not specific or that fails to draw a direct causal relationship between the events in question and the failure to file is not likely to succeed. Document your claims as fully as possible. Documentation should be assigned exhibit numbers and referenced in the body of the letter.

Please also note the final paragraph of Ed's letter. That paragraph declares under penalty of perjury that the facts contained in Ed's letter are accurate. This declaration is tantamount to creating an affidavit.

The failure-to-file penalty is based upon a percentage of the tax owed. It is important to understand how this percentage is determined in order to combat a common error the IRS makes with this penalty. The error is the assessment of the so-called minimum penalty for failure to file.[10] The minimum penalty allows the IRS to collect at least "$100 or 100 percent of the [tax] required to be shown as tax" on the return, whichever is less. Thus, if the tax owed on the return is just $25, the minimum failure-to-file penalty is $25 (100 percent of the tax due).

The mistake is that the IRS asserts the minimum penalty when no tax is owed or a refund is due. The statute provides that the delinquency penalty, including the minimum penalty, be based upon the net amount due after consideration of all withholding and estimated payment credits. Therefore, if the tax owed is $2,000 but the entire amount was paid through wage withholding, there is no underpayment upon which to base the penalty.

Mail your request for abatement using certified mail and include a copy of the original penalty notice for reference. I provide more details on filing the claim at the end of this chapter. As with all IRS correspondence, retain a copy of your letter for future reference together with the postal receipts for certified mail.

Resist the temptation to phone the IRS seeking abatement verbally.

In virtually all cases where citizens seek abatement over the phone, they are told that no abatement is available or that the the penalty is "automatic." Neither of these statements is true. Therefore, to receive full consideration, submit all penalty abatement requests in writing.

What to Do If the IRS Accuses You of Understating Your Tax Bill or Negligence

Code section 6662 allows the IRS to penalize citizens for a number of reasons. The two most common are (1) substantial understatement of income tax owed and (2) negligence or intentional disregard of IRS rules or regulations.

Understatements arise when deductions are disallowed, or unreported income is added to a return. This aspect of the penalty is generally assessed in connection with errors found in a tax return that was filed in a timely manner. The penalty generally accompanies an adverse audit decision or is added to a correction notice such as explained in chapter 2. The negligence penalty is a kind of catchall penalty the IRS uses in virtually all delinquency situations.

Code section 6662(c) defines the term *negligence* as follows:

> For purposes of this section, the term "negligence" includes any failure to make a reasonable attempt to comply with the provisions of this title, and the term "disregard" includes any careless, reckless, or intentional disregard.

The amount of the penalty is 20 percent of the understatement of tax attributable to the negligence or intentional disregard. The idea of negligent conduct is precisely the opposite of good faith or reasonable cause. Code section 6664, which governs nearly all penalty sections in the tax code, sets up the legal defense to most penalties. It states, in part:

> No penalty shall be imposed under this part with respect to any portion of an underpayment if it is shown that there was a rea-

sonable cause for such portion and that the taxpayer acted in good faith with respect to such portion. Code section 6664(c)(1).

Remember, the concepts of good faith and reasonable cause are factual considerations that indicate you acted with good reason, based upon some factual or legal foundation, or because of circumstances beyond your control. When you prove one or more of these factors, the elements of good faith and reasonable cause justify cancellation.

To win the case, you must demonstrate that the underpayment of tax was not due to negligence or disregard of IRS rules or regulations. You do this with specific evidence to support the claim of good faith and reasonable cause, using one or more of the defenses set out above or any other reason that justifies your actions.

The specific language of your letter depends upon the facts and circumstances of your case. The key is to keep in mind that you must provide *evidence* to demonstrate that your actions or failures to act were not part of a deliberate effort to avoid the IRS rules or regulations and that you did not act negligently in connection with your legal duties. Use any relevant evidence, including your own testimony supported by an affidavit, to demonstrate these facts.

More specifically, you must show that your actions or failures to act were occasioned by a good faith belief that your actions were correct. This is to say that you had a reasonable cause to believe that you were acting correctly. Buttress the declaration with facts to illustrate that you did all you could under the circumstances to meet your obligations. Review the good faith defenses set out earlier but do not allow yourself to be constrained by them.

What to Do If the IRS Penalizes You for Paying Late

Your taxes are required to be paid in full on or before the due date of the return. Section 6651 provides a penalty of up to 1 percent of the tax due *per month* for a maximum of twenty-five months when the tax is not paid in full by the due date. The penalty is abated when "it is shown that such failure is due to reasonable cause and not willful neglect."

The standards for winning an abatement of the failure to pay the tax penalty are much the same as those already discussed, with one important exception. In order to prevail on this issue, you must take the showing of good faith a bit further. IRS regulations provide the following guidance:

A failure to pay will be considered to be due to reasonable cause to the extent that the taxpayer has made a satisfactory showing that he exercised ordinary business care and prudence in providing for payment of his tax liability and was nevertheless either unable to pay the tax or would suffer an undue hardship if he paid on the due date. In determining whether the taxpayer was unable to pay the tax in spite of the exercise of ordinary business care and prudence in providing for the payment of his tax liability, consideration will be given to all the facts and circumstances of the taxpayer's financial situation, including the amount and nature of the taxpayer's expenditures in light of the income (or other amounts) he could, at the time of such expenditures, reasonably expect to receive prior to the date prescribed for the payment of the tax. Thus, for example, a taxpayer who incurs lavish or extravagant living expenses in an amount such that the remainder of his assets and anticipated income will be insufficient to pay his tax, has not exercised ordinary business care and prudence in providing for the payment of his tax liability. Further, a taxpayer who invested funds in speculative or illiquid assets has not exercised ordinary business care and prudence in providing for the payment of his tax liability unless, at the time of the investment, the remainder of the taxpayer's assets and estimated income will be sufficient to pay his tax or it can be reasonably foreseen that the speculative or illiquid investment made by the taxpayer can be utilized (by sale or security for a loan) to realize sufficient funds to satisfy the tax liability. A taxpayer will be considered to have exercised ordinary business care and prudence if he made reasonable efforts to conserve sufficient assets in marketable form to satisfy his tax liability and nevertheless was unable to pay all or a portion of the tax when it became due.[11]

The key to defeating the failure-to-pay penalty is showing that you exercised ordinary business care and prudence in providing for your tax liability but were nevertheless unable to pay on time. You must set forth facts to clearly demonstrate the actions taken to provide for your tax liability and the factors or events that made it impossible to pay. Take care to illustrate a causal link between the events alleged to be out of your control and your inability to pay in a timely manner. An example helps to illustrate this.

Chris's otherwise normal world was shattered when her husband, Dennis, suddenly lost his job. Because of major workforce reductions in his industry, there simply was no further work—not only with his current employer but within his entire city. Hoping for the best, Dennis continued to search for work, did odd jobs, and fed his family with their modest savings.

When it came time to file their tax return, the document was mailed to the IRS but without money to pay the tax. Shortly after filing, the IRS assessed the penalty for failure to pay. Chris and Dennis responded with a demand for abatement. Following the lead established by the regulation we just read, Chris drafted her letter setting forth specific facts to demonstrate that she and her husband had exercised ordinary business care and prudence in providing for the payment of their taxes, but through no fault of their own, they were unable to pay on time. Chris's letter painted a picture of the facts and circumstances to clearly illustrate the link between the unfortunate events of life and their inability to pay the tax. Please see Exhibit 4–2.

EXHIBIT 4–2

Dennis and Chris ———
Address
City, State, Zip

Date:
SSN:

Internal Revenue Service
Kansas City, MO 64999

Dear IRS:

On ——— [date] we received notice (copy enclosed) that a penalty for failure to timely pay taxes is assessed against us. This is a protest to the assessment and a request for abatement under all applicable code sections. In accordance with revenue regulation section 301.6651–1(c), this letter contains facts showing "reasonable cause" and "ordinary business care and prudence" justifying abatement of the penalty.

THESE ARE THE FACTS:

For six years, from ——— [date] to ——— [date], I worked as a computer programmer and systems analyst for ——— in ——— [city]. My job was highly specialized, involving only defense contracts.

Every year while employed there, I filed my returns on time and paid all taxes owed. My taxes were paid through wage withholding. Each year I either received a refund or I paid just a few hundred dollars in taxes. I never faced a large tax bill because I was always careful to be sure that wage withholding covered my liability.

Since the mid-1980s, the computer firms in ——— [city] and surrounding areas have steadily decreased their workforces. One by one, each firm, including my employer, laid off workers. On ——— [date], I was laid off and have not worked since.

At the time of the layoff, I made efforts to find other employment. I searched for jobs with every potential employer in my industry. I applied for jobs both directly related and entirely unrelated to my previous employment. I was shocked to learn that there is literally no employment to be had in this area for my particular skills.

From the time of my layoff, I drew unemployment for 26 weeks. After 26 weeks, the unemployment benefits ran out. At the time of my layoff, we had just $2,000 in savings. The unemployment compensation was just $800 per month while the monthly living expenses for my family were over $1,200 per month. We were forced to use our savings to live from month to month. When the savings ran out, we had to borrow money to make up the difference.

At the time of the layoff, because I had no further employment, no withholding taxes were paid on the unemployment compensation. As a result, when our tax return was filed in April, we owed over $3,000. We filed the return without paying the tax because we were told by our tax preparer that we had to.

Our failure to pay taxes in April was not because we failed to provide for the payment of our taxes. We were unable to save enough money because of being laid off. All funds I received from unemployment compensation were used to feed my family, including two young children. We have no equity in our house and so we were unable to borrow against the house to pay the taxes. After our savings ran out, we were forced to borrow money from my father in order to live.

We exercised ordinary business care and prudence in providing for the payment of our taxes. This was done by filing a correct W-4 Form with my employer. I was always careful to be sure that enough money was taken from my check through withholding to cover my taxes. But there was no way to anticipate the timing of being laid off, and even if I had, my income and expenses were such that I could not save more money.

During the period in question, I made every reasonable effort to conserve sufficient funds to pay my taxes, but through no fault of my own, I was unable to do so. The reason is that we simply did not have enough money to pay our necessary living expenses. We were living on unemployment, our small savings that quickly ran out, and money borrowed from my father. We did not squander our funds. All available funds were needed to survive and feed two small children.

Based upon these facts, we submit that "reasonable cause" exists for abatement of the failure-to-pay penalty.

We declare under penalty of perjury that the facts contained in this letter are true and correct in all respects.

Sincerely,

Dennis and Chris ———

Another key to success with this penalty is to illustrate the idea of financial "undue hardship." The general definition of *hardship* is that payment of the tax "will cause an individual taxpayer to be unable to pay his or her reasonable basic living expenses."[12]

To prove this, provide a simple income and expense statement showing your net monthly income after all withholdings and your fixed and necessary monthly living expenses. Include your rent or mortgage payment, transportation costs, child care costs, court ordered payments such as child support or alimony, food and clothing expenses, etc. This financial statement, coupled with a detailed letter of explanation, will help to carry the day on the failure-to-pay penalty.

Chris could have benefited from filing IRS Form 1127, *Application for Extension of Time to Pay Taxes*. However, like many citizens, she was unaware of the form and so she did the next best thing—she filed the return but without paying the tax. Most failure-to-pay penalties can be avoided if you use Form 1127 at or before the time of filing your return, even if the IRS denies the request. The reason is that the process of submitting the application informs the IRS of your problem and clearly illustrates your good faith intent to resolve it. Contrast that with a citizen who simply does not pay and takes no steps to mitigate that fact.

What to Do If the IRS Penalizes You for Underpaying Estimated Taxes

During the course of the year, individuals have an obligation to make estimated payments of their tax liability. Employees make these payments through wage withholding. Under this system, a percentage of your paycheck is withheld by your employer and paid to the IRS. The Form W-2, *Wage and Tax Statement*, is a year-end statement showing both the IRS and the employee the amount of wages paid and the amount of federal and state income tax and social security withheld.

Self-employed persons do not have the "luxury" of a wage withholding program. They must discipline themselves to make quarterly estimated payments. The IRS provides Form 1040ES, *Estimated Payment of Income Tax by Individual,* for this purpose. Estimated payments are due four times per year: April 15, June 15, September 15, and January 15 of the following year. The financial difficulty of making these payments is one reason the estimated tax penalty is the second most commonly assessed penalty, usually behind the failure-to-pay penalty.

Section 6654 establishes the amount of estimated payments required and provides a penalty for failure to pay on time. The statute also creates exceptions to the penalty. The exceptions are somewhat different from the "good faith, reasonable cause" standards presented above but are equally effective. In fact, it might be argued that the exceptions are even broader than the "good faith, reasonable cause" standard applicable in other statutes.

The general rule is that estimated payments must equal 90 percent of the tax due on the current return or 100 percent of the tax paid the previous year, *whichever is less.*[13] To illustrate these requirements, let us assume two hypothetical facts: (1) in 2001, you paid federal income taxes of $6,000, and (2) in 2002, you estimate that your federal tax liability will be $4,000. To avoid the estimated tax penalty, you must pay either $3,600, which is 90 percent of the current liability ($4,000 × .9 = $3,600), or $6,000, which is 100 percent of the previous liability. Because the obligation is to pay the *lesser* of these two amounts, you avoid the penalty if, in this example, your estimated payments total at least $3,600. The balance of the liability is then due at the time of filing the return.

Let me illustrate this with an example. A man I knew once worked for a large corporation. He earned an average income and paid approximately $4,000 in federal taxes. The next year, he struck out on his own and scored with his business. His income rose substantially and his tax liability followed. In that year, he owed federal income taxes in excess of $14,000. During that year, he paid around $5,700 to the IRS in four quarterly installments. He filed his return on time and remitted the balance, approximately $8,300.

Shortly after filing, he received a notice claiming that he owed a penalty for underpaying estimated taxes. The IRS alleged that he was required to make payments equal to 90 percent of his current tax liability, or about $12,600. The IRS assessed a penalty of $630 for the alleged underpayment.

Without delay, the man wrote a letter to the service center that issued the bill. He argued that section 6654(d) requires estimated payments equal to the *lesser* of 90 percent of the current tax liability or 100 percent of the previous tax liability. He attached a copy of his prior year's tax return to the letter. The return showed a tax liability for that year of about $4,000. He also attached copies of estimated tax payment forms and canceled checks for estimated payments made during the next year. The estimated payments totaled about $5,700.

These facts proved that his estimated payments exceeded 100 percent of the prior year's liability. As such, the man complied with the law. The final statement in the letter demanded an abatement of the penalty. The IRS obliged, saving him in excess of $630.

Earlier I stated that there are defenses which, in some cases, may be broader and hence more universally applicable than the defense of "good faith, reasonable cause." The defenses apply when sufficient estimates under either of the above formulas are not made. The law reads as follows:

(A) No addition to the tax shall be imposed under [section 6654] with respect to any underpayment to the extent the Secretary determines that by reason of casualty, disaster, or other unusual circumstances the imposition of such addition to tax would be against equity and good conscience.

(B) No addition to tax shall be imposed under [section 6654] with respect to any underpayment if the Secretary determines that:

  i. The taxpayer (I) retired after having attained the age of 62, or (II) became disabled, in the taxable year for which estimated payments were required to be made or in the taxable year preceding such taxable year, and such underpayment was due to reasonable cause and not willful neglect.[14]

The first of these defenses I refer to as the "equity/good conscience" defense. The second I call the "retired/disabled" defense. I address them in turn.

The equity/good conscience defense is extremely broad. Under this provision, you avoid the penalty upon showing that some type of disaster, such as fire or flood, or "other unusual circumstances" occurred. This might include extensive medical bills that made payment of estimated taxes difficult or impossible. Other circumstances might include loss of job, death or serious illness of a family member, or catastrophic financial problems. Under such circumstances, assessment of the penalty becomes patently unfair, or "against equity and good conscience." That is to say, assessment of the penalty by the IRS becomes nothing more than a cheap shot at an otherwise honest citizen already hobbled by financial problems.

In order to prevail, you need only show that some disaster, casualty, or other unusual circumstance affected your life and seriously disrupted your ability to pay. You then argue that these circumstances render the imposition of the penalty contrary to equity or fundamental fairness and good conscience. In this context, elements of fairness and justice enter the picture. As far as I know, this is the only place in the nearly 18,500 pages of tax code where the IRS is called upon to apply principles of fundamental fairness and justice.

The retired/disabled test is narrower and more clearly defined. If you reached the age of sixty-two and retired during the year in question or became disabled, either in the year in question or in the previous year, you can have the penalty abated. In order to prevail under this test, you must also show reasonable cause for the failure to make estimated payments in addition to the elements mentioned. This requires that there be a link between the facts asserted as reasonable cause and the failure to make the estimated payments. Refer to the list of possible defenses mentioned above for further discussion.

What to Do If the IRS Asserts a Fraud Penalty

There is a fundamental difference between civil fraud and criminal fraud where the IRS is concerned. Criminal fraud can land you in

jail. Civil fraud merely ups the ante of tax liability but does so substantially. There are two types of civil fraud addressed in the tax code
and we examine them both.

The first is found in code section 6663, which contains the general civil fraud penalty. It applies when "any part of the underpayment of tax required to be shown on a return is due to fraud." In that
case, the penalty is 75 percent of the tax. This fraud penalty applies
only to tax returns that are filed.

The second penalty applies if no return is filed. Code section
6651(f) allows for an increase of the normal failure-to-file penalty
from a maximum of 25 percent to a maximum of 75 percent where
the failure to file is "fraudulent." The penalty is graduated in that the
rate is 15 percent per month for a maximum of five months, or 75
percent. Thus a fraudulent failure to file is treated the same as fraud in
connection with a filed return.

What constitutes fraud in connection with the IRS has been the
subject of much debate. However, the courts settled upon a definition
that has stood the test of time. In order to sustain a finding of fraud,
the IRS must prove that the citizen committed an *overt* act in furtherance of an attempt to illegally underpay his income taxes. The *overt*
act—that is, an act of commission as opposed to an act of omission—
must have the effect of deceiving or misleading the IRS with regard
to the citizen's income tax liability.

The fundamental difference between the fraud penalty and virtually all other civil penalties in the code is that *the IRS has the burden of
proof* on civil fraud. Moreover, the allegation of fraud must be supported with "clear and convincing evidence" that you committed an
overt act in furtherance of a scheme to underpay your taxes.

When a fraud penalty is assessed, the IRS may not impose other
civil penalties related to the accuracy of the return. For example, the
accuracy penalty under section 6662 cannot be stacked with the fraud
penalty. This limits the punitive effect of the penalty.

The "intent" element of the penalty is critical. It speaks to the
axiom that ignorance of the law is no excuse. By now I have established the fact that where federal tax laws are concerned, ignorance of

the law is every excuse if you acted in good faith and did not set out deliberately to evade or defeat your obligations. In the case of the fraud penalty, if you did not act with a deliberate intent to violate what you knew to be your legal obligations, the penalty does not apply. The IRS bears the burden to prove that you intentionally and deliberately set out to violate a known legal duty before the penalty can be enforced.

The concepts of bad faith and intent to violate the law refer to your state of mind at the time of the alleged actions. These are difficult elements to prove. In order to infer your intent, the IRS draws from any statements you may have made or activities in which you engaged. Examples of the required overt act, or act of *commission*, necessary to sustain the fraud penalty include:

- Deliberate understatement of income or overstatement of deductions in your return

- Using two sets of records for the purpose of masking income

- Lying to IRS agents during the course of an audit or investigation

- Falsifying documents in order to sustain deductions

- Using only cash as a means of doing business to avoid creating records of income

- Using trusts, shell corporations or offshore entities to conceal income

- Making deliberately false or misleading statements on tax or other forms, such as Form W-4, *Employee's Withholding Allowance Certificate*, or in loan applications

- Placing assets in the hands of third parties or "nominees" to conceal them from the IRS

- Using fictitious names or social security numbers on bank accounts to mislead the IRS.

This is just a partial list of what the IRS and courts refer to as "badges of fraud" considered evidence of fraudulent intent. It is not exhaustive and I do not mean to suggest that each must be present for the IRS to prevail. The agency need only prove *one* act of commission (overt act) to establish the fraud penalty.

Dealing with a civil fraud allegation requires extra effort on your part. It is not enough to simply set forth the facts as I illustrate in the above examples. The first step is to request that the IRS provide—in writing—a detailed statement of the facts and documents it believes support the fraud assertion. Do this by mailing a letter to the IRS office that issued the fraud penalty in the first place. Normally such a penalty comes as a result of the audit process, not from a service center notice.

Your letter produces a statement from the IRS explaining the reasons it believes a fraud penalty is justified. With that in hand, you must respond to the IRS's allegations line by line, providing a good faith explanation for your actions. Keep in mind that the IRS tends to cast your actions or lack thereof in the worst possible light. You must provide information showing that there is an alternative, innocent explanation for your actions. Document your claims to the fullest extent possible as outlined above.

Dale did not fit into any of the molds reserved for those worthy of the fraud penalty. True, Dale did not file tax returns for a number of years. But the simple failure to file, without one or more of the elements of fraud listed above, does not rise to the level of fraudulent behavior. Failure to file is an act of omission. Fraud requires an act of commission. But when the IRS caught up with Dale, it not only computed his tax liability for him, it included the fraud penalty.

Dale requested that the IRS provide an explanation for the penalty and copies of the evidence to support its fraud claim. The IRS's only explanation for the penalty was Dale's "pattern of conduct" in failing to file for several years. As the case developed, it became clear that there was no substantive evidence that Dale committed fraud.

But the law is clear. The mere failure to file a return—an act of *omission*—does not by itself prove fraud. Rather, the IRS must demonstrate that some other affirmative act, the effect of which was to deceive or mislead the IRS, accompanied the failure to file. In Dale's case, there was no affirmative act. He did not file false documents. He made no false statements to investigators. He did not attempt to conceal assets or otherwise conduct his affairs in a criminal or evasive manner.

Dale failed to file his returns chiefly because he did not have the money to pay the tax owed. That, frankly, is the number one reason the vast majority of citizens fail to file. That does not make them subject to the fraud penalty. It makes them delinquent taxpayers—period.

On the basis of the lack of evidence, Dale demanded that the IRS drop the fraud penalty. The IRS obliged, saving Dale several thousand dollars.

For a more detailed discussion of the fraud issue and potential criminal sanctions, please see chapter 3 of my book *How to Get Tax Amnesty* (Winning Publications, 1998).

What to Do If the IRS Accuses You of Filing a False Withholding Certificate

The IRS has the authority to penalize the filing of a false Form W-4, *Employee's Withholding Allowance Certificate*. The W-4 is the form you file with your employer to report the number of withholding allowances claimed. This in turn determines the level of wage withholding. The greater the number of allowances claimed, the less money is taken for federal and state income tax purposes.

In some cases, low-income employees can exempt themselves from withholding entirely. This is not as crazy as it sounds. The situation commonly arises with full-time students who work part-time, and low- to moderate-income citizens with numerous exemptions and deductions. Their financial circumstances are such that they do not have to pay income taxes. As long as they can honestly anticipate that they will have no tax debt in the current year, they can stop withholding by claiming "exempt" on their withholding certificate. I discuss this in more detail later.

As Congress introduces more tax breaks for lower-income citizens, I expect an increase in the number of those who qualify to eliminate withholding. Keep in mind, though, that the withholding certificate is signed under the penalty of perjury, and potentially questionable claims are reviewed and are subject to penalty.

The law provides a penalty of $500 if you submit a Form W-4 that (1) "results in a decrease" in the amount of tax withheld from your paycheck and (2) when "there was no reasonable basis for such statement" at the time it was made.[15]

Your employer is required to send your withholding certificate to the IRS if you claim more than ten withholding allowances or if you claim that you are exempt from withholding. The IRS then reviews the form to determine whether it is justified under the circumstances. To make the determination, it reviews your prior year's tax return and your current income.

If your claim is not justified, the IRS notifies you that the withholding certificate is to be disallowed. This fact is also communicated to the employer, who is told to disregard the certificate and any future certificates until otherwise instructed by the agency. The IRS then asserts the $500 penalty against you. There are two approaches to handling this problem. The first assumes the Form W-4 is accurate, and the second is dedicated to avoiding the penalty if the withholding certificate is in fact erroneous.

The withholding certificate is almost as confusing as Form 1040. That is why so many people underclaim their proper withholding allowances, actually allowing their employers to withhold more money than required. To be sure, all employees are subject to withholding, but it is equally true that you have the right to determine the extent of the withholding. This is done by claiming allowances based upon the financial facts and circumstances of your case.

The number of withholding allowances to which you are entitled is determined by a number of factors. First, you are entitled to claim one allowance for each of your dependent exemptions. If you are married with three children, you are entitled to five allowances (one for yourself, your spouse and each child). Next, you are entitled to take into consideration your itemized deductions. You are also entitled to factor in tax credits and any other tax return item that reduces your tax liability.

Allowances are computed on the work sheet attached to the allowance certificate. Given the broad definition and application of the term *allowance*, it is not at all unusual that a given family with itemized deductions for such things as interest, state and local taxes, and charitable contributions is entitled to ten or more withholding allowances.[16]

And as I stated earlier, the law creates an *exemption* from withholding for low-income individuals, such as full-time students. Qualifying persons may claim "exempt" on the certificate, meaning that they are not subject to the periodic withholding ritual. A person may claim this exemption if he (1) "incurred *no* income tax liability" for the preceding year and (2) "reasonably anticipates" that he will incur *no* income tax liability for the present year.[17] Many low-income citizens qualify for this exemption.

If you claim more than ten withholding allowances or exemption from withholding, you must stand ready to explain the correctness of your withholding certificate if questioned. You must explain:

- How you determined your withholding status

- Specific facts and circumstances justifying your claim

- That your claim was made in good faith, based upon reasonable cause as shown by the facts

- That (most important) to your best knowledge and belief, as shown by the facts, you had a "reasonable basis" for making the claim.

If your form is *in fact* correct but merely questioned by the agency, follow these procedures. In a responsive letter, emphasize that you did not file the form to unlawfully reduce your withholding, or with the knowledge or belief that you had no reasonable basis for making the claim. Mail your letter promptly to the IRS at the address shown on its notice. Be sure to use certified mail. Be careful to identify your letter as being in response to the withholding certificate inquiry and state that you are writing to avoid the penalty under code section 6682.

On the other hand, if your form is *incorrect*, you must act quickly to avoid the $500 penalty. In that case, the statute provides a two-pronged test for determining whether the penalty applies. The first is that the certificate led to a reduction in your withholding. The second is that "at the time the statement was made" there was no "reasonable basis" for making it.

If your withholding statement is incorrect, you may nevertheless avoid the $500 penalty by showing specific facts and circumstances justifying the conclusion that you had a "reasonable basis" for your claim. One such factor may be that an accountant or return preparer completed, or advised you in the completion of, the form. The financial circumstances that affected your determination must be set forth in the letter.

Important language from the statute must be noted. That language provides that the facts considered in determining whether there is a "reasonable basis" for the statement are the facts that existed *at the time* the statement was made. I say this because the IRS is likely to examine your withholding certificate several months or perhaps years after you submitted it. Because of this, the IRS may apply your *current* facts to determine the form's validity. This is not proper. Therefore, in order to establish your "reasonable basis," take care to recite the facts that existed *at the time* of filing the form.

A STANDARD COVER FORM

In chapter 2, I mentioned that whenever a claim is made against the agency, it is good practice to use a standard cover form. Even when seeking abatement of penalties, the best cover form is Form

843, *Claim for Refund and Request for Abatement* (see chapter 2, Exhibit 2-4). Form 843 ensures that IRS employees immediately recognize that you are making a claim against the agency. Merely sending your abatement letter without Form 843 increases the risk that service center personnel will not read or understand enough of your letter to recognize it as a claim.

Complete Form 843 by providing the information requested, and where it asks for the reason the claim should be granted, state "see attached letter." To the form, attach your letter seeking abatement (with copies of your documents—again, *never* mail original documents). Finally, mail the original submission to the IRS via certified mail. Address the package to the Penalty Abatement Coordinator at the service center that issued the penalty.

WHAT TO DO IF THE ANSWER IS NO

I am fond of pointing out that the decisions of IRS examiners are never final. This rule also applies to requests for penalty abatement. Should the IRS deny your request, you will be informed in writing. The IRS should also explain that you enjoy the right to appeal the decision.

The appeal is perfected by drafting a written protest letter within thirty days of the date of the letter denying your abatement request. Address the protest letter to the service center that denied your claim. It must clearly state that you wish to appeal the adverse decision. Exhibit 4–3 is an example of a protest letter.

EXHIBIT 4–3

Michael ———
Address
City, State, Zip

Date:
SSN:

Internal Revenue Service
Kansas City, MO 64999

Dear IRS:

On ——— [date] I submitted a written request for the abatement of civil penalties. By letter of ——— [date], the IRS denied my request.

Therefore, it is my desire to appeal the decision denying my request. I wish to have a conference before an Appeals Officer in ——— [city] relative to this appeal.

The name and address of the appellant is:

Michael ———

Address

A statement of the facts supporting my position is expressed in the attached letter of ——— [date]. The letter sets out facts that demonstrate that I executed reasonable business care and prudence as well as due diligence in connection with this issue. Despite my own efforts and due to factors beyond my control, I was unable to pay my taxes on time.

A statement of the law supporting my position is based upon code section 6651, which stipulates that the penalty does not apply when it is shown that the failure was due to "reasonable cause and not willful neglect."

Reasonable cause exists when it is shown that a person did "what a reasonable and ordinarily prudent person would do under the circumstances." See *Marcello v. Commissioner*, 380 F.2d 509 (5th Cir. 1967). Such a showing has been made in this case.

The facts of this case plainly indicate that I exercised reasonable business care and prudence justifying abatement of all civil penalties.

Under penalty of perjury, I declare that the above facts, as well as those contained in the letter of ———— [date] attached, are true and correct in all respects.

Sincerely,

Michael ————

In all cases I recommend that you attach a copy of your initial request for abatement to the protest letter as an exhibit. This helps to complete the record. IRS Publication 5, *Your Appeal Rights and How to Prepare a Protest If You Don't Agree,* provides more detail on the appeals process. For more discussion of the appeals process, please see chapter 6.

The submission of a written protest in a timely fashion entitles you to a conference before the Appeals Office of the IRS. This can involve an appearance before a local Appeals Officer, but appeals are also routinely handled by phone conference. At your conference, you may present any evidence you believe supports your position. The conference is informal and the purpose is to negotiate a solution to your problem. Most Appeals Officers look for ways to settle amicably with dissatisfied citizens.

There is no reason for you to fall victim to the blizzard of IRS penalties. Though penalty assessments mean big bucks for the agency, precious few citizens ever exercise their right to seek abatement. Even fewer appeal adverse decisions regarding requests for abatement. Understanding these rights provides a sound defense against unjust penalties.

5

Stop Compounding the Problem

An Easy Approach to Canceling Interest

The double-barreled approach used by the IRS to punish citizens comes in the form of penalties *and* interest. The interest problem is especially acute because the IRS assesses interest from the time the tax was *due to be paid*, not from the time the tax was *determined* to be owed. Moreover, interest is charged on the entire unpaid balance of tax, penalties, and previously assessed interest and is compounded on a *daily* basis. No wonder tax bills can easily double or triple over a relatively short period of time.

The Taxpayer Advocate's 1999 annual report summarizes the problem quite succinctly, saying:

> [S]ince interest is charged on virtually every balance due case, we have found that the interest charge itself is a significant problem for a large number of taxpayers. Often the interest (and penalties) due are larger than the original underlying tax due.

Many of the hardship situations that taxpayers face result from the large amount of interest that has accrued. Part of the problem is that the Service, for a variety of reasons, does not resolve (or even address) a taxpayer's particular tax issue for several years. During this time, interest is compounding.[1]

The Taxpayer Advocate's 2000 report ranked delay in processing cases and the corresponding interest assessments as number fourteen on the list of the top twenty problems people faced that year.

What most people do not realize, however, is that some interest assessments may be *abated*. The right to abate interest was created with the first Taxpayers' Bill of Rights Act in 1986 and expanded in 1996 with the second Taxpayers' Bill of Rights Act. In this chapter, I explore both the conditions under which interest may be canceled and the simple steps for achieving cancellation.

A key reason so few people understand the right to cancel interest is that the IRS lied to America about it for so long. Even now, the agency provides little guidance on the subject.

The first version of Publication 1, *Your Rights as a Taxpayer*, appeared in 1989, just after Congress mandated that the IRS prepare a publication clearly and simply explaining taxpayers' rights. Amazingly, Publication 1 outright lied about canceling interest. On page four of the 1989 document, under the heading "Cancellation of Penalties," the IRS declared, "You have the right to ask that certain penalties (but not interest) be cancelled."

In the 1998 version of Publication 1, the IRS dropped the reference to interest, opting to remain silent on the issue. Finally, after I put pressure on the agency about this and other misstatements and omissions in its publications, the agency revised Publication 1 yet again. The August 2000 edition reads, "We will waive interest that is the result of certain errors or delays caused by an IRS employee." This identical statement is found elsewhere in IRS literature, but only recent amendments to Publication 556, *Examination of Returns, Appeal Rights, and Claims for Refund*, provide any definitive guidance on how to go about it.

Inaccurate and incomplete information are chief reasons why

interest assessments are abated so infrequently. The IRS made 13.1 million interest assessments in 1996 and 11.9 million in 1997, of which it canceled just 2.8 million in 1996 and 2.1 million in 1997. Even at that, according to one Treasury Department report,

> The majority of such abatements appear to be the result of adjustments to the underlying tax liability, resulting in a reduction in tax and associated abatement of interest.[2]

This means simply that these were not abatements at all in the context of this discussion. They represented only secondary adjustments to accounts where the underlying tax assessments were corrected. Interest was *not* abated independently for any of the reasons provided for in either of the Taxpayers' Bill of Rights Acts. On the other hand, understanding the right to cancel interest assessments has the potential of saving the American taxpayer billions in unnecessary financial burdens.

HOW INTEREST BALLOONS A TAX BILL

Prolonged delays in processing a case occur for a number of reasons. In recent years, delays are attributable to the massive restructuring of the IRS and the retraining of its employees. Because of this effort, the IRS virtually went to sleep all during 1999, 2000, and into 2001. In addition, the downsizing of the agency's workforce left critical personnel shortages in the areas of audit and appeals. So not only were delays associated with the commencement of new cases, but pending cases were delayed while files were transferred from one office to another and from one caseworker to another.

Another reason for delays is more systemic in nature. The IRS receives well over two hundred million tax returns and in excess of one billion information returns annually. As a general rule, the law provides the IRS with three years from the date a return is filed in which to audit it or otherwise make adjustments. Given the scope of the returns-processing nightmare the IRS faces each year and the fact that the agency moves at the speed of a glacier, it is a wonder it gets *anything* done within the three-year period. Consequently, it is common for more than one and often up to two-plus years to pass before a case is even assigned for examination or other enforcement action.

Another factor leading to interest accumulation is delay associated with protracted litigation. Interest grows on tax bills—to the extent that you actually owe taxes—even while you challenge the IRS. The IRS often uses this fact as a means of dissuading citizens from appeals, but if you can prove that you do not owe the tax, the threat is meaningless. However, in cases where you actually owe the tax, prolonging the inevitable only makes matters worse.

Still another problem is the transient nature of many Americans. We move often, and this poses problems for the IRS in keeping up with us. The IRS sometimes finds it difficult to locate a citizen to communicate with him about a given return until one or more years after he files the return. Parenthetically, I find it fascinating that while the IRS struggles to locate citizens in the audit process, it seems to have no difficulty finding them when it comes time to levy a bank account or paycheck.

The combination of delays and errors leads to terrible results, as illustrated by the story of Kay Council, which appeared in the June 1990 issue of *Money* magazine. The article was entitled "Horribly Out of Control," and related the story of how Kay's husband, Alex, committed suicide as a result of a debilitating IRS battle that dragged on for years. Facing an unjust tax bill of nearly three hundred thousand dollars and no way to pay lawyers to continue the battle, Alex's choice to take his life was purely a "business decision." It allowed Kay to continue the fight with the only remaining resource the family had—Alex's life insurance death benefit.

The lion's share of the tax bill was interest and penalties. Eventually Kay was successful in proving that the IRS's own errors were responsible for the bill. But while she was successful in finally vindicating herself and her husband, the victory was a hollow one, since she lost her husband in the process. In concluding its report on the tragedy, *Money* stated, "Kay Council wants you to believe that the IRS could destroy your family just as it crushed her, her husband of 14 years, and their four children."

This story sticks with me to this day for two key reasons. First, I was interviewed on radio extensively after the story broke. Discussing it repeatedly left me very familiar with the facts. But second and more important, I was grilled on how such a thing could happen and how we might prevent it in the future. I still take issue with the article's suggestion that we are defenseless when it comes to the IRS. While it is true that the events of the Council disaster should never have occurred, it *does not* have to happen to you. If Alex Council knew what you are about to learn, it probably would not have happened to him.

HOW TO CANCEL INTEREST ON PENALTIES

When a penalty is abated for any reason, the corresponding interest on that penalty must also be canceled. If the penalty upon which the interest is based is canceled, no lawful authority remains for the collection of the interest on that penalty.

Consequently, when making an application for penalty abatement, it is a good idea to add a simple paragraph addressing the interest question. That paragraph could read as follows:

> In addition to the abatement of the penalties mentioned in this letter,
> I also request that interest assessed in connection with, and which
> accrued as a direct result of, such penalties also be fully abated.

This language is simple and does not require the submission of a separate demand for abatement.

CANCELING INTEREST FOR WHICH THE IRS IS TO BLAME

Code section 6404(e) provides two circumstances under which interest can be abated. Interest is subject to abatement when it is shown that the interest is attributable "in whole or in part to any unreasonable error or delay by an officer or employee" of the IRS. In short, interest that grows from the IRS's own mistakes or delays in connection with your case can be canceled. The abatement is available when delay occurs in either the act of determining a tax debt (the deficiency process) or the act of collecting taxes.

To win abatement of interest, you must prove three key facts. They are:

1. That the alleged error or delay occurred in connection with "performing a ministerial or managerial act" associated with the case

2. That the error or delay occurred after the IRS contacted you "in writing" with regard to the case

3. That "no significant aspect" of the error delay is attributable to your actions.

I address each of these elements in turn.

1. Ministerial and Managerial Acts

The most crucial element of the test is showing that the error or delay occurred in connection with a ministerial or managerial task. Understanding these two terms and how they apply is the key to winning abatement of interest. Let us examine them carefully.

What Is a "Ministerial" act? IRS regulations define a *ministerial act* as a procedural or mechanical act. These are actions associated with the physical processes necessary to move a case through the system. Error or delay in connection with a ministerial act occurs during the processing of your case after all prerequisites to the act, such as conferences and review by supervisors, have taken place.[3]

Keep in mind that delay that occurs while the IRS is in the act of exercising its judgment or discretion is not ministerial delay. The Senate Finance Committee Report on the Taxpayers' Bill of Rights Act makes it clear that "a ministerial act is a *procedural* action, not a decision in a substantive area of tax law."[4]

To say this another way, the IRS has broad latitude to think about its decisions. While the IRS is considering the case, the interest clock ticks. Only the statute of limitations prevents the agency from sitting on a case indefinitely. However, once a decision is made, the IRS becomes responsible for issuing the opinions and directives necessary to put that decision into effect. At that point, the IRS engages in ministerial acts that are the subject of the statute. If an unreasonable error or delay occurs in connection with carrying out those acts, the interest attributable to the error or delay is subject to abatement.

A common case of delay in connection with determining a tax debt is that which occurs in issuing a notice of deficiency. The notice of deficiency is the IRS's final determination to propose increased tax liability. This act generally follows an audit.

For example, suppose that in the course of your audit you promptly provide to the IRS all documents and explanations necessary for it to pass on the correctness of your tax return. After receiving the information, the IRS fails to issue a prompt notice of deficiency even though it has determined all the issues in the case. The IRS's act of determining how it is going to treat your tax matters is a discretionary act, not ministerial. The act of issuing the notice of deficiency reflecting the decision on the issues is a ministerial act. This delay is grounds for abatement of interest.

Another common example of both error and delay occurs in the collection of tax liabilities that are already assessed. The IRS is required to send its collection notices to the citizen's last known address. This is considered the address shown on the most recently filed tax return. However, the IRS has a persistent problem keeping up with address changes. Thus it is not unusual for collection notices to be sent to old addresses, only to be returned to the IRS as undeliverable.

Often years go by before the IRS catches up with people because of their repeated moves. When the IRS finally locates them, citizens discover to their dismay that thousands of dollars in interest have been added to the bill. In this example, the interest is attributable to the IRS's error in sending collection notices to the wrong address and failing to correct its own records. The process of correctly mailing notices is a ministerial act. The error and delay are grounds for abatement of interest.

Audits are also delayed because of changes in one's residence. Let us say you move prior to the IRS selecting your return for audit. The audit notice is mailed to your old address but forwarded to your new address, which happens to be in another state. You ask the IRS to reschedule the audit date and transfer the case to the IRS office nearest your new residence. The request is approved, but there is a substantial delay in actually transferring the case. The decision of *whether* to transfer a case is not a ministerial act. However, *physically transferring* the case is a ministerial act. This delay is grounds for abatement of interest.

I once worked on a case in which a citizen contacted the IRS seeking information about how much he owed so that he could resolve his debt. He was given a notice saying that he owed X dollars, which he paid. As far he was concerned, the matter was resolved. However, years later, when he was seeking a loan to buy a house, the title company turned up a tax lien showing an additional liability not revealed to him earlier. The process of accessing and providing the most current information to a citizen regarding his account is a ministerial act. While this citizen still had to pay the taxes he owed, the interest that accrued between the time he first contacted the IRS and the time he learned of the additional liability had to be abated.

Another common problem leading to improper interest assessments is the misapplication of payments people make toward their accounts. The IRS receives hundreds of millions of payments every year. And every year the misapplication of payments is ranked among the top twenty problems citizens face. This is such a concern that in 2000 the IRS installed sophisticated and expensive mail-sorting equipment in all its service centers in order to better detect payments. Still the problem of misapplied payments continued to be ranked among the top problems faced by citizens in each of the three years 2000, 2001, and 2002.

The correct application of a payment to your account is a ministerial act. Provided you give the IRS all necessary and accurate identifying information at the time of making your payment, interest attributed to a misapplied payment must be abated. Such information includes your name, current address, social security or other taxpayer identification number, the type of tax, and the year in question. This information should be shown on both the payment device itself and in a simple letter accompanying the payment.

Another problem involves lost or misprocessed tax returns. One of the very first cases I handled concerning ministerial delay involved

Carol and the allegation that she failed to file her 1979 return. While it was true that she filed late, she did file the return, but the IRS did not process it properly. As a result, the IRS treated her as a nonfiler. The agency audited her 1979 income tax return in 1984.[5] But it was not until 1987 that a notice of deficiency was issued and Carol was able to challenge the IRS's tax liability determination. In August 1989, a decision was reached on the merits of her challenges. When Carol received her bill from the IRS, she owed $2,871 in taxes and $6,139 in interest. Carol demanded an abatement of the interest. An example of Carol's letter is shown in Exhibit 5–1 and discussed in more detail later.

What Is a "Managerial" Act? The term *managerial act* is defined in the regulations as

> an administrative act that occurs during the processing of a taxpayer's case involving the temporary or permanent loss of records or the exercise of judgment or discretion relating to management of personnel.[6]

What we are talking about here is the manner in which the IRS handles and administers its internal records, taxpayer files, and the IRS personnel who attend to those items. Let me give you some examples of delay that occurs in connection with a managerial task.

Suppose you are audited, and upon completion, your tax examiner is reassigned for extended training or duty in some other office. The auditor's manager is responsible for reassigning the open cases to other examiners for completion. However, delay occurs in reassigning these cases. This is delay in connection with a managerial task. The interest attributable to that delay is subject to abatement.

Another example involves a completed audit where the auditor's report is mailed as required. The report sets forth proposed changes to your tax return and you disagree with those changes. You request a meeting with the agent's supervisor to discuss the changes and present additional evidence. Delay occurs in setting up the meeting. This is delay in connection with a managerial task. The interest attributable to that delay is subject to abatement.

A third example involves a tax audit that is near completion and the examiner mails out a preliminary report proposing additional taxes. You ask for and receive a conference with the agent's supervisor at which you discuss the proposed changes and provide more information. After a prompt conference, the supervisor supports the auditor's recommendations and agrees to issue a final report so you can exercise your right of appeal. However, delay occurs in assigning the case to the appropriate staff for issuance of the final report because the file is misplaced. The assignment of the case to proper support staff and the responsible management of the file itself are both managerial tasks. The interest attributable to the delay associated with these tasks is subject to cancellation.

Bear in mind that, as in the case of delays involving ministerial tasks, no relief is available in cases where managerial delay involves the exercise of discretion in the application of tax law. For example, consider the case where, after an audit, you request a conference with a manager to present additional material. Where the manager incurs delay because of his acts of *considering* your evidence and *evaluating* your claims in light of the applicable tax law, the interest attributable to that delay is not subject to cancellation.

Likewise, delay that occurs because of the IRS's implementation of new computer systems, structural reorganizations, or the manner in which it prioritizes its caseload or opts to handle a given audit or collection matter is not considered managerial delay. These matters are referred to as "general administrative decisions." The interest attributable to such delays is not subject to cancellation.

2. The IRS Contacted You "in Writing"

The second element of proof you must satisfy is that the error or delay occurred *after* the IRS contacted you "in writing." Until the IRS contacts you in writing, interest is not subject to abatement. This is the safety net the IRS enjoys through the terms of the statute of limitations.

Interest may be abated only when error or delay occurs after the case is opened. A case is opened by means of a written notice to you. This sometimes leads to confusion because the IRS generally has three years from the date you file a return in which to audit that return. Simply because the IRS waits well into the three-year period to contact you does not justify abatement of interest.

3. "No Significant Aspect" of Delay Caused by You

The final element of proof addresses your culpability in dragging the case out. You must prove that "no significant aspect" of the error or delay is attributable to your own actions. That is to say, you must come before the IRS with clean hands regarding the issue of delay. You cannot be responsible for dragging your feet or otherwise hindering the IRS in the disposition of the case.

Examples of situations where the IRS will consider that you did significantly contribute to delay include:

- Requests for audit extensions to gather records or accommodate your schedule

- Failure to make a good faith attempt to resolve a pending case

- Failure to file a return—precludes a claim that the IRS delayed in taking action to procure the return

- Failure to respond to IRS audit or collection notices

- Requests for collection holds (i.e., "uncollectible status") while the IRS pursues collection action

- Failure to pay taxes after the IRS issued preliminary collection notices.

THE INTEREST ABATEMENT WILD CARD

One additional element of the statute bears further discussion. The second Taxpayers' Bill of Rights Act amended code section 6404(e) to include the term *unreasonable* in the definition of errors or delay that give rise to interest abatement. In order to qualify for abatement, *in addition to* meeting the criteria outlined above, the error or delay must be considered unreasonable.

Unfortunately, Congress did not define the term *unreasonable* and simply left the matter for the courts to sort out. This has caused its own set of problems since the lack of objective guidelines in the statute makes it difficult for the courts to determine when the IRS is and is not required to abate interest.[7]

Despite this failing, congressional statements made at the time of enacting section 6404(e) in the first place provide some insight. In the Senate Report on the first Taxpayers' Bill of Rights Act where section 6404(e) was born, Congress stated that the IRS should abate interest where failure to do so "would be widely perceived as grossly unfair."[8] Based upon this, we can say it is grossly unfair to charge you interest if the IRS

- Fails to search its own computer systems for your current address
- Loses your tax return or other documents relevant to your tax liability
- Through its own negligence fails to assign an agent to work your case
- Gives erroneous advice in a substantive area of tax law.

On the other hand, where the IRS is diligent in performing its functions, such as querying its computer systems for a current address and then issuing a notice to the most current address available, and nevertheless commits an error or incurs delay in processing the case, this will probably be looked upon as reasonable.

In your letter seeking abatement of interest, be sure to include an argument grounded in the notion of fundamental fairness. This should be persuasive where the error or delay is plainly attributable to IRS actions and not your own failures.

Exhibit 5–1 is Carol's letter seeking abatement of interest. Notice that she took care to illustrate the timetable of the case. This is critical to alert the IRS as to the specific period of time in which interest is subject to abatement. Carol was also deliberate in showing that she always acted in a timely manner regarding her obligations. As I discuss later, it is essential to establish that the delay in question is not attributable to you. Through Carol's presentation of facts, the IRS was able to conclude that she was entitled to relief under the statute.

EXHIBIT 5–1

Carol ———
Address
City, State, Zip

Date:
SSN:

Internal Revenue Service
Regional Service Center

Dear IRS:

I am in receipt of your statement of tax due dated ———. The bill is for income taxes, penalty and interest in the total amount of $———.

Enclosed you will find a cashier's check in the amount of $———, which represents payment of the income tax and penalty assessments. It should be applied as such. I hereby request an abatement of the interest assessment for good cause as shown below.

My request for abatement of interest is based upon code section 6404(e). In general, that provision requires the IRS to abate "all or part" of any interest assessment when the deficiency is "attributable in whole or in part to any error or delay by an officer or employee of the Internal Revenue Service." As more fully set out here, the facts demonstrate that the IRS is responsible for much of the delay in this case.

My tax return for the year ——— was filed late. It was filed to an IRS collection officer in ——— [office], on ——— [date]. At that time, all tax due was paid. On ——— [date], I received a notice that my return was not filed and that the IRS intended to conduct an examination to determine whether one was required to be filed. At that time, I wrote to the revenue agent and explained that my return was in fact filed. I explained that the file copy of the tax return I have in my possession bears the "received" stamp of the IRS and is dated ——— [date].

On ——— [date], I received a response from the revenue agent indicating that he had no record of receiving my Form 1040. He mentioned that he questioned the revenue officer regarding my claim that it was filed to him, and found that no such return was filed. Nevertheless, my file copy bears the "received" stamp of the IRS dated ———, at the ——— [office]. My copy was stamped by the revenue officer who allegedly stated he did not recall receiving the document. I was told by the revenue agent that he would proceed with the examination as though no return was filed. He stated in his ——— [date] letter that an appointment was set for ——— [date].

At that time I retained a representative to assist me with the case. He requested that I locate my file copy of the income tax return bearing the IRS "received" stamp. This took some time as it had been misplaced. In the meantime, my representative canceled the conference.

After locating my copy of the tax return, I mailed it to the revenue agent. This occurred on approximately ——— [date]. After a copy of the return was mailed to the agent, I heard absolutely nothing from the IRS for over two years.

The next notification I received was on ——— [date]. It was a request by the revenue agent for me to sign Form 872, *Consent to Extend Time to Assess,* for the year in question. Because I was under the impression that the three-year period for assessment had already expired by that time, I did not sign the form, per the advice of my representative. On ——— [date], I received another request to sign Form 872. Again, under the belief that the statutory period for assessment had already expired and per the advice of counsel, I did not sign the form.

The next word I received came on ——— [date], when the IRS mailed a notice of deficiency. A prompt petition was filed with the U.S. Tax Court on or about ——— [date]. It was not until ——— [date] that I was contacted by the Appeals Office and informed of the opportunity to negotiate with Appeals to settle the case.

I took full advantage of the opportunity to settle the case. My representative and I negotiated with Appeals in good faith, and on ——— [date], I was notified that the agreement we reached was approved. Decision documents were signed on ——— [date] and immediately transmitted to the IRS. Two months later, I received a bill for the tax and penalty we agreed to, but that bill included interest well in excess of the tax we agreed to.

As shown from the facts set forth in this letter, the greatest period of delay is directly attributed to the IRS's unreasonable errors. First, the local office lost my tax return and was therefore under the impression that it was not filed. They attempted to conduct an examination solely for the purpose of preparing a return that was already filed long before the audit notice was issued. When they discovered that the return was in fact filed, they delayed well over two years before requesting that I sign a Form 872.

When a notice of deficiency was issued and a Tax Court petition was filed, it was again a matter of well over a year before the case was assigned to the Appeals Office for settlement discussion. At that time, I immediately undertook negotiations with Appeals and reached a settlement with little delay.

Because the interest assessment is based "in whole or in part" upon unreasonable delay directly attributable to the IRS, that interest should be abated in accordance with Code section 6404(e). It would be patently unfair to hold me accountable for various processing errors committed by the IRS.

Under penalty of perjury, I declare that the facts stated in this letter are true and correct in all respects.

Sincerely,

Carol ———

THE ERRONEOUS REFUND CHECK

Over the years, I have spoken with dozens of people who received a tax refund to which they were not entitled. I once spoke with a man in Ohio who received a refund check from the IRS for several thousand dollars. He returned the check to the IRS with a note explaining that he was not entitled to the refund. Like a stray cat, however, the refund check found its way into the man's mailbox a second time. This time the IRS included a letter explaining that he was indeed entitled to the money and that he should deposit the check. So he did.

About nine months later the IRS contacted the man again, but this time singing a different tune. It demanded repayment of the money, now classified as an "erroneous refund." That part was not so bad. The man knew he was not entitled to the funds in the first place and he repaid it.

What was worse is that the agency demanded interest on the money from the date of the initial refund. It was bad enough that the IRS demanded any interest at all. It was particularly troubling that the agency demanded interest during a time when the man did not even possess the money. Remember, he returned the first refund check to the IRS immediately.

Under code section 6404(e)(2), all interest assessed in connection with "any erroneous refund" is subject to abatement. The statute provides for abatement of all interest from the time the check is issued "until the date a demand for repayment is made." In other words, the only interest that may legally be charged is that which accrues *after* the agency demands repayment of the funds. This is an important incentive to act quickly. Keep in mind that if the money is not rightfully yours, the IRS has powerful collection tools available to it. Interest is just the beginning.

In order to win the abatement, you must show that you "or a related party has in (no) way caused such erroneous refund" to be issued. Your tax returns and any potential correspondence to the IRS will be viewed to determine the extent of your role in procuring the refund.

The statute mandates cancellation of interest on erroneous refunds under $50,000. However, the statute itself is unclear on whether the IRS may cancel interest on erroneous refunds of $50,000 or more. To help clear the air, the IRS issued an internal legal opinion stating that it may cancel interest in cases where the facts justify. The following facts are to be considered in deciding the issue:

- Those who fail to return the erroneous refund for a significant period of time after they discover, or reasonably should have discovered, the error are less deserving of abatement since they are considered to have "contributed to the delay and had the opportunity to profit from the IRS's error."

- Whether the citizen returned the erroneous refund "before the IRS notified him of the error," especially if there was substantial delay between the issuance of the refund and notification by the IRS.

- The citizen's level of sophistication, which may indicate whether the person acted reasonably with respect to the error.[9]

A letter demanding abatement of interest assessed due to an erroneous refund must address two elements. The first is the timing issue. You must show the date the refund was received and the date of the IRS notice demanding repayment. All interest accrued prior to the date of the demand for repayment must be abated if the refund was under $50,000. If it is $50,000 or more, the IRS has the discretion to abate interest in appropriate cases.

The second element addresses the question of whether you caused the refund. Your letter must show with an affirmative declaration that you or a related party "in no way caused the refund." When this showing is made, all interest must legally be abated.

ERRONEOUS IRS ADVICE

When you are the victim of erroneous IRS advice, not only can you win an abatement of the penalty attributable to the error, but the interest must also be canceled. This rule is established by code section 6404(f). The law provides that "any penalty or addition to tax" must be abated when the additions are attributable to erroneous advice provided by the IRS.

There are some simple limitations to this rule that must be accounted for in your demand for abatement.

1. You must have received the advice *in writing* and in response to a written request that you submitted to the agency. Your letter must specifically set out the facts of your case and must provide the IRS with all the information needed to render an accurate opinion.

2. You must have reasonably relied upon the written advice. That is to say, you must have followed the advice in the preparation of your tax return. You cannot use the defense of erroneous IRS advice if you never relied on the advice in the first place.

3. You must have provided "adequate and accurate information" to the IRS in your request for advice. Information is considered adequate if it is sufficient to apprise the IRS of all the facts and circumstances of the case and is correct and complete. Obviously, the IRS is not liable for erroneous advice if you did not provide full and accurate information upon which to base the advice.

Your letter demanding abatement of "all additions" to the tax based upon erroneous IRS advice must set forth facts to establish the existence of all the above elements. You must also include a copy of your written request for advice, the IRS's written response, and the report of adjustments to your return that includes the computation of penalties and interest.

If you received verbal advice from the IRS, it is well worth the effort to seek abatement of interest, provided you can prove that you did in fact receive erroneous advice. (This was discussed on p. 75.) Keep in mind that while the statute provides for abatement only in cases where IRS advice is "in writing," the IRS made the administrative determination to allow penalty abatements in cases where its verbal advice is incorrect. It is not an unreasonable stretch to include interest abatements under the same theory. When seeking abatement under these circumstances, include with your submission a copy of your detailed notes of your conversation with IRS personnel, including the name of the person you spoke with, his employee ID number, and the date of the call.

A STANDARD COVER FORM

For the reasons discussed earlier, use Form 843 as a cover form when demanding abatement of interest. The form should reference code section 6404(e) if the demand is based upon IRS error or delay. Use code section 6404(f) if the request is based upon erroneous advice furnished by the IRS. Attach your written demand to the form together with all documentary evidence needed to support the claim. Mail the form via certified mail with return receipt requested, addressed to the Interest Abatement Coordinator at the service center where you file your returns. Retain a copy for your records.

WHEN THE ANSWER IS NO

Demands for abatement of interest are subject to review by the IRS's Office of Appeals. If the answer to your abatement request is no, you have the right to appeal by submitting a written protest letter within thirty days of the date of denial. A written protest letter regarding interest is essentially the same as that covering penalties. Please see Exhibit 4–3 (chapter 4).

The language of the protest letter must be altered to reflect the fact that you are appealing the denial of your interest abatement request. At the Appeals conference, you have the right to present to the agency any additional evidence necessary to support your claim.

The right to demand an abatement of interest is very important. Exercising this right when appropriate assures that you will never pay interest you do not owe.

6

Handling the Tax Audit

How to Keep Your Money in Your Pocket

One of the greatest sources of anxiety for Americans is the idea of an IRS audit. The chief reason for the anxiety is the fact that the agency has gone to great lengths to persuade the public that financial horror will befall them if they run afoul of the IRS. That is why the typical American would rather undergo a root canal than go through a tax audit.

And why not be concerned about an audit? As we learned in chapter 2, former Commissioner Rossotti pointed out that the average face-to-face audit results in an assessment of about $9,500. Who among us can afford to write a check for $9,500 and not miss the money?

Concern over the monetary aspects of the audit is only part of the problem. Nobody wants to go to jail, and when the terms *IRS* and *audit* are used in the same breath, many people conjure up images of prison. The IRS does little to disabuse us of these notions, and in fact, through celebrated cases such as that of Leona Helmsley, the agency does its best to keep America convinced that offending the IRS is much like offending John Gotti.

But the reality is that tax audits need not involve jail, increased taxes and penalties, or beatings from some guy with a three-inch scar on his face. When you understand what your rights are in a tax audit, as well as the IRS's rights and limitations, you can be assured that you will leave the audit with your money in your pocket, where it belongs. To begin our discussion, let us examine exactly what constitutes an audit and how returns are selected for audit.

WHAT IS A TAX AUDIT?

A tax audit is nothing more nor less than the process by which the IRS ascertains the correctness of a tax return. At the outset of the examination, the IRS has no clue whether, for example, your deduction for charitable contributions is correct. The fact that your return was selected because of this claim does not necessarily signal an error. In the strictest sense, selection means only that the IRS questions a claim and is calling upon you to verify it.

Your tax return contains two general categories of claims. The return asserts an amount of income you claim to have earned during the year. And it claims reductions to income that operate to lower the tax. These reductions include, for example, personal dependent exemptions, standard or itemized deductions, business expenses, capital losses, operating losses, and tax credits. The tax code requires that you prove all the claims in your return.

Over the past several years, the IRS has adopted the view that most of the perceived tax cheating occurs with regard to income, not deductions. And because fewer people claim itemized deductions on their tax returns to begin with, the more fruitful audit approach is fast becoming a challenge to your income, not your deductions. This is evidenced by the remarks of former Commissioner Rossotti, discussed in chapter 2, wherein he describes IRS efforts to expand its information returns matching programs.

While in the strictest technical sense the purpose of the tax audit is to ascertain the correctness of your return, in the practical sense the IRS looks upon the audit as a means to get more money. My years of experience dealing with tax audits have taught me that the IRS actually cares very little about whether your return is correct. Its intention is to get the money regardless. This is why it is so important to understand your rights before going into any audit.

HOW THE IRS SELECTS RETURNS FOR AUDIT

The question every citizen asks when discussing the audit process is: "How are returns selected for audit?" Let us start by identifying the two general types of tax audits. First is the correspondence audit, and second is the face-to-face audit. As their names imply, the former is conducted through letter writing and the latter takes place in person. Let us address each in turn.

The Correspondence Audit

IRS computers scrutinize every tax return filed. The computers perform a number of review and comparison tasks, such as determining that your math is correct and ensuring that all necessary supporting schedules are attached. These reviews lead to millions of so-called correction notices, which demand increased taxes and penalties. Though you never saw an IRS agent in the flesh, you were audited, and the results were communicated by correspondence. See chapter 2 for the details.

Correspondence audits also involve much more than just computer checks for math errors. These audits can raise questions about specific items on your return. For example, the IRS may ask you to provide proof of your mortgage interest deduction or real estate taxes. Or, as is very common, the IRS might question your dependent exemptions or the claim of a tax credit, such as the Earned Income Tax Credit.

In such a case, the IRS asks you to provide proof of your claim via return mail. It then evaluates your evidence and passes on the merits of your claim. If your claim is allowed, you are so notified and that ends the matter.

If the claim is disallowed, the IRS sends you a report known as an Examination Report. The report recalculates your tax debt in light of the changes to your return, then asks you to take action. You can either sign the report and accept the changes (which usually means increased taxes) or you can appeal the findings to the IRS's Office of Appeals. This process is discussed in more detail later in this chapter. The Examination Report is often referred to as a thirty-day letter because you have thirty days to either sign it or execute your appeal rights.

The Face-to-Face Audit

The face-to-face audit is the process by which you sit down with a revenue agent (often referred to as a tax auditor) who reviews your return. The decision to conduct a face-to-face examination is based upon several selection criteria. However, the most prevalent is the so-called Discriminate Function System (DIF). Nearly one-third of all returns audited are selected through the DIF scoring process.

DIF is a computer program that compares every line of your return with statistical averages for a person in your same income category and profession. If any line of your return is out of balance with those averages, the difference is scored. The higher the DIF score, the more likely you are to be selected for examination. The IRS reasons that those with higher-than-average deductions are less likely to be able to support their claims. Consequently, these people are more likely to owe money as a result of their audits.

Keep in mind that DIF scores are based only on *averages*. And simply because one or more of your deductions happens to be in excess of the average does not mean you cannot claim the deduction. You are entitled to claim deductions based upon your facts, not averages. Therefore, merely being selected by the DIF program for audit should portend no unwelcome results, provided you can prove that your return is correct.

To update its DIF scores, the IRS has now embarked on a wide-scale random audit program known as the National Research Program.

This program is randomly targeting fifty thousand citizens for audit. The audits will range in breadth from simple correspondence audits to grueling line-by-line examinations. The details of this program are discussed at length in chapter 12.

Although the DIF program is the most widely used audit selection process, it is just one of many. In 1993 the IRS began an audit research program directed squarely at businesses. Known as the Market Segment Specialization Program (MSSP), it is designed to examine and evaluate every aspect of how certain businesses operate within a given market.

As an example, one MSSP project focuses upon gasoline retailers. Let us say the market area is Philadelphia. To start with, the IRS selects for audit a random number of gas retailers in that area— perhaps a dozen. To build a profile of how gas retailers in Philadelphia operate, the IRS audits every element of the business. The audit includes a detailed review of the financial aspects of the business and delves into how the industry itself operates. Auditors contact manufacturers, wholesalers, distributors, trade associations, and others directly or indirectly connected with gasoline retailing. The idea is to learn all that is possible about the industry. After auditing the sample universe of businesses, the IRS develops a manual to guide revenue agents in future audits of similar businesses in that area.

Another common audit selection strategy involves what the IRS calls "compliance initiatives." These are projects based upon the specific claims in a given tax return. For example, since the early 1980s the IRS has targeted certain returns claiming tax-sheltered investments. More recently the IRS has intensified its audits of corporate tax shelters. Other specialized selection classes include trusts, tax protesters, multilevel or direct marketers, and others.[1] When the agency's computer screening mechanism identifies one or more areas of curiosity, the chances of a face-to-face audit grow significantly.

Finally, as explained in Publication 1, *Your Rights as a Taxpayer*, the IRS also uses "information from outside sources" to select returns for audit. These sources "may include newspapers, public records, and individuals." In this regard, the IRS uses tips from disgruntled employees, estranged family members, former spouses, etc., to select returns for audit.

WHAT HAPPENS IN A FACE-TO-FACE AUDIT?

A face-to-face audit usually starts with a letter. The letter explains that your return was selected for examination and tells you the time and date set for the meeting. You are asked to appear at the meeting (with counsel if you wish) and to present evidence to answer the questions raised in your return. In some cases the IRS may announce that it intends to come to your home or place of business to conduct a "field audit."

Sometimes the initial letter identifies the specific questions the IRS has about your return. If so, it tells you, for example, that the agency has questions about your charitable contributions, business expenses, or other deductions. It can raise questions about any of the items in the return, so it is not uncommon for the agent to question more than one item once the audit begins.

In other cases the initial letter is not specific about what is in question. It simply tells you to show up and bring your documents. Either way, the IRS provides a list of the records it expects you to present. The list always includes bank statements, canceled checks, duplicate deposit slips, and copies of tax returns for the years immediately prior to and after the audit year. Be sure to bring with you all the documents needed to support the deductions you claimed.

The audit process may consist of one or more meetings, with either you or your counsel. During the course of the audit, expect the agent to ask questions about your affairs and to seek additional financial information either from you or third parties, such as banks or employers. This process takes place over the course of one or more meetings and spans several months. As the case develops, the auditor may even expand the audit into other years. Keep in mind that the IRS usually has up to three years to audit a return, meaning that it can look at as many as three tax returns at any one time.

When the audit is completed, the agent presents his findings to

you in an Examination Report. The report explains the reasons for
any proposed changes to your return. About 80 percent of those
audited end up owing more money.

It is important to understand that the Examination Report is
merely a *recommendation* for changes to your return. The agent does
not have unilateral authority to impose those changes. In fact, he has
no authority at all to impose those changes. That is why he "asks" you
to sign the report. If you sign it, you accept the changes and waive
your right to challenge the report.

If you disagree with the report and wish to challenge it, you generally have three options:

1. Present more information to the agent to refute his findings.

2. Request a conference with the agent's supervisor.

3. Appeal the agent's findings by submitting a written protest letter
   within thirty days of the date shown on the Examination Report.

If you opt for either (or both) of the first two alternatives, your
additional information is considered and a new report is issued. At
that point, you can either accept the report or appeal the decision.
When you appeal the decision, your case is removed to the Appeals
Office. There the matter is fully reviewed with an eye toward resolving the controversy.

SHOULD I HIRE COUNSEL?

You have the absolute right to counsel at every level of your dealings with the IRS.[2] Counsel can take the form of an attorney, an
accountant, a person enrolled to practice before the IRS (a so-called
enrolled agent), or a return preparer. The costs of representation are
generally indicative of a person's training and experience and you
have to bear that load.

If the audit is a simple correspondence audit or the IRS is looking
at only a narrow swath of issues, it may not be necessary to retain a

tax pro in the first instance. However, if it becomes apparent from the outset that the IRS is embarked upon a far-reaching fishing expedition, you would do well to at least consult experienced counsel, if not retain counsel before meeting with the IRS. You can easily judge this by the scope and breadth of the letter announcing the audit. The more information the IRS is looking for, the broader the fishing expedition.

At the very least, if you used a tax pro to prepare your return in the first place, consult with your preparer and make sure you go over the return so you understand it. Remember, even if you used a pro for return preparation, the burden of proof is on you.

In the garden variety audit situation, assuming you understand what is in your tax return and assuming you have the records needed to support your deductions, it is probably not necessary to hire counsel in the first instance. Keep in mind that you never waive your right to counsel. You can always bring in a pro later if things do not go as smoothly as you hoped. If you decide you want counsel right in the middle of a conversation with the auditor, the audit must be suspended until you obtain counsel.

Bear in mind that not every tax preparer is suited to represent you before the IRS. The worlds of tax preparation and tax litigation are entirely distinct. Frankly, most return preparers have little experience representing clients before the IRS. Look for counsel with this experience, and as an added bonus, find one experienced in dealing with people in your job or profession. This gives the pro a leg up in understanding your financial life.

Also bear in mind that former IRS agents do not automatically make the best representatives. Many former agents claim to have an advantage because of their past work on the "inside." However, I find that those who have worked on the inside tend to be less insightful and aggressive in problem solving than those who have not. And in fact, the longer a person has worked for the IRS, the less likely he is to possess the independent thinking needed to be effective as a taxpayer's representative.

Please note that this is by no means an indictment of all former

IRS agents. I work with several who are top-quality pros. But it is also fair to say—generally—that the more competent they are, the less time they spent with the IRS.

My Web site can help you find experienced, competent counsel to help with your tax problem. To find a tax pro near you, just go to www.taxhelponline.com, click on the Tax Freedom Institute title, and you will see my complete list of members. The Tax Freedom Institute is my association of tax professionals who use the "Pilla techniques" for dealing with the IRS.

DO I HAVE TO ALLOW THE IRS INTO MY HOME OR OFFICE?

In a word, no. Unless an agent obtains a search warrant (which will *never* happen in a routine audit), the IRS must have your *permission* to enter private property, such as your home or the private areas of a public business, such as back offices and warehouses.[3] You do *not* have to give IRS personnel permission to enter your home. I can imagine no circumstances under which I would permit IRS agents into my home for purposes of an audit.

If the auditor states that he wishes to come to your home, simply respond with a polite letter explaining that you do not want the audit to take place at your home. Explain that you (or counsel) will be happy to meet with the agent at his office. Or better yet, consider transforming the audit into a correspondence audit, as I discuss in detail later.

NINE SECRETS TO WINNING YOUR AUDIT

Now that you understand the basics, let me introduce you to the nine key things you need to know about an audit if you are to keep your money in your pocket.

1. Assume You Are Right

One of the first questions asked by those on the threshold of a tax audit is "What did I do wrong?" The feeling is no different from what you experience when you are pulled over by a traffic cop. The assumption underlying the question is that you did, in fact, do something wrong. However, to be successful in an audit, you must dispel this idea.

As we just learned, returns are not necessarily selected for audit because of an error. If a simple mistake is found, the agency generally sends a correction notice to handle it. A face-to-face audit is undertaken to determine the correctness of your return. In every sense, the IRS is asking you to demonstrate that your return is accurate. The IRS cannot determine whether there is an error until your records and data are thoroughly reviewed.

By dispelling the notion that you made a mistake, you place yourself in a significantly more powerful position. Those who believe they made a mistake enter the audit environment believing they must minimize their losses and just get out of there. That attitude will cost you money. The reason is that it is virtually *assured* that the auditor will find some error—real or imagined. For example, in 2001, about 84 percent of those whose returns were audited were found to owe more money.[4] As high as that percentage is, it is actually low compared with historic rates, which are closer to 90 percent.

On the other hand, if you go into the audit believing that your return is correct and then take steps to prove it, your chances of winning increase greatly. The reason is simple. Those who believe they are in the right are more aggressive about asserting their position than those who are uncertain. Your success in an audit depends upon your willingness to assert your position and to document the correctness of your tax return claims. Do not be intimidated. This is your money we are talking about.

2. Know the Issues

Never walk into an audit without knowing the issues. When you are selected for audit, you must demonstrate that all or a targeted portion of your tax return is accurate. You are greatly handicapped if you have no clue what you claimed in the return.

If the audit questions your income, you must prove that you reported all the income you earned. If the audit questions deductions, you must show both that the amount claimed for the deduction is accurate and that the expense qualifies as a legitimate deduction. Neither of these is a particularly difficult process. My book *IRS, Taxes and the Beast* contains the detailed, step-by-step procedures to follow to ensure that you will be able to meet the challenge.

If you use a tax pro to prepare your return, one way of gaining the knowledge you need to handle an audit is to work with your preparer more closely in the preparation process. This means discussing the issue with the preparer before the return is completed and going over the final product before it is filed. In all cases, be sure to store your records in a secure and organized fashion for at least six years from the date the return is filed. This takes much of the pain out of the audit process.

Do not make the mistake of believing that you do not need to know what is in your return just because you used a professional preparer. Please recognize that all a tax preparer does is organize your raw material into the format required by the IRS. Your tax professional cannot create deductions that do not exist, nor will he fabricate explanations for deductions claimed on your return. Make no mistake about it: you are ultimately responsible for the declarations in your return. This burden is *nondelegable*.

3. Realize that You Have Power

Realizing that you have power might be *the* most important key to surviving a tax audit. In general the public is terrified of tax audits and auditors. While there are many reasons for this, a chief reason is that the IRS at least allows (if not causes) the public to believe that the auditor wields great power. This power is believed to include the power to lien, levy, and seize assets—even the power to put you in jail if you do not cooperate.

The reality is, a revenue agent has absolutely no power over you whatsoever. He has no power to lien, levy, or seize your assets. He has no power to send you to jail. More than that, he has no power to even alter your tax return without your consent. Certainly there are IRS employees with such power, but a revenue agent is *not* one of them.

The task of a revenue agent is simple. He examines your return to determine its correctness—period. The unwritten rule, of course, is to collect more money in the process, but that is done only after the examination is closed and you *agree* to pay more money. If you do not agree, the IRS cannot collect more money until all of your appeal rights are exhausted. The first and main appeal is to the Appeals Office.

Most citizens do not realize that they have an absolute right to appeal audit decisions. Those who are aware of a right of appeal believe the appeal process is costly and time-consuming. Likewise, most people believe that when the auditor issues his findings, the matter is closed, and if you want to avoid further trouble, your only option is to sign the audit report and then turn out your pockets. The fact is that none of these beliefs is true.

As I explained earlier, the audit merely makes recommendations concerning your tax liability. The recommendations are presented in the form of an Examination Report. If you do not agree with the report, you have the option to present more information, ask for a conference with the auditor's manager, or submit a protest letter. The protest letter is the catalyst that kicks the case out of the hands of the revenue agent and into the hands of the Appeals Office.

Understanding the right of appeal is critical to success in the audit. The reason is the IRS audit results are wrong 60 to 90 percent of the time. However, precious few people who go through an audit ever appeal the decision. That tells me that the vast majority of audit victims pay taxes they do not owe.

Drafting a protest letter is simple. Just follow the guidance of IRS Publication 5, *Appeal Rights and Preparation of Protests for Unagreed Cases*. According to Publication 5, the protest letter must state:

1. Your name and address.

2. That you want to appeal the auditor's findings to the Appeals Office.

3. The date and symbols from the letter showing the proposed changes. These appear on the bottom of the Examination Report.

4. The tax periods or years involved.

5. An itemized schedule of the changes with which you disagree. Here you must identify the specific changes that you intend to challenge, such as the disallowance of charitable contributions.

6. A statement of facts supporting your position. This can be a simple one or two sentence statement explaining why the adjustment is incorrect.

7. A statement of the law or other authority on which you rely. This is also a simple, one or two sentence reference to the rule that supports your position. The basic rules are easily found in IRS publications that deal with your particular issue.

To be considered, your protest must declare that the statement of facts in paragraph (6) is true under penalty of perjury. Do this by adding the following sentence:

> Under penalty of perjury, I declare that I have examined the statement of facts presented in this protest and in any accompanying schedules and, to the best of my knowledge and belief, it is true, correct, and complete.

Mail the letter via certified mail, return receipt requested, to the "person to contact" shown in the Examination Report.

4. Always Deal with the IRS in Writing

There is nothing unreasonable about seeking a measure of protection, security, and privacy in your dealings with the IRS. The potential for achieving these is heightened when you deal with the IRS in writing. It is not uncommon for audit personnel to solicit information over the phone. I strongly recommend that you never provide sensitive tax data over the phone to anybody, whether they claim to be IRS personnel or not.

IRS Publication 1, *Your Rights as a Taxpayer*, states, "You have the right to know why we are asking you for information, how we will use it, and what happens if you do not provide requested information." Do not be afraid to challenge any IRS communication that does not provide those details in the first instance.

You should never provide information without the benefit of a notice explaining (1) the nature of the inquiry, (2) the year in question, and (3) the intended use of the information. This enables you to determine your legal requirement to provide the material, to consult counsel if you so choose, and to formulate an accurate and correct response to the demand. Additionally, the IRS's written inquiry and your written response make a clear and accurate record of the proceedings.

While it is not common for the IRS to *commence* an audit with a phone call, it is very common for an agent to make requests for additional information or explanations of certain items over the phone in the course of a pending audit. It is in this realm that providing written explanations is important. Agents are given to misunderstanding your statements about your actions. This propensity is reduced greatly if not eliminated when your explanations are in writing.

Anytime the IRS uses phone calls to solicit information, use a letter such as that shown in Exhibit 6–1 to reduce the proceedings to writing.

EXHIBIT 6–1

Your Name
Address
City, State, Zip

Date:
SSN:

Dear Tax Auditor:

On ——— [date] I was contacted via telephone by a person claiming to be a representative of the Internal Revenue Service. That person asked me to provide data regarding my personal affairs. However, I received no written notice from the IRS regarding this matter. I am reluctant to provide sensitive information based merely on a phone call.

IRS Publication 1, *Your Rights as a Taxpayer*, acknowledges my right to privacy and states that I have the right "to know why we are asking you for information, how [the IRS] will use it, and what happens if [I] do not provide it."

In light of the fact that the request for information was made by telephone, I do not know any of the information that Publication 1 says I am entitled to know.

Therefore I request that the IRS provide a detailed statement of the purpose of your request, why the information is requested, the use to which it will be put, and whether I must comply with the request. I also ask that you explain what may happen if I refuse to provide the requested data.

In addition, please provide a detailed statement of the issues in question on my return. You should also explain which years are in question.

Please provide this information at your earliest convenience.

Thank you.

Your Signature

5. Pin Down the Issues

The first cousin to the telephone contact is an audit letter that is vague or general in its requests. If the IRS mails an audit notice that is vague, overly broad, or unspecific as to the issues, respond in writing with a request for specificity. Use a variation of the sample letter shown in Exhibit 6–1. This letter helps you pin down the issues.

This is important because when the initial audit contact is vague, tax auditors often manipulate the examination to best serve the interests of the IRS. They do this by expanding the audit in directions beyond the areas of initial concern. On the other hand, when you have a clear statement of the issues in question, you are in a better position to hold the examination on a tighter course. The process is much like setting an agenda for a meeting.

This point is illustrated by the case of Jan, who was able to greatly reduce the burden placed on her by a vague audit notice. Jan was notified to "appear for an audit" but was provided little other information. She responded by writing a letter similar to the one shown in Exhibit 6–1. When the examiner responded with details, Jan learned that she was to be audited for three tax years. The earliest of the three years involved a return she had filed more than four years prior to receiving the audit notice.

Keep in mind that the IRS has just three years from the date of filing a return in which to audit that return.[5] Jan had filed the earliest of the three returns more than *four* years before she was notified of the audit. As such, the three-year statute of limitations had expired before the audit began. This deprived the IRS of authority to examine the first return. When Jan informed the agent of this fact, he promptly dropped the first year from consideration. By pinning the IRS down on the issues, Jan was able to reduce the burden of her audit by one-third.

6. Do Not Let Yourself Be Pushed Around

A common reason for the IRS's high audit success rate is that too many people allow themselves to be forced into an audit for which they are unprepared. Without the necessary understanding of your return and the records upon which it is based, you cannot hope to succeed in your audit. You also face a problem if you lack records for your deductions, either because they are lost or because you were unable to spend adequate time locating and organizing them.

Do not allow yourself to be forced into a meeting for which you are unprepared. You have the right to postpone your examination until you are satisfied that you can meet your burden of proof. Consider the language of IRS Publication 1, *Your Rights as a Taxpayer,* which declares:

> If we notify you that we will conduct your examination through a personal interview, or you request such an interview, you have the right to ask that the examination take place at a reasonable time and place that is convenient for both you and the IRS.

A common IRS power play is to *demand* that you appear at a given time and place, whether you are prepared or not. But the secret is that the IRS cannot force you to appear at an audit. The agent cannot arrest you if you do not appear, nor can he seize your assets or file a tax lien against you. What he can do is propose to disallow all your deductions, but even that decision is subject to appeal.

The fact is, however, that if you respond in writing in the proper manner, the IRS will not attempt to disallow your deductions and you will be afforded adequate time to prepare. Valid reasons for rescheduling the conference include:

- Conflicts due to prior personal or work commitments

- Time needed to locate and organize records

- Medical problems with yourself or a family member

- Time needed to consult counsel.

This list is by no means exhaustive. Any good faith reason for needing additional time can be asserted. Your letter must explain that you are unable to appear as scheduled. You should suggest alternative times and dates that are more convenient. It is helpful if you politely refer to the language of Publication 1 in making your request.

Even if the agent ignores your letter and disallows your deductions, simply appeal the decision by filing a protest letter. The Appeals Office will return the file to the Examination staff with instructions to "develop the case." That is to say, Appeals will tell the auditors to do their job and not play games.

7. If You Are Not Comfortable, Stay Away

Many IRS audit techniques revolve around asking questions and seeking information designed to trap the citizen. That is, the agent knows in advance the purpose of a particular line of questioning but does not reveal his purpose to you. Instead, he merely asks questions and demands answers. Not only is this unfair, but it has the effect of rattling an ignorant citizen. If you are easily rattled or intimidated, or concerned that you talk too much, staying out of danger is simple. Just *stay away* from the audit. The IRS cannot compel you to participate in a face-to-face audit.

Though you have the obligation to prove that your return is accurate, you can meet that burden through means other than a personal appearance. The alternative is a correspondence audit—the process of handling your audit through the mail. The IRS routinely uses correspondence audits to verify returns. Consider the following statement from Publication 1, *Your Rights as a Taxpayer:*

> We handle many examinations and inquiries by mail. We will send you a letter with either a request for more information or a reason why we believe a change to your return may be needed. You can respond by mail or you can request a personal interview with an examiner. If you mail us the requested information or provide an explanation, we may or may not agree with you, and we will explain the reasons for any changes. Please do not hesitate to write to us about anything you do not understand.

The correspondence audit offers you every opportunity to prove the correctness of your return but without subjecting you to a potentially intimidating confrontation.

To illustrate this, consider Larry's audit. He was naturally nervous, and the last thing he wanted was to face an auditor. Consequently, when he received an audit notice, he was adamant about not appearing personally. In a responsive letter, Larry demanded a correspondence audit. The letter was careful to point out that he:

- Was not refusing to be audited or to meet his burden of proof

- Had all necessary records and would provide copies

- Would—in writing—answer all questions and provide whatever additional explanations were necessary.

An example of Larry's letter is shown in Exhibit 6–2.

As the audit progressed, Larry was asked to provide bank statements, canceled checks, and other relevant data. In each case he responded in writing by submitting the applicable material together with explanations. When Larry's audit was completed, he had reached an agreement with the IRS and never set foot in an IRS office. He never laid eyes on a tax examiner and never lost one hour of work. Most important, Larry never placed himself in a situation where his own fear or ignorance could come back to haunt him.

Even if you are more than willing to take on the challenge of a face-to-face audit, there is another reason to consider the correspondence audit. Remember, the typical face-to-face audit nets the IRS about $9,500 in increased taxes, while the typical correspondence audit nets just $2,500.[6] And though there are a number of reasons for this, one significant factor is that it is more difficult to orchestrate a holdup through the mail than in a face-to-face confrontation.

EXHIBIT 6–2

Larry ———
Address
City, State, Zip

Date:
SSN:

Dear Sir:

On ——— [date] I received notice from you that my return for ——— [year] is under audit. The notice indicated that the following deductions [list them] are under examination. Your letter asks that I appear on ——— [date] to discuss these issues.

Please be advised that it is my desire and intent to fully cooperate to resolve each of your questions. I am in possession of records and testimony to prove that my return is correct in all respects. I stand prepared to present that evidence in order to resolve this matter. I am aware of my responsibility to present adequate proof of deductions and income.

However, I am also aware, as explained in IRS Publication 1, that many tax examinations are conducted via correspondence. For various reasons, not the least of which is a grueling work schedule that will not permit any time off [or list all other appropriate reasons], I will not be able to meet with you face-to-face. Nevertheless, I stand ready and willing to provide all necessary information and will answer all relevant questions through the mail.

Pursuant to your request of ——— [date] I am enclosing copies of all records [do not send originals] that pertain to the following items [list items of income or deductions flagged by IRS]. The records consist of ——— [provide explanation for each document, including issue to which it relates].

If you have any questions regarding these matters, please write to me at the above address. I will provide prompt responses by return mail.

Sincerely,

Larry ———

8. Stop the Steamroller

The goal of the IRS is to complete audits in the first interview. The faster it closes cases, the more audits it performs—simple as that. Unfortunately, a *fast* examination is not always *accurate*, particularly if you are not prepared. If you need time to obtain requested information or hire counsel, do not be shy about your right to suspend the interview. Keep two overarching principles in mind as you cope with audits: (1) the IRS cannot force you to attend a given conference, and (2) even if the agent disallows your deductions, you have the absolute right to appeal the decision.

I was once involved in an audit with a woman who was asked to provide evidence of the purchase price of stocks she had sold. The IRS wished to determine whether she had reported all profit from the sale. As proof, we offered the woman's ledger, which she used to record the purchase and sale price as well as the dates of all her holdings.

Unfortunately, the agent was not impressed. He wanted to see copies of the broker's confirmation slips for each transaction. The confirmation slips would contain the date, purchase or sale price, the number of shares involved, and the total amount of the trade. We explained that the confirmation slips were not saved. The woman's only record was the contemporaneous ledger she created to memorialize these very facts. The agent responded that if no confirmation slips existed, he would disallow the claimed basis, asserting that she realized 100 percent profit in the sale of each stock. "That assumes she obtained the stocks free of charge," I argued. "You know that didn't happen."

"That may be true," he replied, "but you have the burden to prove your basis and I don't accept this ledger." At that, I indicated that we wanted the examination suspended until such time as confirmation slips could be produced. "You said you didn't have them. What would be the use of suspending the audit?" he countered. "I intend to make the adjustment."

I responded, "The purpose of this audit is to determine the correctness of the tax return. Clearly, we cannot determine its correctness by merely drawing the assumption that she obtained expensive stocks free of charge. Obviously that is ridiculous and that did not happen. In the interest of fairness, you must provide an opportunity to present adequate proof on this point."

Because the IRS could not force us to continue, we opted to suspend the audit unilaterally. We then gathered the needed information from the library and through her brokerage house. Before long, we returned to face the agent. This time the audit was concluded, but on our terms. He accepted our proof, and there was no change as to the stock transactions. If we had not stopped the steamroller when the agent threatened to disallow the claimed basis, my client would have faced a bill for tens of thousands of dollars in additional taxes she did not owe.

9. Prevent Audit Abuse

My trade secret for preventing audit abuse and keeping the IRS firmly under control is very simple—tape-record the audit. When I suggest this, most people surprisingly say, "I didn't know I could do that." Let me draw from IRS Publication 1, *Your Rights as a Taxpayer*, to respond. The document reads:

> You may make sound recordings of any meetings with our examination, appeal, or collection personnel, provided you tell us in writing 10 days before the meeting.

Recording the audit provides the simplest way to (1) keep the IRS agent in line and (2) make a permanent, accurate record of what transpires. This also helps you in the note-taking process, ensuring that you do not misunderstand the agent's suggestions or demands. Moreover, when your recorder is running, the agent is far less inclined to deliberately intimidate, deceive, or mislead you.

You must notify the IRS ten days before the meeting of your intention to record the audit. The notice must be in writing. Exhibit 6–3 is an example of a simple letter informing the IRS that you will record the audit. By submitting this letter, you ensure your right to record the audit.

EXHIBIT 6–3

Your Name
Address
City, State, Zip

Date:
SSN:

Dear Auditor:

On ——— [date] I received notice from you that my return for ——— [year] is under audit. According to my rights as explained in IRS Publication 1, I wish to record the examination that is to take place on ——— [date]. I will bring my own recording equipment. Please note that this request is made within the time period required.

Thank you.

Your Signature

USING AFFIDAVITS TO WIN YOUR AUDIT

Chapter 3 demonstrates how to use affidavits to prove compliance with your legal obligations. Not only are affidavits valuable tools in proving, for example, that your return was filed or your taxes were paid on time, they are equally beneficial in solving audit disputes. In fact, in some situations affidavits are the *difference* between winning and losing an audit.

To prove deductions, auditors generally look for documentation, such as canceled checks or invoices. However, paperwork is not always available, and even when it is, it is not uncommon to supplement paperwork with detailed explanations. Affidavits are important tools for proving deductions when paperwork is missing or incomplete or when you must provide supplemental explanations for your documents.

Although the IRS rarely says so, it is not necessary to produce a slip of paper in order to establish your entitlement to a deduction. The law requires only that you *prove* you expended the money claimed as a deduction and that the deduction be allowed by the code. Only in rare cases does the law define what records are necessary to prove a given deduction. Most often, the manner of proof is left up to you.

Affidavits to Verify Income

The IRS is challenging income at a growing rate. If it believes you underreported your income, it adds phantom income to your return and computes the additional tax. Phantom income is income the IRS "believes" you earned, whether or not you actually did. The burden falls on you to establish a foundation of evidence to support your initial income claim. This defeats the IRS's claim. The only way to do this is with an affidavit. Let me illustrate.

Paul was a commissioned salesman who came under audit. Among the questions asked of Paul was, "How did you live on just $18,300 per year?" Paul's answer was simple: "I couldn't. That's why I got another job."

But the IRS examiner was not satisfied. She wanted Paul to prove that he earned no more than the $18,300 claimed in the return. "Please provide copies of your bank statements," she said, intending to compare his bank deposits with the income claimed. If your bank deposits are greater than the declared income, the IRS assumes the difference is unreported taxable income. But Paul could not provide bank statements because he did not have an account during that period.

Upon completion of the audit, the agent arbitrarily tacked $3,900 of additional income onto Paul's return. She claimed that he "must have" earned that income in order to live. Paul used an affidavit to defeat the claim.

Paul's affidavit declared that the income shown on the return was all the income he earned during that period. The affidavit was presented with a matching declaration from the owner of the company for which Paul worked. Confronted with the two statements, the IRS agent lacked any authority to increase Paul's income. An example of this affidavit is found in Exhibit 6–4.

When the affidavit was mailed to the agent, we accompanied it with a demand that the alleged unreported income be dropped from the audit report. The agent agreed, and all corresponding penalties were similarly abandoned.

EXHIBIT 6–4

AFFIDAVIT OF PAUL ———
SSN:

STATE OF ———
COUNTY OF ———

My name is Paul ———. During the year ———, I was employed by ——— [name of company] as a commissioned salesman. I was paid solely on the basis of the sales that I made. I did not receive a fixed salary or an hourly wage.

During ——— [year], my total commission income was $18,300. This amount was determined by adding all the commission checks paid to me by ——— [name of company] during ——— [year]. Attached to this affidavit is the affidavit of ——— [name], the owner of ——— [name of business]. That affidavit verifies that my total commissions during ——— [year] were $18,300.

I filed a timely federal income tax return for ——— [year]. On the return, I accurately reported all income earned by me from all sources. The total gross income shown in the return is $18,300. I did not earn any income from any other source. I did not earn in excess of $18,300 during ——— [year].

Paul ———

Date: ———

Notary Public:_____

My Commission Expires: ———

Another illustration of how this works is Dennis's case. Dennis operated his own small business. He kept his own records, handled his own billing, and prepared his own tax returns. During the course of Dennis's audit, the auditor believed she discovered a discrepancy, but she never discussed the issue. In the Examination Report, we learned that the auditor believed that Dennis underreported his income by several thousand dollars. She added phantom income to Dennis's return and calculated the corresponding tax and penalties. Naturally, we appealed the decision.

At the appeal, we did two things to challenge the phantom income. First, we presented the bookkeeping ledgers Dennis prepared contemporaneously with his receipt of income over the course of the year. The ledgers showed income consistent with that reported on the tax return. Second, Dennis submitted an affidavit similar to Paul's (Exhibit 6–4) in which he testified (1) that the ledgers were true and correct reflections of his income, (2) that they were made contemporaneously with receiving the income, and (3) that all of the income earned by him was reflected in the ledgers.

The affidavit was submitted to the Appeals Officer together with copies of the ledgers. After reviewing the affidavit and ledgers, the Appeals Officer modified the Examination Report, dropping 100 percent of the phantom income. Using the affidavit, Dennis proved that the income reported in his tax return was true and accurate. The few minutes it took to draft the simple affidavit and have it signed and notarized saved Dennis countless thousands of dollars in taxes, interest, and penalties he did not owe.

Affidavits to Prove Deductions

Lost records are a big problem for many people. As I discuss in chapter 3, there are countless reasons why people lose expense records. Whatever the reason, you are at a distinct disadvantage in a tax audit without your records. That is why you have to know about using affidavits as the basis for reconstructing lost records.

A reconstruction is nothing more than the process by which you retrace your steps involving a particular expenditure. On paper, you show how much you spent, when you spent it, and the items for which it was spent. The affidavit is the means of presenting *testimony* describing your expenses and supporting the reconstruction. This procedure applies to any expense you must prove. However, the success of a reconstruction depends upon the starting point. You must have some type of fixed reference point to provide the raw material upon which the reconstruction is built. Let me show you how this works.

Kathy was a traveling sales representative for several clothing manufacturers. The IRS audited tax returns for three years during which she was heavily engaged in this activity. Unfortunately, Kathy did not have one scrap of paper for the years under audit. She had to reconstruct records to prove that her travel expense deductions were legitimate.

Kathy used a charge card extensively in her travels. For her, this was the starting point for reconstructing her expenses. Her first step was to send a letter to the card issuer requesting copies of all monthly statements for the years in question. In addition, Kathy had an address book showing the names and addresses of the companies and persons on whom she called during the course of business. The charge statements told us the cities that Kathy traveled to, and the address book revealed whom she called upon while there. From this information, we were able to ascertain how much time was spent in each city and how much money was most likely spent on meals, hotels, and gasoline.

To be sure, not each and every expense Kathy incurred was paid for with plastic. But we were able to fill in the gaps based upon her usual practices. Those details were presented to the IRS in the form of an affidavit.

When completed, Kathy's reconstruction was lengthy but simple. In spreadsheet format, the reconstruction consisted of a document that presented the following information:

- The date and duration of travel

- The place of travel

- The business purpose of the travel

- The person or organization visited

- The relationship to Kathy's business of the person or organization visited

- The amounts expended for gasoline, food, lodging, and miscellaneous expenses.

Where Kathy had one or more charge slips to support these facts, they were referenced with exhibit numbers, and copies were provided to the IRS. Every penny of Kathy's expenses as shown in the reconstructions was allowed.

Another case illustrates what can be done even when you do not have as much of a starting point as Kathy did. Dan was a stockbroker, and like some people, he preferred to use cash rather than checks or credit cards to conduct his business. While it certainly is not illegal to use cash, it can be more difficult to prove deductions if you do not collect receipts.

Dan's tax return contained a number of areas for which the IRS sought verification. Dan showed business expenses to the tune of several thousand business miles, with fees for parking, and over a thousand dollars in meals and entertainment expenses. He also showed some miscellaneous expenses associated with his brokerage activities. With the exception of a handful of restaurant receipts, Dan had no documentation to show his mileage, his business expenses, or the charitable contributions.

In Dan's case, the starting point was his appointment book for the year in question. From the notations in his book, he determined the clients he met and where they met. For example, from a notation showing that he was to meet client X at ABC restaurant, Dan was able to determine that:

- He drove to the restaurant from his office, resulting in deductible business miles.

- He paid for lunch (something he always did for clients), thus resulting in a deductible entertainment expense.

- The purpose of the discussion was solely business because there was no other reason to meet that person during business hours.

From the appointment book, Dan reconstructed a mileage log showing his business miles and the purpose of the travel. Using the few receipts he had and the notations in his book, he was able to determine how much money was spent on the business lunches. Based upon the particular establishment in question and its location, he could determine whether he also incurred parking fees.

The reconstructions took the same form as Kathy's. Dan's accompanying affidavit explained how the expenses were arrived at. The affidavit stated clearly and plainly that the expenses shown in the work sheets, copies of which were attached to the affidavit, were expenses incurred in the ordinary course of Dan's business. He explained that as a stockbroker, he regularly entertained clients and incurred business miles to do so. He also explained the business purpose of the entertainment. An example of Dan's affidavit is shown in Exhibit 6–5.

EXHIBIT 6–5

AFFIDAVIT OF DANIEL ———

STATE OF ———

COUNTY OF ———

My name is Daniel ———. This affidavit is made to verify certain business expenses claimed as deductions for ——— [year].

During ——— [year], I was employed by ——— [company] as a stockbroker, paid on a commission basis. A requirement for continued employment and steady sales was to entertain existing and potential clients. I did this on a regular basis. The entertainment was solely for the purpose of discussing investment opportunities and providing answers to clients' questions and concerns.

On Form 2106, *Employee Business Expenses*, I claimed entertainment expenses of ——— [amount], business mileage of ——— [amount], and fees for parking of ——— [amount]. Attached to this affidavit and made a part hereof are reconstruction work sheets reflecting the computations of these amounts.

Entertainment expenses were reconstructed from my appointment book. I determined the persons entertained each week and the place of the entertainment. A copy of the appointment book is attached. With that information, I determined the amounts expended for entertainment. These amounts were added to arrive at the total of ——— [amount].

Mileage reconstructions were determined by computing the round-trip distance from my office to the various meeting places identified in my appointment book. The miles were then added to arrive at the total of ——— [number] miles.

Parking fees were determined by ascertaining whether the meeting occurred within the downtown area or outside it. I did this by referring to the meeting location shown in the appointment book. Meeting locations within the downtown area necessarily involved parking fees. Those outside it did not. The number of meeting places within the downtown area totaled ———. The parking fees associated with meetings were added to arrive at the total of ——— [amount].

The expenses shown were ordinary and necessary business expenses incurred for the purpose of earning income. Entertaining clients is an essential aspect of my business. I was required to incur these expenses. None of the expenses were reimbursed by my employer.

Daniel ———

Subscribed and sworn to before me on ——— [date].

Notary Public: _____

My Commission Expires: ———

The auditor carefully reviewed the affidavit and the reconstructions and he asked Dan questions. The questions focused on the *merits* of the reconstructions, how the facts were arrived at, and the business purpose of the expenses. Dan was careful to answer each question specifically and fully, making sure that all the details were clear. At the conclusion of the audit, Dan was given the benefit of every dime of deductions supported by his reconstructions and affidavit. Despite the fact that Dan did not have contemporaneous records to back up the claimed expenses, the reconstructions and affidavit provided all the proof needed to settle the audit dispute in his favor.

My final example involves charitable contributions. Bruce's tax return contained a deduction of $750 for contributions to his church. Bruce did not have receipts because, as many do, he donated cash by dropping it into the collection plate each week. To prove the deduction, we structured a simple affidavit.

The affidavit declared specifically that Bruce and his wife attended church every week—fifty-two weeks per year. It expressly declared that each week, they gave $15 in cash by dropping it into the collection plate. Next the affidavit explained that on Friday of each week, after depositing one-half of her paycheck into the bank and taking the remaining portion in cash, Bruce's wife did the grocery shopping. Upon completion, she had money for the weekend, which included the weekly church contribution.

The simplicity, clarity, and lack of ambiguity of these claims are the keys to success. You cannot expect to achieve success if your affidavit is vague or ambiguous. It must state the facts clearly, simply, and to the point. It must avoid equivocation and generalities. Lastly, it must draw the ultimate conclusion based upon the facts presented. In Bruce's case, the ultimate conclusion was that he did in fact contribute $750 to his church during the year in question.

HANDLING ERRONEOUS INCOME CLAIMS BY THIRD PARTIES

One of the most common problems I see stems from information returns filed with the IRS that are incorrect. With more than 1.3 billion information returns filed each year, it does not take a large error rate to create substantial problems for millions of citizens. And even if the IRS were free of errors in the processing of these returns, the reality is that citizens and businesses alike regularly make mistakes with these returns. And as if that is not bad enough, fraudulent information returns are filed each year for various reasons, including their use as a means of retaliation by one citizen against another.

Unfortunately, the IRS's general attitude is to take information returns at face value, forcing the citizen to prove he did not earn the income alleged in the information return. Proving a negative can be difficult. However, section 6201(d) provides help in this situation.

In general terms, the statute requires the IRS to conduct an investigation into the facts of the case when a citizen "asserts a reasonable dispute with respect to any item of income reported on an information return." In order to trigger the investigation into the validity of an information return, you must "fully cooperate" with the IRS by providing "access to and inspection of all witnesses, information, and documents" within your possession or control.

When you do that, the IRS cannot rely blindly upon the claims of income in an information return. Rather, it must produce "reasonable and probative information" to justify its claim that you in fact earned the income alleged in the information return. If the return is indeed erroneous or even fraudulent, the agent will be able to garner no proof to support the return.

If you receive an information return that is erroneous, immediately write to the issuer of the form and demand that it be corrected. Send the letter via certified mail. Point out that code section 7434 provides authority for you to recover damages from any person who "files a fraudulent information return" with the IRS.

Retain a copy of your letter with your certified mail receipts. These documents provide powerful evidence in your favor if the IRS attempts to include the alleged income in your return. Also, providing copies to the IRS helps you meet the burden to "fully cooperate" to sort out the issue. Finally, an affidavit expressly declaring that you did not earn the income alleged in the information return helps seal the deal in your favor.

WHY PAY TAXES YOU DO NOT OWE?

Tax audits can be fearful and intimidating. However, if you understand the nature of the examination process, your obligations and rights throughout, and that you have substantial power, no tax audit should ever produce a bill that you do not owe. If you cannot afford to pay taxes you do not owe, you must understand your rights and the power of the affidavit process.

7

The Million-Dollar Precaution

Audit-Proof and Penalty-Proof Your Tax Return

Because the idea of a face-to-face tax audit is so terrifying to most people, a prevailing question is "How can I avoid a face-to-face audit?" The answer offered by many tax experts always disturbs me. Too often, tax preparers suggest that you simply fail to claim all the deductions to which you are entitled. The theory is that by reducing your deductions, you in turn reduce the chances of being selected for examination. Stated another way, you should—in effect—*buy* audit protection by ignoring your legitimate deductions.

Another oft-cited technique for limiting the potential bite of an audit requires you to hold back deduction items at the time of filing. The theory is that if you are audited later, those items can then be thrown on the table to negate the effect of any disallowed deductions. This too amounts to the purchase of audit protection insurance at the price of increased taxes. The notion is specious and the process wholly unnecessary.

Even worse is the fact that neither of these techniques is at all sound. In the first place, the IRS examines 100 percent of the returns filed through the computer process. There is nothing you can do to prevent that scrutiny, including failing to claim legitimate deductions. Second, we know that historically about 90 percent of the people audited are found to owe more money. The average assessment after face-to-face examination is nearly $9,500. Therefore, the tactic of holding back deductions at the time of filing, only to spring them on the auditor later, simply does not work.

Each of these techniques is based upon two fundamental misunderstandings. The first concerns how returns are selected for audit. The second concerns what it means to be audited. In the last chapter we examined both those questions at length. We learned that being selected for an audit does not mean you did anything wrong, and we learned that most returns are selected for audit on the basis of the Discriminate Function System (DIF) computer program. This is the program that compares your deductions with the averages. The higher your DIF score, the more likely you are to be audited.

Using that premise, I answer in this chapter the question of what can be done to avoid being dragged through a face-to-face tax audit *without* losing one dime of deductions in the process. My million-dollar precaution allows you to claim with confidence all your legitimate deductions.

A valuable by-product of this strategy is the introduction of a new level of financial privacy. My technique enables you to rest assured that you meet your legal obligation to prove the correctness of your tax return, but at the same time it minimizes the extent to which you must bare your financial soul to the IRS. Truly, this system allows you to close the IRS's spying eyes as it attempts to criticize each detail of your financial affairs.

WHY OTHER SYSTEMS DO NOT WORK

The so-called audit-proofing strategies discussed above are designed primarily with the DIF program in mind. Theoretically, if you reduce the total of your deductions, those remaining fall below the averages. That way you are allegedly assured that your return will not be selected for a face-to-face examination.

There are two great flaws in this theory. First, because we do not know from year to year what the average deduction amounts are, we have no way to know how much to reduce a given deduction to bring it into alignment with the averages (or even if a given deduction exceeds the average to begin with). Second and more important, arbitrarily cutting your deductions only guarantees that you pay more taxes. Most of us pay plenty in taxes to begin with. We do not have to make matters worse by failing to claim the legal deductions to which we are entitled.

Furthermore, the philosophy behind these audit-proofing techniques is all wrong. The techniques are propagated by people who *do not* understand the audit process. As we learned in the last chapter, an audit is nothing more than the process the IRS uses to determine the correctness of a tax return. The fact that your return was *selected* for audit is no indication that there is an actual *error* in the return. Selection indicates only that there is a *question* raised by one or more claims in the return.

The audit is the process of obtaining answers to those questions. Provided you can demonstrate the accuracy of your return and you understand your rights, the audit holds absolutely no hidden danger or financial risk.

HOW MY SYSTEM WORKS

How can we take what we know about the audit selection process and use it to audit-proof a tax return? The answer lies in the selection process itself. Here is how it works. Returns flagged by the DIF program are first assigned to a reviewer at the service center. Only after a reviewer sees a need for a face-to-face exam is the return handed off to a local office for audit.

My audit-proofing technique takes effect at the point of the service center review and prevents the return from being forwarded for audit. The key here is to provide sufficient information with the return *at the time of filing*. The information must answer any potential questions raised by the return itself. The hard evidence makes the return as audit-proof as it can be. The result is that you avoid the hassle, anxiety, and trauma of a face-to-face audit—not to mention the average $9,500 tax bill that accompanies it.

Let me offer an example. Suppose you are entitled to claim a deduction for 20,000 business miles. To audit-proof the claim, make a copy of your mileage log (the contemporaneous record of the mileage) and attach the copy (never send originals) directly to the tax return at the time of filing. In addition, provide an affidavit to verify that all miles were legitimate business miles incurred solely to earn income. Review chapter 3 on drafting affidavits and see chapter 6, under the heading "Using Affidavits to Win Your Audit."

If your return is kicked out because of the apparently high mileage claim, IRS service center reviewers find before them the information they need to verify your claim. There is no need to pursue additional information through an audit. To the extent that you do so at all, you interact with the IRS strictly through the mail, avoiding the face-to-face confrontation—even if a given claim is in fact *incorrect*.

A properly audit-proofed return contains the following attachments:

1. An explanation of the nature of the claim. For this purpose, use IRS Form 8275, *Disclosure Statement*. I refer to this as the audit-proof form because it is the foundation of your audit-proofing package. An example of Form 8275 is shown here as Exhibit 7–1.

2. A complete explanation of the purpose of the expense (if a business expense, your explanation should include a statement as to why the expense is "ordinary and necessary" to the operation of your business). This should be presented in the form of an affidavit.

3. Copies of all documentary evidence available to support the deduction.

EXHIBIT 7–1

Form **8275** (Rev. May 2001) Department of the Treasury Internal Revenue Service	**Disclosure Statement** Do not use this form to disclose items or positions that are contrary to Treasury regulations. Instead, use Form 8275-R, Regulation Disclosure Statement. See separate instructions. ▶ Attach to your tax return.	OMB No. 1545-0889 Attachment Sequence No. **92**
Name(s) shown on return		Identifying number shown on return

Part I   General Information (see instructions)

	(a) Rev. Rul., Rev. Proc., etc.	(b) Item or Group of Items	(c) Detailed Description of Items	(d) Form or Schedule	(e) Line No.	(f) Amount
1						
2						
3						

Part II   Detailed Explanation (see instructions)

1 _____

_____

_____

2 _____

_____

_____

3 _____

_____

_____

Part III   Information About Pass-Through Entity. To be completed by partners, shareholders, beneficiaries, or residual interest holders.

Complete this part only if you are making adequate disclosure for a pass-through item.

Note: A pass-through entity is a partnership, S corporation, estate, trust, regulated investment company (RIC), real estate investment trust (REIT), or real estate mortgage investment conduit (REMIC).

1 Name, address, and ZIP code of pass-through entity	2 Identifying number of pass-through entity
	3 Tax year of pass-through entity to
	4 Internal Revenue Service Center where the pass-through entity filed its return

For Paperwork Reduction Act Notice, see separate instructions.   Form **8275** (Rev. 5-2001)

ISA

4. If the IRS has a particular form covering the deduction, such as Form 4684 for Casualty and Theft Losses or Form 8283 for Non-Cash Charitable Contributions, complete the form and attach it to the return.

As you ponder the merits of this strategy, keep in mind that over 125 million personal tax returns are filed each year. Only about 1 percent are assigned for face-to-face examination, though that will increase. Which return do you suppose the IRS will spend its limited time auditing, your documented return or one of the millions of undocumented returns?

THE PENALTY-PROOFING BENEFIT

Disclosing your facts as described above has a second benefit. That is, should a claim be disallowed for some reason, you avoid being penalized. The reason is that the law does not permit the IRS to assess penalties when you make "full disclosure" of all facts, provide supporting documents, and offer some reasonable justification for making the claim.

IRS regulations provide that disclosure is adequate if a statement is attached to the return that includes all of the following:

- A caption identifying the statement as a full disclosure of facts

- The identification of the tax return item in question

- The amount of the item in question

- The facts affecting the tax treatment of the item, which apprise the IRS of any potential controversy concerning the item.[1]

IRS Form 8275, *Disclosure Statement*, meets all these requirements. I referred to it earlier as the audit-proof form, but it also penalty-proofs the return.

Another key to penalty-proofing the return is that you must be able to demonstrate that your position has a *reasonable basis* in law and fact. This standard requires that you exercise due diligence prior to making any potentially troublesome claim. That is, you must make a reasonable effort to ascertain the correctness of your claim before asserting it. Provided you discover sufficient evidence to persuade a reasonable person of the correctness of the claim, the penalty is avoided if the claim is properly disclosed to the IRS and supported as shown above.

Here is an example of how beneficial this strategy can be. Hester received a lump sum distribution of $44,000 from her employer as part of an early retirement incentive package.[2] According to documents provided by the employer, the distribution was from a pension plan. Both Hester and her employer believed that the distribution did not constitute severance pay.

When the employer issued a W-2, however, it identified the distribution as *wage income*, whereas on her tax return, Hester treated the money as a *pension distribution*, not wage income. Moreover, she elected to income-average the payment over ten years as allowed by law at the time.

On the face of her tax return, Hester added this language, "Lump sum distribution erroneously reported by employer on W-2 and reportable on Form 4972 [relating to pension distributions]." In addition, she attached to the return a statement prepared by the employer plainly describing the payment as a pension distribution. She certainly had a reasonable basis for her treatment of the distribution as pension, not wage income.

Later, the IRS determined that Hester had in fact received severance pay, not a pension distribution. As it turned out, the agency was correct according to the fine print in her contract. It should have been treated as wage income not subject to the ten-year income-averaging right. As a result, she owed more income tax. However, the IRS's claim did not end there. The IRS ordered Hester to pay a $2,244 penalty.

Hester challenged the IRS, claiming she was not liable for the penalty because on the face of the return she made full disclosure to the IRS of the facts surrounding her claim. The IRS was on notice of the nature of her claim. At the time of filing, she provided documentation sufficient to allow the IRS to pass upon its merits.

Interestingly, Hester *did not* use the IRS's disclosure statement, Form 8275. Rather, she simply added an explanation to the return and attached her supporting documents. Because of this, the IRS argued that she failed to make a proper disclosure and insisted that the $2,244 penalty should apply. The Tax Court rejected the IRS's argument, ruling that even though she did not use the agency's disclosure form, she did provide "facts sufficient to enable the IRS to identify the potential controversy, if it analyzed that information."[3]

After analyzing Hester's disclosure, the court held:

> We conclude that the disclosure on [Hester's] return was adequate to disclose the controversy. [Hester] did not try to hide the position she had taken on her tax return as is often done by those attempting the "audit lottery." [Hester] not only made a notation on the tax return that indicated the position she had taken, but also attached a copy of the explanation of the payment which indicated the potential controversy. We, therefore, hold that [Hester] is not subject to the penalty.[4]

Hester saved $2,244 by penalty-proofing her tax return. The key to avoiding penalties is simple. Do not attempt to hide your claim from the IRS. When making a potentially controversial claim, disclose the facts to the IRS, allowing it to pass upon the merits of the claim. By doing so, if it transpires that you are not entitled to the tax treatment elected, as was the case with Hester's distribution, you avoid the penalties associated with the claim.

You may be thinking that the Form 8275, *Disclosure Statement,* is a way to call attention to yourself. "Why file the form," you ask, "if all it does is trigger an audit?" The form itself does not trigger an audit. An audit is triggered when the computer flags a potential trouble spot in your return. More pointedly, the DIF scores trigger the audit. By not using the disclosure form, you are virtually assured that the return will be handed off for a face-to-face examination if a complex or questionable item appears or if your deductions are well above the averages.

Using the disclosure statement and providing supporting documentation as outlined here assures that there is no need for face-to-face scrutiny. Rather, the IRS need only pass upon the merits of your claim. If the IRS disallows your deduction, you have the right to appeal the decision. The important key is that even if you lose on the merits of the deduction, you *prevent the assessment of very costly penalties*. In Hester's case, the extra few minutes she spent penalty-proofing saved exactly $2,244.

AFFIDAVITS AS AN AUDIT- AND PENALTY-PROOFING TOOL

Affidavits play an important role in the audit-proofing and penalty-proofing scenario. There are some cases in which the propriety of a deduction turns on information that cannot be provided through documentation obtained from third parties. This is what I refer to as the "intangible" element of a deduction. Such information is essential to proving the deduction but must be presented in some other fashion.

For example, a home office claim is acceptable only if the space in the home is used "regularly and exclusively for business purposes." No deduction is allowed when office space is used for personal, nonbusiness purposes such as an evening TV room. Thus, proof must be presented in the form of testimony to establish the "intangible" element of business use. Use an affidavit to achieve that goal.

Of course, unless you are an outright tax criminal, the IRS generally does not offer evidence to refute your claims. It simply does not have to. You must prove that your return is correct. If you are unable to do this for any reason, you lose without the IRS lifting a finger. That is what makes an affidavit so effective. The agency rarely, if ever, refutes it with evidence to the contrary.

However, do not read this as license to submit fictional statements to the agency to support bogus deductions. You sign your tax return under penalty of perjury, and all attached documents comprise integral elements of your submission. Any statement that is known to be false as to a material matter at the time you make it could give rise to a felony charge of willfully filing false statements with the IRS. The potential for stiff fines and jail time is simply not worth the risk.[5]

In the home office example, an affidavit must unequivocally declare that the office space is used regularly and exclusively for business purposes. It should state that no personal, nonbusiness use occurs within the space. To be effective, your affidavit must establish that you meet all the elements of the deduction you intend to claim. Review chapter 3 for all the details on crafting sound affidavits.

AN INCREASED MEASURE OF FINANCIAL PRIVACY

With all the IRS's ability to demand the production of information, it is difficult to understand how anybody has any degree of financial privacy remaining. The truth is that measured against the yardstick of what may be considered constitutional standards, we have little or no financial privacy. The IRS's ability to demand records, access your bank account, and obtain data from other third parties makes absolute financial privacy a thing of the past.

But understanding your requirements under the law can help to restore some measure of privacy. Bear in mind your legal burden of proof with regard to your tax return. You must prove the correctness of all claims regarding income and expenses. If you claim to have earned $15,000 income, you must show the claim to be accurate. If you claim to have paid $5,000 in charitable contributions, you must prove the accuracy of that claim.

It is important to understand the limits of the IRS's reach. The agency has the right to demand proof of any item claimed in the return. However, its power does not extend beyond that point. Stated another way, the IRS has no authority to delve into every aspect of your financial life if those issues have no bearing upon the correctness of your tax return.

For example, if you make no claim of any charitable deduction, the IRS has no right to question you regarding your charitable giving.

This distinction is important because during the course of a typical audit, especially audits that target the question of your income, agents routinely demand the production of all canceled checks, bank deposit slips, monthly bank statements, documents concerning loans and repayments of loans, and so on. But if these issues have no bearing upon the truthfulness of the claims in your return, they are entirely irrelevant.

A clear example arises with regard to the demand for "all canceled checks." If you were to examine the checks you write during the course of an average month, you would find payments for groceries, haircuts, recreational activity, restaurants, car payments, gasoline, day care, theater tickets, maybe even a parking ticket. However, the vast majority of these expenses are of a personal nature and are therefore *nondeductible*. Moreover, unless you are a tax criminal, you probably made no effort to deduct them.

Consequently, the nature, amount, and purpose of such expenses are simply of *no legitimate concern* to the IRS. Stated more pointedly, it is *none of their business* how you spend your money on nondeductible expenses. Therefore the agency has no right to demand, and you are under no obligation to produce, records having no bearing upon the issues raised in your return.

This reality closes the door on more than 50 percent of what the IRS demands to see in a given audit. By using the audit-proof and penalty-proof techniques outlined here, what the IRS has a right to see is readily organized, easily understood, and probably already provided with the return. Under such circumstances, the agency has no legitimate claim to more information.

By using these techniques, you eliminate the need to sift through every document you own to respond to a steady stream of IRS demands. In fact, you most likely eliminate the need to deal with an auditor altogether because the documentation necessary to prove the claims in your return is submitted with the return. This gives you the legitimate right and power to say no to further demands.

In essence, you have the right to terminate an audit when it exceeds the legal limits. You have the right to stop an agent from pry-ing or attempting to pry into issues that have no bearing upon the correctness of the return. You have the right to assert your financial privacy and can make it stick when adequately prepared. Indeed, if you do not assert that right, you surely will enjoy no right to financial privacy. To be sure, the IRS recognizes no limits to its own power.

While the right to financial privacy certainly exists, few exercise it, because they are afraid of the purported power of the tax auditor. But as we have learned, tax auditors have no power; too much of the audit process hinges on tactics of bluff and intimidation, misinformation and disinformation. When you understand these facts, you become more willing and able to exercise your rights. The result is that your level of privacy naturally increases.

8

Common Problems Businesses Face

Heading Off Challenges That Could Ruin Your Business

Businesses face unique and varied IRS problems. In the first place, the duty of collecting income taxes falls mostly to businesses. Four of every five dollars paid in taxes are collected not by the IRS but by businesses through wage withholding. For this reason alone, businesses face a mountain of regulations and incur countless billions of dollars in compliance fees and costs.

Second, while about 70 percent of individuals file short forms to simplify their reporting obligations, businesses have no such luxury. Businesses with employees must file *five* employment tax returns over the course of the year—four covering the wage withholding on employees and the fifth covering unemployment taxes. These are Forms 941 and 940, respectively. What's more, businesses must file income tax returns that are always substantially more complicated than individual returns. And finally, businesses face a staggering burden to file information returns, particularly Forms W-2 and 1099. We already know that businesses file more than 1.3 billion such returns each year.

The combination of these and other problems was addressed in testimony to the Senate Small Business Committee on April 12, 1999, by Margaret T. Wrightson, the associate director, Tax Policy and Administration Issues, General Government Division of the General Accounting Office. Wrightson explained that small businesses are subject to multiple "layers of filing, reporting and deposit requirements." She pointed out that:

> By our count, there are more than 200 requirements—which we grouped into four layers—that may apply to small businesses as well as large businesses and other taxpayers.[1]

To be sure, not all two hundred requirements apply to every business. However, it is equally true that the list of requirements grows annually and so do the consequences for compliance failures. This is perhaps best illustrated by the fact that of the 32.49 million penalties assessed by the IRS in 2001, nearly 30 percent were assessed against businesses, though businesses accounted for just over 16 percent of the total returns filed that year.

That is why I dedicate specific attention to the common problems faced by businesses, in respect to both penalties and audit challenges.

THE TRIPLE THREAT OF EMPLOYMENT TAX PENALTIES

Employment taxes make up the lion's share of penalties most businesses face. There are two elements of employment taxes. The first is the employee's share of withheld income and social security taxes. Known as "trust" taxes, these are withheld directly from the employee's check and paid to the IRS by the employer. They are referred to as trust taxes because the employer holds the employees' income taxes in trust until paid to the IRS. The second element is the employer's matching share of social security and unemployment taxes. Known as "nontrust" taxes, these are the taxes for which the employer himself (not the employee) is responsible. Simply stated, trust taxes are taken from the pocket of the employee, and the nontrust taxes come directly from the employer.

Employers are required to report substantial information regarding their relationship with their employees. First is the amount of wages paid. Second is the amount of trust and matching social security nontrust taxes owed. This information is submitted on a quarterly basis using Form 941, *Employer's Quarterly Federal Tax Return*. Form 940, *Employer's Annual Federal Unemployment (FUTA) Tax Return*, is the tax return used to report and pay nontrust Federal Unemployment Tax Act (FUTA) taxes. The latter is filed once a year. Even though Form 941 is due quarterly, employers must make *deposits* of trust fund taxes on a *monthly* basis if the tax liability exceeds $2,500 for any one quarter, more often if the tax burdens are higher.

It is from the pages of these requirements that three common penalties surface. I address them in turn.

1. *Failure to deposit withheld taxes.* The failure-to-deposit penalty contains a graduated scale under which the rate of penalty increases in relation to the length of time trust tax deposits are delinquent. The scale was implemented to provide an incentive to correct underpayments as quickly as possible *prior* to IRS enforcement action.

   This is the graduated scale:

   • 2 percent if the failure is not more than five days

   • 5 percent if the failure is more than five days but not more than fifteen days

   • 10 percent if the failure is more than fifteen days.[2]

   If the tax is not deposited by the time the IRS begins issuing written demands for payment, the penalty increases to 15 percent, its maximum level.

2. *Failure to file trust tax returns, Form 941.* The same failure-to-file penalty discussed in chapter 4 is used to penalize the failure to file employment tax returns. The penalty is assessed at the rate of 5 percent per month for a total of five months.

3. *Failure to pay employment taxes.* The penalty for failure to pay employment taxes is assessed in the same manner as the penalty for failure to pay income taxes. The penalty grows at the rate of 5 percent per month to a maximum of 25 percent.

HOW TO CANCEL EMPLOYMENT TAX PENALTIES

The penalties for failure to deposit, failure to file, and failure to pay are canceled when you show that the failure was due to "reasonable cause and not due to willful neglect."[3] The reasonable cause standard used here is the same as that discussed in chapter 4. To quickly review, *willful negligence* is the intentional disregard of, or reckless indifference to, your legal duties. The idea implies that you took no action to attend to your responsibilities or acted (or failed to act) in a manner that you knew or should have known would jeopardize your ability to comply.

On the other hand, penalties do not apply when your failure to act was due to some "reasonable cause." This idea implies that unforeseen circumstances beyond your control prevented compliance, provided you were proactive in attending to your tax duties.

When dealing with employment taxes, the IRS is stricter in its evaluation of what constitutes reasonable cause than when dealing with income taxes. The reason is that employment taxes are largely withheld from others. The agency views the failure to pay trust taxes with a jaundiced eye, believing that you used the tax revenue to operate your business.

Moreover, the IRS assumes that managing tax matters is an integral aspect of business. This creates a presumption that you know your obligations and must act to fulfill them. But this presumption is overcome by factors evidencing that the failure to comply was due to reasonable cause, not willful negligence. Let us look at some reasonable cause concepts specifically related to businesses.

Cancellation of employment tax penalties is common for those new in business with no history of compliance failures. Those with little or no understanding of these rules can often make a case of "ignorance" justifying cancellation of the penalties. When you prove that you made a reasonable effort to determine your duties but were innocently unaware of one or more of these obligations, or erred in connection with fulfilling them, reasonable cause exists. This is especially true of failure to comply with the deposit rules, which are complicated and change often. For more on the ignorance defense, please review chapter 4, under the heading "What is Good Faith?"

The defense of "reliance" is also effective with employment tax penalties. The key to the reliance defense is to show that you engaged a tax professional, company bookkeeper, or other person to handle your tax obligations, but due to circumstances beyond everyone's control, you were unable to comply. It is not enough merely to delegate your duties to a third party who failed to perform. The failure must be accompanied by some reasonable cause.

I was once involved in the case of a family business, the patriarch of which engaged a professional bookkeeper to handle the business affairs. The bookkeeper fell ill but carried on with her responsibilities to keep records and prepare and file returns. However, as the bookkeeper's condition grew worse, her attention to detail waned. Soon she was making accounting errors that led to errors in deposits and employment tax returns. Although the business owner monitored her actions, the errors were not readily apparent until the IRS contacted him regarding two delinquent trust tax returns. Because he exercised responsibility in attending to his affairs and because the failures were due to the illness of the bookkeeper, the failures were due to reasonable cause and not willful neglect.

A case for reasonable cause can often be made where the business faces substantial financial problems. Although the IRS expects trust taxes to be paid ahead of all other claims, failure to pay may be excused when severe financial hardship threatens the life of the business. Though the IRS disputes this, a growing legion of court decisions plainly hold that financial problems can constitute reasonable cause for not paying employment taxes.[4] Contrary to its litigation stance, the IRS's own regulations support this idea. Specifically, regulation section 1.6161–1(b) excuses the failure to pay on time when doing so would cause significant "undue hardship."[5] Undue hardship is more than just inconvenience; it is the kind of financial pressure that jeopardizes the viability of an ongoing business. The idea implies substantial financial loss, such as might arise by:

- Selling property at a sacrifice price

- Loss of operating equipment or facilities if rent or lease payments are not made

- Losing key suppliers if outstanding invoices are not paid

- Inability to perform on the terms of binding contracts.

When seeking abatement of the failure-to-pay penalty, take extra care to establish that you exercised ordinary business care and prudence in providing for your tax liability, but through no fault of your own, you were unable to pay.

To win abatement of employment tax penalties, your reasonable cause showing must be presented in writing with as much supporting documentation as possible. Provide detail on the causal relationship between the events alleged as reasonable cause and your failure to act. Follow the examples in chapter 4 to guide you in the process.

FAILURE TO FILE INFORMATION RETURNS

The law requires the filing of information returns in dozens of circumstances. The most common situation applies to employers required to report wages paid to employees using a wage statement, Form W-2. Businesses also file tens of millions of Form 1099, reporting payment of nonemployee compensation such as dividends and interest. The tax code penalizes those who fail to file information returns or who file erroneous returns. The law generally creates a penalty of $50 for each failure, with a maximum penalty of $250,000 for any single tax year.[6]

This penalty also contains an incentive to correct erroneous filings before they become a problem. The law contains an escalation provision that operates in this fashion:

- If any error or omission is corrected within thirty days after the return's filing date, the penalty is $15 per return with a yearly maximum of $75,000 ($25,000 for small businesses—defined as those with less than five million dollars in average annual gross receipts for the "most recent three taxable years" prior to the year for which the penalty is assessed).[7]

- If any error or omission is corrected between the period beginning thirty-one days after the due date and ending August 1, the penalty is $30 per return with a yearly maximum of $150,000 ($50,000 for small businesses).

- If the error or omission is corrected after August 1, the penalty is $50 per return with a yearly maximum of $250,000 ($100,000 for small businesses).

When the failure to file is "due to intentional disregard," the penalty jumps to $100 per return and there is no benefit of the graduated system.[8] However, this penalty does not apply when the failure is due to reasonable cause and not willful neglect. The standards and elements of reasonable cause addressed above and in chapter 4 apply here.

FILING INFORMATION RETURNS IN ELECTRONIC FORMAT

The IRS is constantly pushing more requirements on businesses and tax professionals to file tax and information returns in electronic format. In this way the IRS not only requires private businesses to do the agency's bookkeeping, reporting, and tax collection, but also burdens businesses with the government's data processing. The chief requirement here is that certain businesses must submit information returns in machine-readable form.

The law presently requires the use of magnetic media when a business submits "at least 250 returns during the calendar year."[9] The penalty for not filing on magnetic media applies to returns *in excess* of 250. The penalty is assessed under precisely the same scheme as discussed in the previous section (p. 177). Thus the penalty does not apply when "it is shown that such failure is due to reasonable cause and not to willful neglect."[10]

In addition to the generally applicable reasonable cause standard, the law contains a directive instructing the IRS to "take into account (among other relevant factors) the ability of the taxpayer to comply at reasonable cost" with these regulations.[11] Instances of undue hardship, such as temporary equipment breakdowns or destruction of magnetic media equipment, must be considered in granting one-year or multiyear exemptions from this requirement and in determining good faith in connection with a failure to comply.

Another exception is the so-called low-volume exception. Simply stated, if you filed fewer than 250 information returns in the previous calendar year and "reasonably expect to file fewer than 250 returns" for the current calendar year, you are considered a "low-volume" filer and may submit the returns in "paper form."[12]

From these rules we can distill several grounds upon which businesses may obtain relief from the penalty. They are:

- The returns did not exceed 250, or if they did, the penalty is applicable only to the number *in excess* of 250.

- You filed fewer than 250 returns last year and reasonably expected to file fewer than 250 in the current year.

- You are entitled to a single- or multiyear hardship extension because of excessive cost or equipment problems.

- The failure to file was due to reasonable cause and not willful neglect.

A letter requesting abatement of this penalty can incorporate any or all of the above defenses. At the very least, you must make a good faith, reasonable cause argument, since that standard is universally applicable while the other defenses are fact-specific.

TRUST TAX ASSESSMENTS OF A FAILED CORPORATION

The IRS collects trust taxes from a failing or failed corporation through a vehicle known as the Trust Fund Recovery Penalty (TFRP). When a corporation becomes delinquent with trust taxes, collection personnel first attempt to collect the tax from the corporation's assets. If that fails because the corporation has no assets or is defunct, the IRS assesses the TFRP penalty against the corporation's "responsible persons."

Responsible persons are the company's employees or owners who were required to withhold, truthfully account for, and pay the trust taxes but who "willfully failed" to do so.[13] The TFRP assessment transforms a corporate liability into the personal liability of the responsible persons. The penalty is collectible from the personal assets of those individuals.

Two factors must be present before a TFRP assessment is considered legitimate. First, the person against whom the penalty is assessed must be a "responsible person." This is a person with the right to exercise ultimate control over the corporation's income and assets. To be responsible, that person must have made the decision not to pay the taxes at a time when they were due. There can be more than one responsible person. However, a person lacking control over the corporation such that he could not make *binding* decisions over financial matters cannot be held a responsible person.

Next, the responsible person must have acted "willfully." This definition is narrower in the context of the TFRP than elsewhere in the tax law. In this context, willfulness exists when one made a conscious and knowing decision to favor other creditors at a time when he knew that trust fund taxes were delinquent. Absent a showing of willfulness, even a responsible person cannot be subjected to the penalty assessment.

How does the IRS determine who is responsible? The process

begins with an "investigation" by a revenue officer. This is done with Form 4180, *Report of Interview with Individual Relative to the Trust Fund Recovery Penalty*. This form is a detailed questionnaire that addresses the roles of the corporation's various officers and employees. All officers and key employees are asked to complete the form. The form undertakes to learn, among other things:

- The names of all officers and shareholders

- Who was responsible for signing corporate checks

- How decisions were made to pay or not pay various creditors

- Who was responsible for tax return preparation and filing

- Your particular role in the company.

From this information, the revenue officer decides who was responsible for the failure to pay and proposes a TFRP assessment. The "dirty little secret" about the so-called investigation is that it is not really an investigation at all. Because the IRS is so serious about collecting trust taxes, investigators shotgun the assessment against as many people as possible. The questionnaire is really used merely as a means of obtaining names and addresses. Once the penalty is proposed against *all* officers, the IRS stands back while the individuals fight over who truly is responsible. Unfortunately, most people have no idea how to challenge a TFRP. As such, the IRS ends up with multiple erroneous assessments and works to collect each one.

How to Challenge a Proposed TFRP Assessment

The revenue officer communicates the proposed assessment in a letter to the targets. The letter states that efforts to collect from the corporation failed and the IRS is now looking to the responsible persons to pay the tax. The letter gives you thirty days to either sign and accept the assessment or submit a protest letter appealing the decision. The contents of the protest letter are described on p. 136.

Your protest letter must set forth facts that enable the IRS to conclude either (1) that you were not a responsible person or (2) that the failure to pay trust taxes was not willful. The protest letter leads to an Appeals conference. Here, be prepared to submit a detailed affidavit describing your duties and responsibilities with the company. If you contend that you were not responsible, you must prove that you did not have the power to dispose of company assets and did not direct the company's financial activities. If you contend that the failure to pay was not willful, you must prove either that you did not know about the delinquent taxes or that you did not pay other creditors at a time when you knew the taxes were unpaid.

Because of the IRS's prejudice regarding unpaid trust taxes, this penalty is a tough nut to crack. Therefore you must document your presentation to the fullest extent possible and be very specific in your fact showing. It helps greatly to have the testimony of other witnesses, such as former employees, who can support your version of the facts. Documentation is also important, especially if it proves that someone else ran the financial aspects of the company.

Janet faced a TFRP when her medical services company failed. She was a 30 percent shareholder in the corporation. Her two partners owned 70 percent of the company. The company fell behind on payroll taxes when Medicare stopped paying full price for the company's medical testing services. The IRS assessed the penalty against all three owners.

But Janet had nothing to do with the management of the company. Although she owned 30 percent, she was effectively locked out of management by the 70 percent owners, who also happened to be married to each other. They handled all the books, wrote all the checks, made all the financial deals, negotiated with all suppliers and other creditors, and hired and oversaw the accountant who prepared the company tax returns. Janet was—for all practical purposes—nothing more than another employee.

When she was assessed the penalty, we appealed the assessment. We then drafted a very specific affidavit showing in detail all the above facts. In addition, we obtained an affidavit from the accountant explaining that all his dealings were with the husband-and-wife team, that he never spoke with Janet, and that she was never involved in any financial meetings he had with the others. His testimony lent substantial weight to Janet's claim that she had nothing to with, and indeed had no power to make, decisions binding the company. This showing was sufficient to cancel the assessment against her.

RECLASSIFIED INDEPENDENT CONTRACTORS

One way that businesses try to manage growing costs and administrative burdens is to use independent contractors (IC) for service needs. An independent contractor is a self-employed person who provides goods or services to the business community. Because ICs are self-employed, businesses using them do not bear the costs associated with employees. There is no requirement to withhold taxes on payments to ICs, and you need not account for ICs in connection with other nontax federal employment regulations.

There is an ongoing dispute between the IRS and businesses as to what constitutes a legitimate IC, and there has been abuse on both sides. In the late 1980s, the IRS cracked down through increased employment tax audits, scrutinizing thousands of businesses. Many ICs were reclassified as employees. Many reclassifications were flat wrong.

While it is true that the IRS does not like ICs, it is also true that there is nothing illegal about using them *legitimately*. A legitimate IC is not an employee masquerading as a self-employed person. A legitimate IC is a person who truly is self-employed. He operates his own business. He makes his services available to the general public or other businesses. He owns his own tools and maintains his own office—home office or otherwise. He probably advertises his business. And he probably works for a number of other clients. He works on his own time, subject only to the terms of the contracts he enters into freely. The contracts are usually in writing. He can hire and fire his own employees. In the final analysis, he can gain or lose on a given contract, depending upon his own actions. He files a tax return using the sole proprietor tax form, Schedule C, to report his business income and expenses.

On the other hand, an improper IC is really someone's employee. The employee must report to work at a given time. He works only for a wage, salary, or commission. He does not control the place of work or the manner in which the work is performed. He does not advertise his services to others and does not work for others. He owns no equipment of his own, and all work is done using his employer's equipment. He has no office of his own. He cannot hire others to do the work for him. In the final analysis, he cannot lose in a given situation, because he is paid a salary or wage. Even if the business owner loses money in a given transaction, the employee still gets paid his wage.

The difference can be boiled down to a simple question: Who has the right to control (whether or not that power is used) the workplace, including tools and equipment, the worker, and the manner in which the work is performed? If the worker controls those things, he is a legitimate self-employed IC. If the employer controls those things, the worker is his employee.

Because ICs fall outside the IRS's safety net of wage withholding, the agency is often tough on the question of who is an IC. Unfortunately, Congress has balked at providing a bright-line test. Consequently, the matter is often subject to court decisions and IRS regulations. To determine who is and who is not an IC, the IRS developed a list of twenty fact considerations it calls the "20 Common Law Elements."[14] These factors focus heavily upon the control issues outlined above.

A challenge to your ICs begins with an employment tax audit. During the course of the examination, the IRS asks both you and your workers to complete a detailed questionnaire, IRS Form SS-8, *Determination of Worker Status for Purposes of Federal Employment Taxes and Income Tax Withholding*. Through the questionnaire and from discussions with workers and company officials, the examiner determines whether the workers are in fact employees. If the determination is affirmative, the IRS reclassifies the workers as employees and imposes a host of back taxes and penalties. The heavy costs growing from a reclassification make it mandatory that you understand how to avoid reclassification in the first place and how to appeal if workers are reclassified. You must also understand the so-called safe harbor rules. I address these presently.

How to Avoid Reclassification

The first rule here is simple. DO NOT rely solely on the IRS's questionnaire to communicate the facts. The form is too superficial, asking for many yes or no answers rather than facilitating a detailed recitation of the facts. Instead, submit a detailed affidavit with documentation. This is not to say that you should refuse to complete the IRS questionnaire. A better idea is to submit it along with a supplemental affidavit to ensure that you cover all the necessary bases.

Affidavits from the workers themselves are also very helpful. They should document critical facts that weigh in favor of IC status. Such facts include:

- Maintenance of their own office

- Purchasing their own tools and equipment

- Control of the workplace and how the work is performed

- Advertising their services to the public

- Performance of services for others

- Hiring their own workers.

All your evidence must concentrate on the control elements I explained above. When you prove that the IC is in control, you avoid reclassification.

How to Appeal When Workers Are Reclassified

You have thirty days from the date of the IRS's letter in which to appeal its decision. The appeal is executed through a written protest letter (see p. 136). Your protest letter must set forth facts to support the idea that your workers are legitimate ICs, not employees. The protest letter leads to an Appeals conference where you have the opportunity to present evidence on the merits of the case. To challenge the merits of the

IRS's determination, use affidavits and documents as outlined above. If you win on the merits, you do not have to treat workers as employees.

But also know that the law provides an escape hatch even if you do not win on the merits. Referred to as a "safe harbor," this remedy kicks in if, in good faith, you in fact misclassified your workers but at the same time followed all the correct procedures for reporting them as ICs. The safe harbor protects you from back tax and penalty assessments that can crush a business. Here is how it works.

If a worker was treated as an IC for a given tax period, the IRS *cannot* retroactively convert the worker. This means there are no back taxes, penalties, or interest. However, to qualify for safe harbor treatment, you must have had a "reasonable basis" for treating the worker as an IC.[15] The trade-off is that you must begin treating the worker as an employee for future tax periods. This rule effectively overlooks prior classification errors, but again, only if you had a reasonable basis for treating workers as ICs.

A reasonable basis exists if, in establishing the IC status, you relied upon any of the following:

- Judicial precedent, published IRS rulings or technical advice, or a letter ruling from the IRS directed to your business

- A past IRS audit of your business in which the status of your workers was not challenged by the IRS

- A long-standing, recognized practice of a significant segment of your industry.

The courts add another factor establishing reasonable basis. That is where you relied in good faith on the advice of counsel concerning the use of ICs.[16]

There are two further conditions to meet to enjoy safe harbor protection. First, the company must have filed all tax returns, including information returns, required by law. Second, your treatment of the workers must have been consistent with the tax returns filed. Thus, a failure to file information return Forms 1099 might vitiate the safe harbor protection. Likewise, if Form W-2 was filed instead of 1099s, this too weighs against the company, as does altering the treatment of the worker during the period in question.

How to Avoid Reclassification Problems

If you use ICs, you can avoid reclassification problems and strengthen your position by:

- Using written contracts to specify the nature of the relationship and spell out the critical elements of control. The IC must have control as outlined above.

- Ensuring that the IC uses his own tools and equipment. If he uses your tools and equipment, he should pay rent.

- Ensuring that the IC pays his own insurance where applicable.

- Ensuring that the IC *understands the relationship* and his obligations. Provide written notice of the fact that he is obligated to report his earnings on a tax return and pay self-employment taxes.

- Filing Form 1099 to report all payments. If the payments are less than $600 per year, you have no legal obligation to report, but do it anyway. It shows good faith and could be an important step in avoiding problems.

- Not disguising your employees as illegitimate ICs. It will not work and could cost you a fortune.

THE HOBBY LOSS RULE

One of the most common problems faced by small, start-up businesses is that the IRS often classifies them as "hobbies." In that case they are denied business expense deductions. This happens because the IRS often misstates the applicable rules to its own advantage. This is a risk if your small business has lost money for several consecutive years. When this happens, the IRS is wont to claim that your activity is not engaged in for profit. You may deduct only those expenses associated with a business operated *for profit*. You cannot deduct expenses for activities carried on primarily for sport, hobby, or recreation. If your business is reclassified as a hobby, you are asked to pay taxes on all the receipts without the benefit of any expense deductions.

At the outset of this discussion, it is important to understand that there is *no* legal provision requiring you to earn a profit in a set number of years. This runs contrary to popular belief, but it is nevertheless true. There are, however, two specific provisions of the law that we must address to understand the issue. Let us turn to them.

The first is code section 162, the code section that allows deductions for business expenses. It reads, in pertinent part,

> There shall be allowed as a deduction all the ordinary and necessary expenses paid or incurred during the taxable year in carrying on any trade or business.

Two rules emerge. First, expenses are deductible if they are "ordinary and necessary." Second, they are deductible if incurred while carrying on a "trade or business." Expenses not related to a trade or business operated for profit are nondeductible personal expenses.

The second relevant code section is the source of the confusion. It is code section 183 and reads, in part,

> In the case of an activity engaged in by an individual or an S corporation, if such activity is not engaged in for profit, no deduction attributable to such activity shall be allowed except as provided in this section.

When engaged in a trade or business, you may deduct all ordinary and necessary expenses. But if your activity is not engaged in *for profit*, the related expenses are not generally allowed as deductions. That might seem simple, but the confusion arises after reading section 183(d). That section reads as follows:

If the gross income derived from an activity for 3 or more of the taxable years in the period of 5 consecutive taxable years exceeds the deductions attributable to such activity . . . then, unless the Secretary establishes to the contrary, such activity shall be presumed for purposes of this chapter for such taxable year to be an activity engaged in for profit.

Section 183(d) creates a presumption. The *presumption* is that the activity is *in fact* engaged in for profit if it produces profit in any three of five consecutive years. In that case, all proper deductions are allowed under code section 162.

That is what the law *says*. Now let us look at what it *does not* say.

It *does not* say that if no profit is realized in three of five years, you are not entitled to claim deductions. If you fail to earn profit in at least three of the five years, what happens is that the *presumption* of a profit motive dissolves. That means you must *prove* a profit motive. And as long as you can prove a profit motive, you can lose money ten out of ten years and still claim your deductions.[17]

The reason is that the test in section 162 for allowing deductions has nothing to do with whether your business *actually* earns a profit. The test is whether you engaged in the activity with an *honest objective* of making a profit. It boils down to a question of intent. Did you undertake to earn a profit, or did you intend to play and have fun? If the former, you are entitled to the deductions; if the latter, you may not be.

The expectation of profit need not be *reasonable*. That is to say, your activity need not necessarily be a smart or savvy business move. Instead, you need only have a good faith objective of making a profit. When a good faith profit objective exists, you are entitled to your deductions even if actual profit does not.

How Do You Prove a Profit Motive?

IRS regulations identify several criteria used to evaluate your profit motive.[18] Let us discuss them.

1. *How you carry on the activity*. Carrying on in a "businesslike manner" indicates a profit motive. The following factors are considered businesslike operations:

- Keeping careful books and records

- Adopting new operating techniques to replace nonprofitable ones

- Emulating the practices of profitable businesses

- Seeking to improve and upgrade the quality of your product or service

- In general, making attempts to cut costs and to improve income and hence profit.

2. *Your personal expertise or that of your adviser*. Venturing into an area of business in which you have absolutely no expertise may indicate lack of a profit motive. But if you pursued a given hobby for years, you might reasonably convert that hobby to a profitable business. The law recognizes several means by which you can educate yourself. They include:

- Self-education through study of books and periodicals

- Attendance at seminars, trade meetings, and shows

- Memberships in trade organizations and associations

- Consultation with known experts.

3. *The time and effort you spend in the business*. This is an important factor. A profit motive is definitely indicated when you spend substantial time carrying on the day-to-day affairs of the business. This is particularly true if you quit a steady job to pursue your business. Spending full time in the operation, either personally or through employees, is strong evidence of a profit motive.

I once had a client who operated a photography business out of his home. The IRS tried to call his business a hobby and disallowed all his deductions. In addition to the other factors discussed here, we focused on this element to prove his profit motive. He spent full time in this business, and in fact it was the sole source of his income. He worked ten-hour days, six days a week, and traveled throughout the state to take wedding photos. Given the time spent and his reliance on the business for his livelihood, it was irrational to suggest he was doing it for the "fun of it."

4. *The expectation that business assets will appreciate.* Some businesses require a substantial investment in assets. While no profit may be realized in the yearly operation of the business, a profit motive exists if you actually and honestly expect to earn profit through the appreciation of assets.

   An example is the rental real estate business. Many rental properties actually lose money due to high maintenance costs, mortgage interest, and real estate taxes. But at the same time, rental property usually appreciates, often outpacing the negative cash flow over time. Anticipated appreciation of assets evidences a profit motive.

5. *Your success in carrying on past activities.* The IRS looks to past success as evidence of intended success in the present undertaking. A history of success in your ventures weighs in favor of a profit motive.

6. *The history of income or loss with respect to the activity.* This sole element is responsible for the IRS's view that lack of actual profit indicates no profit motive. The IRS says that a "continuing lack of profits, other than in the initial stages of a venture, *may indicate* that an activity is not engaged in for profit."[19]

   Note that the regulation *does not* state that the lack of profits "proves" lack of a profit motive. The courts have long recognized that lack of profit in the start-up stages of an operation does not evidence lack of a profit motive. New businesses need time to develop and mature before realizing consistent profits.

You must also consider unforeseen and unfortunate circumstances that impact profitability. These might include conditions such as the health of the owner or a key employee, disease (as in livestock), weather, and other casualties, unforeseen market conditions, or other elements over which you have no control.

7. *The amount of occasional profits.* Occasional profit earned in prior years evidences a profit motive. Courts are inclined to believe that profits, even small ones sufficient only to support your family, strongly indicate a profit motive. Standing alone, however, this element does not tip the scale one way or another. When the other key elements point to a profit motive, even the absence of profits does not tip the balance in favor of the IRS. The potential for future profits also indicates a profit motive.

8. *Your financial status.* The IRS often argues that if you earn substantial and steady income from other sources, this indicates a lack of profit motive in the activity. But it does not necessarily follow that citizens with reliable incomes from other sources fail to meet the profit motive test. The courts recognize that independent wealth or income is almost a prerequisite to financing a start-up business, especially one with heavy initial capital demands. This is especially true in today's financial climate where obtaining bank financing is at best difficult.

9. *The elements of personal pleasure or recreation.* This is one of the most critical of the points. If the business affords opportunities for substantial personal pleasure, this is strong evidence of lack of a profit motive. Take, for example, the pilot who purchased a small airplane for use in a rental business. He loses money in the rental business but regularly uses the plane for his own recreational purposes. The courts are not likely to find any profit motive in this business.

On the other hand, if the asset is seldom or never used for personal purposes, that weighs in favor of an honest profit motive. Lack of personal use or pleasure, combined with the businesslike manner of the operation, weighs heavily in defeating the IRS's claim that an asset was purchased only for personal use.

10. *Other factors.* In addition to these nine criteria, court decisions add other factors to the list. They are:

- Methods of advertising and promotion. When the business is advertised and promoted in a businesslike manner, this is strong evidence of a profit motive.

- Business plan. A business plan or design to build profitability is also strong evidence of a profit motive. Consideration is given to how the plan is carried out.

- Use of a hired manager with profit sharing. Courts have recognized a profit motive when the citizen hired a manager who participated in a profit-sharing arrangement. This indicates that at least one other party believes in the business's profit potential.

Present your evidence in the form of a detailed affidavit addressing each of these elements to the extent that they are relevant to your case. Although it is important to affirmatively declare that you "honestly intended to make a profit," your bald declaration will not carry the day. You must buttress your statement with objective facts to support the conclusion that you had a profit motive.

For example, if you have a written business plan and have used it to seek financing (whether or not approved), these are important indicators of a profit motive. While you may not have a written business plan, you may have proceeded systematically to advertise and market your business. In this case, document the steps you took and provide copies of your marketing tools. These might include print ads, a Web site, phone directory ads, and mailers.

Applying the above elements to your business will easily defeat an IRS claim that your business is a hobby. By doing so, you sustain your deductions and insulate yourself from a big tax bill. Not every one of the above elements applies to every business. They do not have to. No single element will tip the scales one way or the other. The issue is decided on the basis of a preponderance of all the evidence.

What If You Cannot Prove a Profit Motive?

Even if your business is in fact a hobby, all is not lost. By making the IRS follow the law, you can defeat the potential negative effects of losing your deductions. There are two critical rules that apply in this situation, both of which are often overlooked by tax auditors. Let us examine them.

The first is that even if you lack a profit motive, you are entitled to deduct expenses that are legally deductible in any event, regardless of a profit motive. These expenses include state and local taxes and interest on a home mortgage. Also included are casualty and theft losses, nonbusiness bad debts, worthless securities, tax counsel expenses, medical expenses and charitable contributions.[20] These are all allowed under other provisions of the code without regard to a profit motive. Therefore, even if you are not in business to make a profit, you get the benefit of these deductions.

The second point is that even if the activity is not engaged in for profit, you are entitled to deduct expenses up to the amount of the income earned. This is where the IRS often misleads people. When the IRS claims your business is a hobby, it disallows *all* deductions. The effect is to force you to pay taxes on 100 percent of your income.

However, the code clearly entitles you to claim otherwise deductible expenses up to the amount of gross income derived from the activity.[21] For example, suppose you earned $5,000 in income and claimed $7,000 in expenses, thus creating a $2,000 loss. If you are not in business for profit, you may nevertheless claim $5,000 in deductions for the expenses. This eliminates any tax on the income. Moreover, you can preserve the remaining $2,000 of loss and carry it forward to subsequent years when there is profit. If you have no profit motive, you cannot claim a loss, but that does not mean you must shoulder the burden of the tax on the income.

What to Do If Your Profit Motive Is Attacked

If your profit motive is attacked, you must present a detailed affidavit to prove that you engaged in the activity to earn a profit. Applying the facts and circumstances of your case, address each of the elements outlined above. Provide documentation to the fullest extent possible. Be prepared to execute an appeal if the auditor rules against you. Do not forget that regardless of your profit motive, you have the right to claim deductions up to the extent of your income. This way, at least you avoid paying taxes on the income. Do not be bluffed into paying taxes you do not owe just because you cannot prove a profit motive.

DON'T TAKE NO FOR AN ANSWER

I state repeatedly in this treatise that the word of a tax examiner is not final. If you understand the rules outlined here and never lose sight of your right to appeal an adverse decision, you can be assured that you will never pay business taxes you do not owe. The appeals process is discussed in chapter 6.

9

Paying Taxes on Your Terms–Not Theirs

Minimizing Wage Levies, Bank Levies, and Tax Liens

Of all the IRS problems you might encounter, the worst by far are collection problems. People customarily think of *everything* involving the IRS as related to collection, but this is not true. Just about everything we discussed to this point actually involves the *ascertainment* of tax liability. Only *after* your liability is determined and assessed does the collection process begin.

For example, computer notices determine errors in tax returns and impose assessments based upon correcting the alleged errors. Likewise, audits are the process of determining the correctness of a tax return. When delinquencies are ascertained, additional taxes are assessed. So too with penalties and interest—these are added to tax delinquencies only after determining the underlying tax. But once a tax is assessed, the IRS has the right to forcibly collect it if the bill is not paid "voluntarily."

To this end, the IRS is empowered with a potent arsenal, including the ability to lien assets, levy wages, and seize bank accounts and other assets. Because collection problems are so onerous, preventing them is always better, cheaper, and easier than curing them. But prevention requires proactive involvement from the outset because the process is largely automated.

When the IRS undertakes to collect a delinquent account, its computers instigate the first wave of attack through a series of computer-generated notices. The process is dangerous because, if not managed properly, the automated collection function resorts to tax liens and wage levies without human interaction.

This chapter addresses the procedures for:

- Avoiding and releasing wage and bank levies

- Challenging improper assessments

- Minimizing the destructive impact of tax liens

- Obtaining emergency assistance in the worse-case scenario.

We begin with the basics—a discussion of the difference between a tax levy and a lien.

LEVY VERSUS LIEN

A levy is the process by which the IRS takes ownership of your assets, whether bank accounts, wages, or other property. For example, through a levy notice served on your employer, the IRS stands in your shoes, usurping your right to receive your paycheck. Rather than allowing you to collect the check yourself, the IRS collects it and applies the proceeds to your delinquent taxes.

A lien does not alter the ownership status of your property. That is to say, a tax lien does not transfer to the IRS your interest in, say, your home. Rather, the lien *secures* the IRS's claim to your property by publicly recording the fact that the agency maintains a legal claim against your assets. The lien is the process by which the IRS protects its interest in your property. This prevents your selling or disposing of assets without paying the assessment.

In short, liens do not transfer property rights; levies do.

WHEN TO EXPECT A LEVY OR LIEN

The collection process begins with a written notice requesting immediate payment. The notice is mailed within about five to eight weeks after the return is processed and the tax is assessed. Subsequent notices are mailed if the tax is not paid in full in the first instance.

The first notice is an "urgent reminder" that you have not paid your taxes. The IRS asks for payment and calculates interest and penalties through the period ending ten days from the date of the letter. This letter is often mistaken for a final notice because it says you must pay "within ten days." However, careful examination reveals that it actually instructs you to make payment within ten days to "avoid further accumulations of interest and penalties." In other words, the ten-day period is the period for which penalties and interest *have already* been added. Once the ten days expire, the debt amasses further accruals. This first letter is *not* a final notice, notice of intent to levy, since it *does not* fulfill the statutory requirements of a final notice.[1]

After a series of like notices, the IRS completes the cycle with a final notice, notice of intent to levy. We often refer to this letter as the thirty-day letter because it clearly states that collection will commence after thirty days from the date of the letter if the tax is not paid. Only a final notice triggers the IRS's enforced-collection rights. The final notice is clearly marked with the words "final notice" and plainly mentions your right to a so-called Collection Due Process Hearing (discussed later in this chapter). An example of a final notice is reproduced here as Exhibit 9–1.

Unless you stabilize collection as I outline in detail in this chapter, you can expect enforcement action anytime after the thirty days expire—without further notice.

EXHIBIT 9-1

SB E

 Department of the Treasury
Internal Revenue Service
P.O. BOX 145566
CINCINNATI, OHIO 45214

Date:
FEB. 17, 2003

Taxpayer Identification Number:

Caller ID:

Contact Telephone Number:
TOLL FREE: 1-800-829-3903
MON. THRU FRI. 8:00AM TO 8:00PM

CALL IMMEDIATELY TO PREVENT PROPERTY LOSS
FINAL NOTICE OF INTENT TO LEVY AND NOTICE OF YOUR RIGHT TO A HEARING

WHY WE ARE SENDING YOU THIS LETTER

We've written to you before asking you to contact us about your overdue taxes. You haven't responded or paid the amounts you owe. We encourage you to call us immediately at the telephone number listed above to discuss your options for paying these amounts. If you act promptly, we can resolve this matter without taking and selling your property to collect what you owe.

We are authorized to collect overdue taxes by taking, which is called levying, property or rights to property and selling them if necessary. Property includes bank accounts, wages, real estate commissions, business assets, cars and other income and assets.

WHAT YOU SHOULD DO

This is your notice, as required under Internal Revenue Code sections 6330 and 6331, that we intend to levy on your property or your rights to property 30 days after the date of this letter unless you take one of these actions:
. Pay the full amount you owe, shown on the back of this letter. When doing so,
  . Please make your check or money order payable to the United States Treasury;
  . Write your social security number and the tax year or employer identification number and the tax period on your payment; and enclose a copy of this letter with your payment.
. Make payment arrangements, such as an installment agreement that allows you to pay off your debt over time.
. Appeal the intended levy on your property by requesting a Collection Due Process hearing within 30 days from the date of this letter.

WHAT TO DO IF YOU DISAGREE

If you've paid already or think we haven't credited a payment to your account, please send us proof of that payment. You may also appeal our intended actions as described above.

Even if you request a hearing, please note that we can still file a Notice of Federal Tax Lien at any time to protect the government's interest. A lien is a public notice that tells your creditors that the government has a right to your current assets and any assets you acquire after we file the lien.

We've enclosed two publications that explain how we collect past due taxes and your collection appeal rights, as required under Internal Revenue Code sections 6330 and 6331. In addition, we've enclosed a form that you can use to request a Collection Due Process hearing.

We look forward to hearing from you immediately, and hope to assist you in fulfilling your responsibility as a taxpayer.

Enclosures: Copy of letter, Form 12153, Publication 594, Publication 1660, Envelope

Automated Collection System

Letter 1058 (Rev. 05-2002)(LT-11)

AVOIDING WAGE AND BANK LEVIES

In the following pages, I examine three wage levy scenarios, the first two of which are the most common. The first involves filing a return *but* without fully paying the tax owed. When you file a return, the IRS automatically assesses the tax shown on the return. If you do not pay in full at the time of filing, the IRS may use enforcement action to collect.

The second scenario involves ways of dealing with the IRS's initial mail contacts demanding payment. These contacts could be based upon either (1) a tax return filed without full payment or (2) an audit or penalty assessment. Prior to an actual levy, the agency uses correspondence to announce its intentions. Your reaction to these letters dictates the agency's subsequent tactics.

The third scenario involves *releasing* levies the IRS already has in effect. Every year, millions of people suffer levies because they failed to follow the strategies I outline in the first two scenarios. But even if you are under levy right now, these procedures will help you immensely.

HOW TO HANDLE YOUR TAX RETURN WHEN YOU CANNOT PAY IN FULL

There are two strategies for dealing with the fact that you do not have the money to pay your taxes in full at the time of filing. Which you use depends on the seriousness of the problem. If you can pay the taxes within six months, you must attempt to win an extension of time to pay the taxes. If you cannot pay within six months, seek an installment agreement.

Requesting an Extension of Time to Pay

One of the IRS's best-kept secrets is the fact that the law provides for an extension of time to *pay* taxes.[2] While the IRS denies this, the agency has nevertheless gone to the trouble of creating a form on which to make the application. It is Form 1127, *Application for Extension of Time for Payment of Tax* (Exhibit 9–2). (I have always found it peculiar that the agency has a form to engage a procedure the agency says does not exist.)

Unlike Form 4846, the filing extension, the payment extension *is not* automatic. Most payment extensions are denied because the few people who file them do not know how to prove they are entitled to an extension.

To win the extension, you must demonstrate that you exercised reasonable business care and prudence in providing for your taxes, but through no fault of your own and due to circumstances beyond your control, you are unable to pay on time. You must also show that paying on time will cause an economic hardship. Hardship exists when, because of enforcement action, it is impossible to pay necessary living expenses. See p. 209 for more details on this idea. Finally, you must agree to give the IRS security for the unpaid tax. The IRS achieves this by filing a tax lien. Although that might not sound like a good idea, the fact is that when you do not pay in full, the IRS almost always files a lien anyway. But even the effect of a lien can be minimized, as I explain later.

If the extension is granted, you may receive up to six additional months to pay your taxes—without penalties. Interest accrues during the extension period. However, by avoiding penalties, you cut in half the amount of additions the IRS imposes. More important, while on the payment extension, the IRS cannot execute enforcement action. This means no levies as long as you pay the tax by the extended due date.

If the agency denies the request, you can still avoid enforcement action by obtaining an installment agreement. Moreover, just submitting the request puts you in a better position to seek abatement of failure-to-pay penalties later. This is because filing the extension is the quintessential act of good faith. You put the IRS on notice of the problem and take affirmative steps to resolve it rather than waiting for the IRS to chase you down for payment.

EXHIBIT 9-2

Form 1127
(Rev. 11-93)
Department of the Treasury
Internal Revenue Service

APPLICATION FOR EXTENSION OF TIME FOR PAYMENT OF TAX

(ATTN: *This type of payment extension is rarely <u>granted</u> because the legal requirements are so strict. Please read the conditions on the back carefully before continuing.)*

Taxpayer's Name (include spouse if your extension request is for a joint return)	Social Security Number or Employer Identification Number
Present Address	Spouse's Social Security Number if this is for a joint return
City, Town or Post Office, State, and Zip Code	

District Director of Internal Revenue at _____
(Enter City and State where IRS Office is located)

I request an extension from _____ , 19 _____ , to _____ , 19 _____ ,
(Enter Due Date of Return)

to pay tax of $ _____ for the year ended _____ , 19 _____ .

This extension is necessary because *(If more space is needed, please attach a separate sheet):* _____

_____

_____

_____

I can't borrow to pay the tax because: _____

_____

_____

To show the need for the extension, I am attaching: (1) a statement of my assets and liabilities at the end of last month (showing book and market values of assets and whether securities are listed or unlisted); and (2) an itemized list of money I received and spent for 3 months before the date the tax is due.

I propose to secure this liability as follows: _____

_____

_____

Under penalties of perjury, I declare that I have examined this application, including any accompanying schedules and statements, and to the best of my knowledge and belief it is true, correct, and complete.

_____   _____

SIGNATURE (BOTH SIGNATURES IF YOUR EXTENSION REQUEST IS FOR A JOINT RETURN)   (DATE)

The District Director will let you know whether the extension is approved or denied and will tell you if you need some form of security. However, the Director can't consider an application if it is filed after the due date of the return. We will send you a list of approved surety companies if you ask for it.

(The following will be filled in by the IRS.)

This application is ☐ approved   for the following reasons:
☐ denied

_____

_____

Interest _____   Date of assessment _____   Identifying no. _____

Penalty _____   _____   _____
                                      (SIGNATURE)   (DATE)

ISA

EXHIBIT 9–3

Form **9465**
(Rev. December 2002)
Department of the Treasury
Internal Revenue Service   (99)

Installment Agreement Request

▶ If you are filing this form with your tax return, attach it to the front of the return. Otherwise, see instructions.

OMB No. 1545-1350

Caution: *Do not file this form if you are currently making payments on an installment agreement. Instead, call 1-800-829-1040.*

1	Your first name and initial	Last name	Your social security number
	If a joint return, spouse's first name and initial	Last name	Spouse's social security number
	Your current address (number and street). If you have a P.O. box and no home delivery, enter your box number.		Apt. number
	City, town or post office, state, and ZIP code. If a foreign address, enter city, province or state, and country. Follow the country's practice for entering the postal code.		

2 If this address is new since you filed your last tax return, check here . . . . ▶ ☐

3			4			
	Your home phone number	Best time for us to call		Your work phone number	Ext.	Best time for us to call

5	Name of your bank or other financial institution:	6	Your employer's name:
	Address		Address
	City, state, and ZIP code		City, state, and ZIP code

TIP *If you are filing this form in response to a notice, do not complete lines 7 through 9. Instead, attach the bottom section of the notice to this form and go to line 10.*

7 Enter the tax return for which you are making this request (for example, Form 1040) . . . . ▶ **7**

8 Enter the tax year for which you are making this request (for example, 2002) . . . . ▶ **8**

9 Enter the total amount you owe as shown on your tax return **9**

10 Enter the amount of any payment you are making with your tax return (or notice). See instructions . . . **10**

11 Enter the amount you can pay each month. **Make your payments as large as possible to limit interest and penalty charges.** The charges will continue until you pay in full **11**

12 Enter the date you want to make your payment each month. **Do not** enter a date later than the 28th . ▶ **12**

13 If you want to make your payments by electronic funds withdrawal, see the instructions and fill in lines 13a, 13b, and 13c.

▶ **a** Routing number ☐☐☐☐☐☐☐☐☐ ▶ **c** Type: ☐ Checking ☐ Savings

▶ **b** Account number ☐☐☐☐☐☐☐☐☐☐☐☐☐☐☐☐☐

I authorize the U.S. Treasury and its designated Financial Agent to initiate a monthly ACH electronic funds withdrawal entry to the financial institution account indicated for payments of my Federal taxes owed, and the financial institution to debit the entry to this account. This authorization is to remain in full force and effect until I notify the U.S. Treasury Financial Agent to terminate the authorization. To revoke payment, I must contact the U.S. Treasury Financial Agent at **1-800-829-1040** no later than 7 business days prior to the payment (settlement) date. I also authorize the financial institutions involved in the processing of the electronic payments of taxes to receive confidential information necessary to answer inquiries and resolve issues related to the payments.

Your signature	Date	Spouse's signature. If a joint return, both must sign.	Date

General Instructions

Section references are to the Internal Revenue Code.

Purpose of Form

Use Form 9465 to request a monthly installment plan if you cannot pay the full amount you owe shown on your tax return (or on a notice we sent you). Generally, you may have up to 60 months to pay. But before requesting an installment agreement, you should consider other less costly alternatives, such as a bank loan. If you have any questions about this request, call 1-800-829-1040.

Guaranteed Installment Agreement. Your request for an installment agreement cannot be turned down if the tax you owe is not more than $10,000 and all three of the following apply.

1. During the past 5 tax years, you (and your spouse if you are making a request for a joint tax return) have timely filed all income tax returns and paid any income tax due, and have not entered into an installment agreement for payment of income tax.

2. The IRS determines that you cannot pay the tax owed in full when it is due and you give the IRS any information needed to make that determination.

3. You agree to pay the full amount you owe within 3 years and to comply with the tax laws while the agreement is in effect.

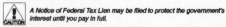 *A Notice of Federal Tax Lien may be filed to protect the government's interest until you pay in full.*

Bankruptcy or Offer-in-Compromise. If you are in bankruptcy or we have accepted your offer-in-compromise, do **not** file this form. Instead, call 1-800-829-1040 to get the number of your local IRS Insolvency function for bankruptcy or Technical Support function for offer-in-compromise.

For Privacy Act and Paperwork Reduction Act Notice, see back of form.

Form **9465** (Rev. 12-2002)

ISA
GTF FFD7050F 1

Requesting an Installment Agreement

If the IRS denies a request for extension of time to pay or if you need more than six months to pay, use Form 9465, *Installment Agreement Request*. This form can be submitted with the return at the time of filing. The installment agreement request sets the wheels in motion to establish an installment agreement. Once that process begins, you greatly reduce the likelihood of enforced collection. Moreover, under the circumstances listed below, the IRS *must* approve an installment agreement without question. Exhibit 9–3 is an example of Form 9465.

The IRS *must* grant an installment agreement if all of the following criteria are met:

- The amount owed (not including interest and penalties) is not more than $10,000.

- Within the last five years, you have not (1) failed to file any required tax return, (2) failed to pay any previous tax, or (3) entered into a prior installment agreement.

- You prove that you are financially unable to pay tax by the due date.

- You agree to pay in full within three years.

- You meet all tax obligations while the agreement is in effect.[3]

The IRS has the right to determine whether you are financially unable to pay. To make the determination, the IRS asks you to complete a financial statement. This is Form 433-A, *Collection Information Statement for Wage Earners and Self-Employed Individuals*. You do not have to submit the financial statement, but if you refuse, the agency will not consider an installment agreement.

The financial statement reveals your income, expenses, assets, and liabilities. From there, the IRS determines your "disposable income." Disposable income is ascertained by subtracting your necessary living expenses from net take-home pay, after withholding for all current taxes. The difference is your disposable income, which is the amount of the installment payment. Unfortunately, the IRS uses predetermined expense standards for housing, utilities, food, clothing, personal care, and miscellaneous items to arrive at your disposable income. These standards are artificially low, having the effect of increasing the amount demanded beyond your ability to pay.

The installment agreement precludes the IRS from enforcing collection in any other manner not specifically provided for in the installment agreement document (IRS Form 433-D). This rule applies both during the period the agreement is being negotiated and once it is accepted.[4] However, should you default, the IRS may revoke the agreement and enforce collection anytime after thirty days from the date of revocation.

Even if you do not qualify for a mandatory installment agreement, you can still achieve an installment agreement by proving that you cannot pay in full and that enforcement action will cause a serious financial hardship.

What to Do If You Cannot Afford an Installment Payment

If you are living paycheck to paycheck, you may not be able to afford *any* payment because of your necessary living expenses. In this case the IRS can freeze collection action and forego the necessity of an installment agreement. This is known as "uncollectible status." It occurs in cases where you are either unemployed or underemployed.

If you cannot make a payment because of your financial condition, ask for uncollectible status, both in your letter and on the face of the installment agreement request, Form 9465. Where the form asks for a monthly payment amount, write in the number zero. Then note at the bottom of the form that you seek "uncollectible status." In your letter, explain clearly that you cannot make a payment because of your harsh financial circumstances. To illustrate your condition, include a brief sketch of your current income and all monthly expenses. The IRS will most likely follow up with a request for a more detailed financial statement as discussed above.

If the IRS agrees that you cannot afford a payment, it freezes collection, putting the case on hold. Keep in mind, however, that in the vast majority of cases, neither an installment agreement nor uncollectible status *solves* the underlying tax delinquency problem. The reason is that penalties and interest continue to accrue, even when collection is frozen. Therefore you must take some other action to resolve your underlying debt.

There are numerous strategies to resolve the underlying debt. For example, if you do not legally owe the tax, you can challenge the underlying debt through the process of audit reconsideration. This allows you to reopen a closed examination case to present evidence that the tax assessment is incorrect.

If you do legally owe the debt, an Offer in Compromise (OIC) gives you the opportunity to negotiate a settlement for less than you owe. This way, you settle the delinquency for an amount equal to your *ability* to pay, rather than by paying the entire liability.

If all else fails, bankruptcy can help. One of the best-kept legal secrets in the country is the fact that income tax debts are dischargeable in bankruptcy. Your debt must meet certain rules, but those that do are wiped out. For more details on these procedures, which are outside the scope of this discussion, see my book *How to Get Tax Amnesty* (Winning Publications, 1998).

HOW TO RESPOND TO THE IRS'S INITIAL COLLECTION CONTACTS

Most people are unaware of both the payment extension (Form 1127) and the installment agreement request (Form 9465). Consequently, many file tax returns without full payment *and* without seeking either of the two remedies discussed above. In this case, the IRS undertakes collection immediately after assessing the tax.

The best approach is to take decisive steps to head off enforcement action *prior* to receiving the final notice. Respond promptly to the IRS's first notice. If you failed to respond, respond to any subsequent notice. The key is to respond *at any point* along the way but not to wait until you receive the final notice. Your response should be in writing and directed to the address shown on the top of the letter (see Exhibit 9–1). Always send your letters via certified mail with return receipt requested.

Your response must explain that you do not have the capacity to pay the tax in full and that you need an installment agreement. Ideally, include an installment agreement request (Form 9465) with your letter, indicating how much you can pay each month. This sets in motion the process of establishing the agreement and stabilizing collection, which in turn averts enforcement action.

It is important to be clear about your request. Do not use vague references or unspecific terminology. Be concise and succinct. Be sure to state clearly that you cannot endure enforcement action. The language I recommend reads, "I do not have the income or assets to be able to pay the bill in full, and enforcement action will cause an undue economic hardship by making it impossible for me to pay my living expenses." Ask for an installment agreement at a level you can afford. If the agency needs additional information to make a decision, it will send you a form seeking financial information.[5]

If you have already waited too long and the IRS has issued the final notice, take quick action to head off a levy. Immediately contact the Taxpayer Advocate's office in your local area rather than correspond with a service center. The TA's office responds faster. Now, keep in mind that when the IRS says you have thirty days to pay "or else," it does not mean it will take enforcement action on the thirty-first day. However, it is equally important to understand that the IRS *has the right* to enforce collection *anytime* after thirty days. Therefore, *do not* delay.

The Taxpayer Advocate (TA) is a liaison between the IRS and the citizen. The TA can step in when there is a problem the citizen cannot resolve through normal channels. The TA's management structure is separate from other IRS functions and completely divorced from any of the agency's enforcement arms. See chapter 1 for more details.

The TA can order the IRS to refrain from action it is about to take or terminate actions it has already commenced, if those actions will cause a financial hardship.[6] The TA can be very helpful, both in heading off levies and in winning release of levies already in place.

The Taxpayer Advocate Service has a representative in every main IRS office and within each of the ten service centers.

To reach the TA, address your letter to the Taxpayer Advocate at the address of the IRS's main office in your state. The letter should be much the same as that outlined above. Include a copy of the final notice and give the date you received it. Explain pointedly that you cannot endure enforcement action and must have an installment agreement. The TA will consider your letter and assign the case for negotiation of an installment agreement. Once you come to terms, no levy action will proceed.

HOW TO RELEASE WAGE AND BANK LEVIES

Once a levy is in place, it is imperative to move quickly. A wage levy attaches to your next paycheck and transfers to the IRS all money beyond current tax withholdings and minimum exemption amounts, which are not generous. The first step is to complete the exemption form provided with Form 668-W, *Notice of Levy on Wages, Salary or Other Income*, the levy form issued to your employer. If you do not, the IRS ends up with half your take-home pay. This is a simple form that asks only for your tax return filing status and your dependents. The exemption amounts are based on these two factors. However, do not stop there.

A bank account levy is not so immediate, but neither is there a minimum exemption amount. The IRS can and will take the entire bank balance. However, the law provides a twenty-one-day waiting period before the bank may surrender your account. The waiting period begins with the date of the levy.[7] This gives you time to work with the IRS before losing your money. In the meantime, the bank will not clear any outstanding checks until the IRS releases the levy.

Generally, the IRS releases wage and bank levies in the following cases:

- The tax was paid or is legally unenforceable because the collection statute of limitations expired.

- Releasing the levy will facilitate tax collection.

- An installment agreement was in effect prior to the levy and you are not in violation of the agreement.

- The levy is creating a financial hardship.

- The fair market value of the property levied exceeds the tax owed, and release of the levy on that property will not hinder collection.[8]

Some of these points are self-explanatory, such the one dealing with installment agreements. Others warrant more discussion. Let us consider them.

Releasing the Levy Will Facilitate Collection

This is broad language that applies in any situation where the levy will do more harm than good to the IRS's prospects of collecting. One example is where a company has an employment policy against enforced creditor collections. If you can show that the levy will lead to sanctions, such as losing your job, such ramifications do not "facilitate collection." Obviously, you are less likely to pay the tax if you have no job. A few other examples include:

- Levy of IRA or 401(k) accounts that create a tax liability in the year of the levy as a result of the early withdrawal of retirement funds.

- Levy of bank account proceeds while several checks are outstanding. The levy causes the checks to bounce, affecting your credit and good standing with other creditors, in turn affecting your ability to conduct business and ultimately to pay the tax.

- Levy of assets jointly owned by other persons who do not owe the IRS. Levy of these assets requires compensation to the nondebtor joint owner. This reduces the IRS's levy proceeds and diminishes the value of the levy action.

Anytime you can show that collection will not be facilitated by the presence of the levy, it should be released.

Levy Is Causing Economic Hardship

This provision applies when the levy is causing an economic hardship due to your financial condition. To increase the chances of obtaining relief from the levy, always argue this point, either alone or in conjunction with others. However, it is not enough merely to *allege* economic hardship. You must prove that your overall financial condition is such that the levy stands to ruin you.

The IRS regulations provide some guidance as to what constitutes "economic hardship." Consider the following:

> This condition applies if satisfaction of the levy in whole or in part will cause an individual taxpayer to be unable to pay his or her reasonable basic living expenses. The determination of a reasonable amount for basic living expenses will be made by the director and will vary according to the unique circumstances of the individual taxpayer. Unique circumstances, however, do not include the maintenance of an affluent or luxurious standard of living.[9]

To win release of the levy under this provision, be prepared to submit a detailed financial statement, usually on Form 433-A. This statement provides the information the IRS needs to determine your ability to pay. As I stated earlier, the IRS evaluates your living expenses in light of its fixed standards and generally attempts to squeeze as much from you as possible. To mitigate this, be prepared to document all your living expenses.

In addition, the regulation provides that the IRS must take into consideration the following information in determining whether your living expenses are "reasonable":

- Your age, employment status and history, ability to earn, number of dependents, and status as a dependent of someone else

- The amount reasonably necessary for food, clothing, housing (including utilities, home-owner insurance, home-owner dues, and the like), medical expenses (including health insurance), transportation, current tax payments (including federal, state, and local), alimony, child support or other court-ordered payments, and expenses necessary to earn income (such as dues for a trade union or professional organization, or child care payments that allow you to work)

- The cost of living in the geographic area where you reside

- The amount of property exempt from levy that is available to pay your expenses

- Any extraordinary circumstances such as special education expenses, a medical catastrophe, or natural disaster

- Any other factor that you claim bears on economic hardship.[10]

To make this presentation, submit a letter via certified mail to the local office of the Taxpayer Advocate. Be specific and detailed and provide the information outlined above. Be very clear and specific about the nature of the harm the levy is doing. It is not enough to make the conclusory allegation that the levy is causing economic hardship. You must give examples, such as that you are unable to make a mortgage or auto payment or that you have several outstanding checks that will bounce, thereby destroying your good standing with merchants and creditors. Make a specific and clear request that the levy be lifted immediately. Ask the TA to fax a Release of Levy to your bank or payroll department to ensure a prompt release. Provide the name and fax number in your letter.

Keep in mind that if you withhold information regarding your financial status and ability to pay, you will at the least delay the process, and most likely your request to release the levy will simply be denied. Moreover, IRS regulations require that you act in good faith. Examples of failure to act in good faith include (but are not limited to) falsifying financial information, inflating actual expenses or costs, and failing to disclose all your assets.[11] Therefore, *do not* withhold information or misstate your financial condition and expect the IRS to release a levy. An example of the letter discussed here is shown in Exhibit 9–4.

EXHIBIT 9–4. Letter Seeking Release of Levy

Your Name
Address
City, State, Zip
Phone:

Date:

Office of the Taxpayer Advocate
Internal Revenue Service
Address
City, State, Zip

Tax Year ———
SSN:

REQUEST FOR RELEASE OF LEVY

Dear Taxpayer Advocate:

On ——— [date] my employer, ———(name), received a Notice of Levy on Wages. This levy will go into effect with my next paycheck, which is to be issued on ——— [date].

Please note that this levy will cause a serious economic hardship by making it impossible for me to pay my necessary living expenses. My current income and expenses are such that without my full paycheck, I will be unable to pay bills that are necessary to meet my current, mandatory living expenses for myself and my family. The chart below shows my current income and expenses.

INCOME	MONTHLY LIVING EXPENSES
List total monthly gross income	List all living expenses. Be sure to include wage withholding for current taxes, other payroll deductions, and expenses that do not occur every month, such as auto insurance

As you can see, the levy will make it impossible for me to pay these expenses. Given that I have ——— children/dependents living at home with me, this wage levy will put me into a position where I cannot pay the expenses necessary to provide for my family. The levy should be released immediately.

[List any other grounds for release of levy, such as employment policies regarding collection action that will jeopardize your employment. Also present facts on other financial demands, such as medical conditions or educational concerns.]

On the basis of these facts, I hereby request an immediate release of this levy. My next paycheck will be issued on ——— [date]. Therefore the levy should be released before that time. I request that you fax a release of levy to my employer at ——— [fax number]. The release should be addressed to ——— [name of company payroll clerk].

In addition, I request that the IRS establish an installment agreement to pay these taxes. I can afford to pay $——— per month. [Alternatively, ask for uncollectible status if you cannot afford any payment.]

If you need additional information, I can be reached at the above address and phone number. Otherwise, please issue the release of levy without delay.

Thank you.

Sincerely,

Your Signature

Send your letter via certified mail with return receipt requested. Keep a copy for your records.

RELEASING TAX LIENS

Though tax liens do not transfer title of property to the IRS, they certainly can mess up your credit. In fact, the lien itself is usually the very reason a person cannot borrow the money necessary to pay the outstanding tax. Generally the IRS releases liens only if the tax is paid or is legally uncollectible due to lapse of time. However, there are a number of circumstances when liens are removed even before paying the tax in full. Because of the financial handicap imposed by liens, it is necessary to examine a couple of strategies for winning their release.

The Lien Withdrawal

The law contains a tool useful to override tax liens that do more harm than good in the collection process—in other words, most of them. The tool is known as the "lien withdrawal." There are four possible reasons for withdrawing a lien. They are:

1. The lien filing was premature or in violation of IRS procedures.

2. You entered into an installment agreement that does not specifically provide for a lien.

3. Withdrawal of the lien will facilitate the collection of the tax.

4. The Taxpayer Advocate determines that withdrawal of the lien would be in the best interests of both you and the IRS.[12]

Let me explain these points in more detail, beginning with the first. There are two key administrative procedures the IRS must follow before it can file a lien. First, the deficiency procedures (explained in chapter 2) require a notice and the opportunity to appeal before an assessment can be made. If the deficiency procedures are not followed, the assessment is invalid and the IRS does not have the legal right to collect. That means the lien is likewise invalid. Second, once a tax is properly assessed, the IRS cannot collect until after issuing a final notice, notice of intention to levy, as explained in the opening pages of this chapter. Believe it or not, the IRS often fails to send the proper notices, or mails them to an incorrect address. A violation of either procedure warrants withdrawal of a lien.

Now let us address point two, installment agreements. As I explained earlier, the formal installment agreement, IRS Form 433-D, generally allows the IRS to file a lien when the agency deems it necessary. However, the right to file a lien must be stated in the agreement. It is common for installment agreements not to allow for a lien. This happens, for example, when a citizen makes it clear that he is working to obtain a loan against or to sell property to pay the tax. Of course, the presence of a lien messes up the opportunity to carry out either act. If the agreement does not provide for a lien and one is filed anyway, you have the right to get it withdrawn.

The third and fourth points present the broadest opportunities to win withdrawal. Point three gives the IRS the authority to withdraw a lien when withdrawal will "facilitate tax collection." This is a broad, undefined phrase that often operates to your advantage. A tax lien not only encumbers your property, thus preventing sale, but it destroys your credit as well. That often makes it impossible to get a loan to pay the taxes. This works against your efforts to pay.

Suppose, for example, that you have substantial equity in your home sufficient to pay your tax. However, almost all lenders refuse to lend money when a tax lien is involved. The bank may be perfectly willing to lend money—*if* the lien is removed first. But the IRS will not release its lien unless the tax is paid—first. Of course, you cannot pay the tax unless the lien goes away, since the source of funding is the loan. The standoff creates a situation where tax collection is *not* facilitated, because the lien makes it impossible to obtain financing to pay the bill. Under the circumstances, withdrawal of the lien "facilitates tax collection."

Another example involves a person wishing to sell his home. Substantial equity in the home makes it possible to pay off the debt, but the lien prevents a clear title from passing to the buyer. Therefore the title company will not close the sale unless the lien is removed. Even if money is escrowed to pay the tax, the buyer cannot be assured of a clear title unless the lien is removed, because the lien attaches to the property itself, *not* just the person who owes the tax. The lien therefore *follows* the property if title is transferred. But if the lien is withdrawn, title may pass to the new owner, allowing the title company to close the sale. Under the circumstances, withdrawal of the lien "facilitates tax collection."

Point four allows the lien to be removed when the Taxpayer Advocate agrees that withdrawal is in the "best interests" of both you and the IRS. This too is broad, undefined authority that operates to your advantage. The TA often forces collection officers to do what they are otherwise unwilling to do. If you prove that the lien is doing more to prevent collection or otherwise cause financial hardship than it is to protect the IRS's interests, the TA will order its withdrawal.

How to Seek Withdrawal of a Tax Lien. An application for withdrawal of the lien must be made in writing. It should be directed to the Chief, Special Procedures, in the main local IRS office. Special Procedures is an adjunct to the collection function and handles the legal paperwork, such as lien releases. The application must contain:

- Your name, address, social security number, and other contact information.

- A copy of the tax lien in question.

- A description of the property encumbered by the lien.

- A statement of the reasons the lien should be withdrawn. Refer to the above list of four possible reasons. Keep in mind that any or all of these may be used as grounds to withdraw a lien.

- An argument supporting your claim. The argument must be specific and documented to the fullest extent possible. For example, if you are seeking a loan to pay the tax, provide all the documents surrounding the loan process. Also, support your argument with an affidavit to the extent possible. For example, if you claim that you never received a final notice or that the IRS agreed during installment agreement discussions not to file a lien, these claims must be set forth in a detailed affidavit.

- The names and addresses of anyone you wish the IRS to notify that it is withdrawing the lien. This process helps to correct damage done when the lien was filed.

- Any other information you believe should be considered.

Sign the application and include a declaration that, "under penalty of perjury," the application and all its exhibits, including documents, affidavits, etc., are "true and correct." The application must be filed in triplicate.[13]

When the IRS agrees to withdraw, the agency must file a notice in the same local government office where the lien was filed. You must be given a copy of the notice. What is more, when you ask *in writing*, the IRS must "promptly make reasonable efforts to notify credit reporting agencies and any financial institution or creditor whose name and address is specified in such request, of the withdrawal of such notice."[14]

This feature helps to repair credit damage done by the lien. You have the duty to provide the IRS with the names and addresses of those you want notified. Thereafter, it is the agency's duty to send the notice expressly vindicating you from the damaging lien.

The Lien Subordination

Another effective method of dealing with tax liens is the process known as "subordination." Use this method instead of withdrawal when there is no question about the legality of the lien, but rather you are attempting to sell or borrow against property to pay off the tax. Under this technique, the IRS agrees to make its lien subordinate, or secondary, to that of another creditor, such as a bank. This strategy often prevents the IRS from selling your property for pennies on the dollar.

The IRS can subordinate a lien if (1) the IRS is paid an amount equal to its lien or interest in the property in question, or (2) the IRS will ultimately collect more by subordinating the lien, and collection of the tax is facilitated by subordinating the lien.[15]

IRS regulations governing this process state in part as follows:

For example, if a notice of Federal tax lien is filed and a delinquent taxpayer secures a mortgage loan on a part of the property subject to the tax lien and pays over the proceeds of the loan to a district director after an application for a certificate of subordination is approved, the district director will issue a certificate of subordination. This certificate will have the effect of subordinating the tax lien to the mortgage.[16]

The IRS requires a written application before it will subordinate a lien, but there is no preprinted IRS form for the application. However, IRS Publication 784, *Application for Subordination of Federal Tax Lien,* provides guidance. The application must contain the following information:

- Your name, address, social security number, and contact information

- Whether the subordination is sought to secure the "payment of the amount subordinated" or to "facilitate tax collection"

- A detailed description of the property for which the subordination is sought, including the street address and legal description

- A copy of the tax lien in question and the date and place of its filing

- A copy of the proposed documents that create the liability to which the tax lien will be subordinate (for example, a mortgage for a bank loan), a description of the transaction (such as "mortgage to pay tax"), and the date the transaction is to be completed

- If other encumbrances exist upon the property, they must be disclosed, including the name of the lien holder, the date it was created, the amount due, and a description of the encumbrance

- An estimate of the fair market value of the property (This can be obtained from real estate tax records, an experienced local realtor, or a recent appraisal of the property.)

- When seeking the subordination to obtain a mortgage, the amount of money to be paid to the IRS if the subordination is granted

- When seeking the subordination in order to "facilitate collection," a statement showing why you believe the IRS is more likely to collect by granting the subordination

- Any other information that has a bearing

Sign the application declaring that "under penalty of perjury, all facts contained in the application and documents attached are true and correct" and specifically request that the application be granted.

File the application with the local office of Special Procedures. The application must be made in triplicate, and you should use certified mail whenever sending any documents to the IRS.

Jim's case provides a perfect example how the subordination process works. It would have saved him unimaginable heartache. Jim was a brilliant psychiatrist and his practice was successful until his business and personal tax returns were audited. At the conclusion of the audit, the IRS claimed that Jim owed $550,000 in taxes. It was later proved that the IRS made more than $500,000 in "mistakes" and that the most he could have owed was $23,000. Still, after all the arguing, the IRS held fast to a claim for $53,000 in taxes and penalties.

Jim owned a home worth about $250,000 on which the bank held a $100,000 mortgage. The equity was more than adequate to pay the bill, and Jim made arrangements with his banker to borrow the money. The sole proviso was that the IRS must agree to lift its lien so the bank would rest in the first position as a security holder.

Hoping to put the matter behind him, Jim phoned the revenue officer and presented his plan. He would pay the tax in full "within three days" if the IRS would simply lift the lien. The revenue officer's answer was as short as it was unreasonable: "No." Jim was eventually pushed into bankruptcy by a combination of IRS incompetence and IRS unwillingness to find a solution.

The revenue officer failed to explain the formal subordination process to Jim. However, in a case such as Jim's, the agency most certainly would have subordinated the lien if only he had filed his request *in writing*—to the proper office—and with the correct supporting information as outlined above. Jim's only downfall was that he did not know what you just learned. His ignorance cost him his home.

Expiration of the Lien

In general the IRS has just ten years from the date a tax is assessed in which to collect it. At that point the tax becomes unenforceable due to lapse of time unless the collection statute is extended for some authorized reason. Once the assessment expires, regulations require the IRS to release its lien.[17] (See my book *How to Get Tax Amnesty* for more details on the collection statute of limitations.)

If your collection statute is expired, file an application for release of the tax lien. Although there is no IRS form on which to make the application, IRS Publication 783, *Instructions on How to Apply for a Certificate of Discharge*, provides the following guidance:

- Make the request in writing to Special Procedures staff in your main local IRS office.

- Give your name, address, social security number, and contact information.

- Include a copy of the lien in question.

- State "the grounds upon which the issuance of a release is sought." In this case, seek release on the grounds that the collection statute of limitations has expired. To prove this, obtain a copy of your Individual Master File (discussed in chapter 1), which shows, among other things, the tax assessment date. Use that as the basis for arguing that the agency's right of collection has expired.

- Sign the statement, include a declaration that "under penalty or perjury, all facts contained in the application are true and correct," and specifically request that the application be granted.

As is the case with nearly all the lien release procedures, the ultimate responsibility for obtaining a lien release lies on your shoulders. You must make the application, or the IRS is not likely to remove any lien. This is true even if the tax is paid and even if the collection statute of limitations has expired.

THE COLLECTION DUE PROCESS HEARING

The IRS Restructuring Act created two new rights that have come to be known as the "collection due process rights." They grow from a long and tortured process of complaining about what was viewed by many proponents of taxpayers' rights, including myself, as summary and often arbitrary collection powers. The first right addresses tax liens, and the second addresses levy and seizure actions.[18] These are probably the most important gains in taxpayers' rights in two decades. Unfortunately, Congress is now moving to limit these rights.

These rights apply to all liens and levy action. The rights give you the opportunity to challenge the IRS's intended collection action *before* it takes place. By filing IRS Form 12153, *Request for a Collection Due Process Hearing,* as outlined below, your case is removed from the collection function and placed into the hands of the Appeals Office. Here, honest efforts are made to find an amicable solution short of enforced collection action. This is how to use these important rights.

Appealing a Newly Filed Tax Lien

The IRS must notify you that it has filed a lien not more than five days after its filing. You then have thirty days from the day *after* the five-day period expires in which to file an administrative appeal of the lien. The appeal gets you a hearing before the Appeals Office.[19] I discuss the hearing process in detail later in this chapter.

Appealing Levy and Seizure Actions

Once the IRS issues a final notice, notice of intention to levy (see Exhibit 9–1), a thirty-day waiting period begins. The IRS cannot take collection action until those thirty days expire. During that period, you may file an administrative appeal of the intended levy or seizure action.[20] File the administrative appeal of either a lien or intended levy action using IRS Form 12153, *Request for a Collection Due Process Hearing.* An example of Form 12153 is shown in Exhibit 9–5. File the form within the thirty-day window and be sure to give your reasons for challenging the collection action. Some common reasons are outlined later in this chapter. Once you file that form, collection action immediately ceases until the Appeals Office rules on your challenge.

EXHIBIT 9–5

Request for a Collection Due Process Hearing

Use this form to request a hearing with the IRS Office of Appeals only when you receive a **Notice of Federal Tax Lien Filing & Your Right To A Hearing Under IRC 6320,** a **Final Notice - Notice of Intent to Levy & Your Notice of a Right To A Hearing,** or a **Notice of Jeopardy Levy and Right of Appeal.** Complete this form and send it to the address shown on your lien or levy notice for expeditious handling. Include a copy of your lien or levy notice(s) to ensure proper handling of your request.

(Print) Taxpayer Name(s): _____

(Print) Address: _____

Daytime Telephone Number: _____ Type of Tax/Tax Form Number(s): _____

Taxable Period(s): _____

Social Security Number/Employer Identification Number(s): _____

Check the IRS action(s) that you do not agree with. Provide specific reasons why you don't agree. If you believe that your spouse or former spouse should be responsible for all or a portion of the tax liability from your tax return, check here ☐ and attach Form 8857, Request for Innocent Spouse Relief, to this request.

_____ **Filed Notice of Federal Tax Lien (Explain why you don't agree. Use extra sheets if necessary.)**

_____ **Notice of Levy/Seizure (Explain why you don't agree. Use extra sheets if necessary.)**

I/we understand that the statutory period of limitations for collection is suspended during the Collection Due Process Hearing and any subsequent judicial review.

Taxpayer's or Authorized Representative's Signature and Date: _____

Taxpayer's or Authorized Representative's Signature and Date: _____

IRS Use Only:

IRS Employee *(Print)*: _____ IRS Received Date: _____

Employee Telephone Number: _____

Form **12153** (01-1999)   Department of the Treasury - Internal Revenue Service

When the Appeals Office takes control of the case, an Appeals Officer is required to verify that the IRS has met all the requirements of the tax code in executing the specific collection action. This includes verifying that the IRS followed all the proper administrative procedures requisite to obtaining a valid assessment. This is critical, especially in the case of computer notices, since so often the IRS fails to follow the proper deficiency procedures in making its assessments. Review chapter 2.

The collection due process hearing is not at all like a court hearing. It is a very informal conference held with an Appeals Officer in his office. Just you and the Appeals Officer will attend, unless you opt to have counsel represent you. You should determine in advance whether to utilize counsel, since counsel will have to file a power of attorney ahead of time.

The hearing gives you the opportunity to raise "any relevant issue relating to the unpaid tax" or the proposed collection action. This means you have broad latitude to challenge both the tax assessment and the IRS's intended collection action. Specifically, you can:

1. Raise spousal defenses such as the innocent spouse or injured spouse defense. I discuss these defenses in detail in chapter 10.[21]

2. Question the appropriateness of the collection action, that is, whether the IRS is justified in filing a lien or levying assets given all the facts and circumstances of the case. You might argue that a wage levy will cause serious economic hardship by making it impossible to pay necessary living expenses, or that the seizure of a bank account will cause checks to bounce, thereby ruining your good standing with other creditors.

3. Offer collection alternatives such as entering into an installment agreement, establishing uncollectible status, or submitting an Offer in Compromise. Your plan should illustrate how the IRS is better served under your plan than it is by enforcing collection.

4. Challenge the merits of the underlying tax liability if you never received a notice of deficiency or otherwise never had an oppor-

tunity to challenge the tax. You have the burden to present a foundation of evidence to support your claim that you never received a notice of deficiency. An affidavit is important to establish these facts.[22]

The fourth point is critical in that it offers the opportunity to challenge tax assessments if you did not previously have such a chance. This is especially important to tax return nonfilers victimized by the IRS's "substitute for return" (SFR). Those who fail to file tax returns in a timely manner are often introduced to the IRS's own calculation of their tax liability through an SFR. Although an SFR determination is subject to the deficiency procedures, the IRS rarely follows them. As a result, the citizen has no opportunity to challenge the assessment despite the fact that such assessments are almost always erroneous. The collection due process hearing affords such an opportunity prior to suffering the wrath of enforced collection. For more details on the SFR process, see chapter 3.

If the Appeals Office renders an unfavorable decision, you have thirty days from the date of the ruling in which to make a second appeal. That appeal goes to either the Tax Court or the U.S. District Court, depending upon which court has jurisdiction over the underlying tax liability. In this way you actually have the opportunity for judicial review of the agency's intended collection action. While the judicial process is outside the scope of this discussion, I cover it in my book, *Taxpayers' Ultimate Defense Manual* (Winning Publications, 1989).

For two key reasons, the collection appeal provisions are by far the most pointed tax collection appeal statutes Congress ever created. First, unlike other provisions, these do not limit the issues you can raise on appeal. As stated, you may raise "any relevant issue," including the merits of the underlying tax if that has not been previously decided. Second, and perhaps more important, the courts have jurisdiction to review the IRS's determination in a separate appeals process. This opens judicial doors that were previously shut tight.

ENFORCED COLLECTION MEANS BUSINESS

There is no doubt that enforced collection truly is the business end of tax law enforcement. And unfortunately, tens of millions of citizens face this action every year. In order to keep the IRS from running you over in the collection process, you must understand the basic rights outlined above.

In almost every case, wage and bank levies can be avoided or their negative impact minimized when you act promptly and correctly. However, when you ignore the problem, hoping against hope that it will go away, the situation only grows worse. And to add insult to injury, you almost always lose your appeals rights by waiting.

10

Divorcing Yourself from Tax Problems

Coping with Spousal Tax Bills

Few things are more frustrating than having a current or former spouse's tax debt follow you around. Often, IRS collection efforts seem irrational and unfair when the debt is clearly attributable to the actions or failures of one spouse but the IRS looks to the other spouse for payment, even in cases where a divorce has seemingly cleaved the interests and liabilities of the parties. But as in every area of tax law administration, there are solutions to these problems. When properly executed, these solutions divorce you from the tax problem. The solutions are known as "injured spouse relief" and "innocent spouse relief," and I address them here.

PROTECTING YOURSELF FROM YOUR SPOUSE'S DEBTS

Over time, Congress has given the IRS broad power to collect the debts of other government agencies. The IRS collects back due child support and spousal alimony, delinquent student loans, and debts owed to various federal and state agencies. The primary means of doing this is to engage a process known as the "offset," which is a euphemism for seizing your tax refund. Unfortunately, nondebtor spouses are routinely injured as a result of this action.

A nondebtor spouse is the spouse who does not owe a delinquent debt. That spouse is injured when her share of the tax refund is seized to pay the separate, nontax debt of her spouse. As an example, suppose a married couple files a joint tax return and is owed a $1,500 refund. However, the husband has past due child support from a prior marriage. The IRS seizes the entire refund and applies it to the debt. The wife is "injured" because a portion of the refund belongs to her, and though she does not owe child support, she loses her share of the refund.

However, while signing a joint income tax return creates a joint tax liability, it *does not* create joint ownership of the tax refund unless you live in a community property state. Consequently, only the portion of the overpayment actually belonging to the debtor spouse can be offset. If your refund is offset against your spouse's separate debt, the law provides a means of recovering the money.

The rule is different in community property states. Under community property rules, each spouse has a vested one-half interest in the property of the other spouse. This includes both wages and other property, including a tax refund. State law, not the IRS, determines the extent to which community property can be offset for the separate or premarital debts of one spouse.

In Texas, California, Idaho, and Louisiana, state law generally allows complete offset. In those states, the IRS will not issue refunds. However, in Arizona, Nevada, New Mexico, Washington, and Wisconsin, state law provides that community property is *not* subject to the separate or premarital debts of one spouse. In those states, the IRS must issue refunds to the injured spouse.

If you live in a community property state, check the status of your law before pursuing an injured spouse claim. The question to answer is whether community property can be used to satisfy the separate or premarital debts of one spouse. You must also examine whether assets acquired *prior* to marriage become part of the community estate upon marriage. In many cases, such assets are treated differently from those acquired *during* marriage.

Seeking a Refund of Your Money

The first step to recovering your money is to establish the fact that you are an "injured spouse." To meet this burden, you must prove that:

- You do not owe the delinquent, nontax debt.

- You earned and reported income on the joint tax return.

- You made and reported tax payments on the joint return.

- You do not live in a community property state.

If the IRS notifies you that your refund is to be offset, use IRS Form 8379, *Injured Spouse Claim and Allocation*, to establish the four points outlined above and to make the injured spouse claim for refund. Mail the form by certified mail to the service center where you filed the joint return. Keep a copy of your submission and the postal service receipts for certified mail.

You can also use the injured spouse claim to recover offsets against IRS debts that are owed by just one spouse. This situation is common in cases involving second marriages, where one party enters the marriage with a prior tax delinquency. The IRS cannot collect the existing debt from the separate assets of the nondebtor spouse, including her share of the tax refund.

The amount of your refund is based on your share of the joint income tax liability and on the payments you personally made against the liability. For example, suppose your husband owes delinquent child support debts. If your joint return shows tax payments made solely through his wage withholding, there will be no injured spouse refund because his money alone created the overpayment. You face a similar result if the joint return shows income earned solely by your husband.

To compute the injured spouse refund, first calculate your income tax liability separately. This process is referred to in the injured spouse claim, Form 8379, as "allocating" income and expense items. Set forth both the income and deductions that are attributable to either spouse. The income you personally earned should be allocated to you. If you claimed a standard deduction, each spouse is entitled to one-half the deduction. However, according to the instructions for Form 8379, itemized deductions can be allocated "in any manner." This means you can ascribe all the itemized deductions to the nondebtor spouse. This has the effect of increasing the amount of the injured spouse refund you are likely to receive.

Dependent exemptions must be allocated as whole numbers. That is, if you have three exemptions, you cannot allocate 1½ to each spouse. Each spouse must claim the exemptions they would have been entitled to claim if separate returns were filed.

Allocate your deductions on the injured spouse claim form in the spaces provided. If you do not, they cannot be allocated later when the IRS examines your claim. If you fail to allocate on the form, the IRS will do it for you and the result will not be favorable. Exhibit 10-1 is an example of IRS Form 8379, *Injured Spouse Claim and Allocation*.

After allocating income and deductions, compute your share of the joint tax liability. For purposes of the refund, your share is figured using "married filing separately" rules. That is not to say, however, that you are now subject to the married filing separately tax *rate*. The applicable rate continues to be the married filing jointly *rate*. It is only *your share* of the tax that is computed under the married filing separately rules.[1]

The next step is to allocate payments against the tax. Wage withholding payments are allocated to the spouse who paid them. Similarly, separate estimated tax deposits are allocated to the spouse who made them. However, estimated payments made with the return or payments made with a filing extension may be allocated between the spouses at their discretion. As is the case with itemized deductions, it is in your best interest to allocate these payments to the nondebtor spouse since that increases your injured spouse refund.

EXHIBIT 10-1

Form **8379**	**Injured Spouse Claim and Allocation**	OMB No. 1545-1210
(Rev. December 2002) Department of the Treasury Internal Revenue Service		Attachment Sequence No. **104**

Are You an Injured Spouse?

You are an injured spouse if you file a joint return and all or part of your share of the overpayment was, or is expected to be, applied (offset) against your spouse's past-due Federal tax, child or spousal support, Federal nontax debt (such as a student loan) or state income tax. Complete Form 8379 if **all three** of the following apply and you want your share of the overpayment shown on the joint return refunded to you. **But** if your main home was in a community property state (see line 6 below), you may file Form 8379 if only item 1 below applies.

1. You are not required to pay the past-due amount.
2. You reported income such as wages, taxable interest, etc. on the joint return.
3. You made and reported payments such as Federal income tax withheld from your wages or estimated tax payments, or you claimed the earned income credit or other refundable credit, on the joint return.

Do not use this form if you are requesting relief from liability for tax that you believe should be paid only by your spouse (or former spouse). Instead, file **Form 8857**, Request for Innocent Spouse Relief.

How Do You File Form 8379?

● If you have not filed your joint return, attach Form 8379 to your return in the order of the attachment sequence number. **Enter "Injured Spouse" in the upper left corner of the return.** Because the IRS will process your claim before an offset occurs, filing Form 8379 with your original return may delay your refund by 6 to 8 weeks.

● If you have already filed the joint tax return, mail Form 8379 by itself to the Internal Revenue Service Center for the place where you lived when you filed the joint return. See your tax return instruction booklet for the address. **Be sure** to include copies of all W-2 and W-2G forms of both spouses and any Forms 1099-R showing income tax withheld. The processing of your claim may be delayed if you do not include these copies. Please allow at least 8 weeks for the IRS to process your claim.

● If you later file **Form 1040X**, Amended U.S. Individual Income Tax Return, requesting an additional refund, you should attach a revised Form 8379 if you want the refund allocated between you and your spouse.

Note: *The Treasury Department's Financial Management Service (FMS), not the IRS, is authorized to apply (offset) all or part of the joint refund to past-due child or spousal support, Federal nontax debt, or state income tax. If you also owe past-due child or spousal support, Federal nontax debt, or state income tax, the FMS will apply all or part of your share of the refund to the debt. If an offset occurs, you will receive a notice from the FMS.*

Part I	**Information About the Joint Tax Return for Which This Claim Is Filed**

1 Enter the following information exactly as it is shown on the tax return for which you are filing this claim. The spouse's name and social security number shown first on that tax return must also be shown first below.

First name, initial, and last name shown first on the return	Social security number shown first	If Injured Spouse, check here ▶ ☐
First name, initial, and last name shown second on the return	Social security number shown second	If Injured Spouse, check here ▶ ☐

Note: *If you are filing Form 8379 with your tax return, skip to line 5.*

2 Enter the tax year for which you are filing this claim (for example, 2002) ▶ _____

3

Current home address	City	State	ZIP code

4 Is the address on your joint return different from the address shown above? .... ☐ **Yes** ☐ **No**

5 Check this box only if you are divorced or separated from the spouse with whom you filed the joint return and you want your refund issued in your name only .... ☐

6 Was your main home in a community property state (Arizona, California, Idaho, Louisiana, Nevada, New Mexico, Texas, Washington, or Wisconsin) at any time during the year entered on line 2? .... ☐ **Yes** ☐ **No**
If "Yes," which community property state(s)? _____
Note: *Overpayments involving community property states will be allocated by the IRS according to state law.*

Go to Part II on the back.

Privacy Act and Paperwork Reduction Act Notice. Our legal right to ask for the information on this form is Internal Revenue Code sections 6001, 6011, 6109, and 6402 and their regulations. You are required to give us the information so that we can process your claim for refund of your share of an overpayment shown on the joint return with your spouse. We need it to ensure that you are allocating items correctly and to allow us to figure the correct amount of your claim for refund. If you do not provide all of the information, we may not be able to process your claim. We may give this information to the Department of Justice for civil and criminal litigation, and to cities, states, and the District of Columbia to carry out their tax laws. We may also disclose this information to other countries under a tax treaty or to Federal and state agencies to enforce Federal nontax criminal laws and to combat terrorism.

You are not required to provide the information requested on a form that is subject to the Paperwork Reduction Act unless the form displays a valid OMB control number. Books or records relating to a form or its instructions must be retained as long as their contents may become material in the administration of any Internal Revenue law. Generally, tax returns and return information are confidential, as required by Code section 6103.

The time needed to complete and file this form will vary depending on individual circumstances. The estimated average time is: **Recordkeeping,** 13 min.; **Learning about the law or the form,** 10 min.; **Preparing the form,** 59 min.; and **Copying, assembling, and sending the form to the IRS,** 25 min.

If you have comments concerning the accuracy of these time estimates or suggestions for making this form simpler, we would be happy to hear from you. You can write to the Tax Forms Committee, Western Area Distribution Center, Rancho Cordova, CA 95743-0001. **Do not** send the form to this address. Instead, see **How Do You File Form 8379?** above.

ISA

Form **8379** (Rev. 12-2002)

EXHIBIT 10–1 (cont.)

Form 8379 (Rev. 12-2002)   Page **2**

Part II	Allocation Between Spouses of Items on the Joint Tax Return			
	Allocated Items	**(a)** Amount shown on joint return	**(b)** Allocated to injured spouse	**(c)** Allocated to other spouse
7	**Income.** Enter the separate income that each spouse earned. Allocate joint income, such as interest earned on a joint bank account, as you determine. But be sure to allocate **all** income shown on the joint return.			
a	Wages			
b	All other income. Identify the type and amount ▶ _____ _____ _____ _____ _____ _____			
8	**Adjustments to income.** Enter each spouse's separate adjustments, such as an IRA deduction. Allocate other adjustments as you determine			
9	**Standard deduction.** If you itemized your deductions, go to line 10. Otherwise, enter in both columns **(b)** and **(c)** $\frac{1}{2}$ of the amount shown in column **(a)** and go to line 11			
10	**Itemized deductions.** Enter each spouse's separate deductions, such as employee business expenses. Allocate other deductions as you determine			
11	**Number of exemptions.** Allocate the exemptions claimed on the joint return to the spouse who would have claimed them if separate returns had been filed. Enter whole numbers only (for example, you **cannot** allocate 3 exemptions by giving 1.5 exemptions to each spouse)			
12	**Credits.** Allocate any child tax credit, child and dependent care credit, and additional child tax credit to the spouse who was allocated the dependent's exemption. **Do not** include any earned income credit here; the IRS will allocate it based on each spouse's income. Allocate business credits based on each spouse's interest in the business. Allocate any other credits as you determine. .			
13	**Other taxes.** Allocate self-employment tax to the spouse who earned the self-employment income. Allocate any alternative minimum tax as you determine			
14	**Federal income tax withheld.** Enter Federal income tax withheld from each spouse's income as shown on Forms W-2, W-2G, and 1099-R. **Be sure to attach copies of these forms to your tax return or to Form 8379 if you are filing it by itself.** (Also include on this line any tax withheld on any other Form 1099 or any excess social security or tier 1 RRTA tax withheld.)			
15	**Payments.** Allocate joint estimated tax payments as you determine			

Note: *The IRS will figure the amount of any refund due the injured spouse.*

Part III	Signature. Complete this part only if you are filing Form 8379 by itself and not with your tax return.

Under penalties of perjury, I declare that I have examined this form and any accompanying schedules or statements and to the best of my knowledge and belief, they are true, correct, and complete. Declaration of preparer (other than taxpayer) is based on all information of which preparer has any knowledge.

Keep a copy of this form for your records	Injured spouse's signature		Date	Phone number (optional)
Paid Preparer's Use Only	Preparer's signature ▶	Date	Check if self-employed ☐	Preparer's SSN or PTIN
	Firm's name (or yours if self-employed), address, and ZIP code ▶			EIN
				Phone no.

Form **8379** (Rev. 12-2002)

Your portion of the overpayment becomes the refund amount. To find that amount, simply subtract your share of the joint tax liability from your contribution to it. For example, suppose your share of a $5,000 total tax bill is $2,000. Suppose you contributed $2,500 to the joint tax bill. Your share of the refund is $500 ($2,500—your contribution—minus $2,000—your share of the tax bill).

Avoiding Offsets in the First Place

If you know before filing your tax return that there is a potential for the IRS to offset your refund, a simple precautionary measure can save you a lot of trouble. The best part is, this strategy does not cost you any of the benefits of joint filing. Simply submit the injured spouse claim form with your joint return *at the time of filing*. Place the form on top of your tax return and mail the package to the service center using certified mail, return receipt requested. Be sure to keep a copy of your entire submission.

INNOCENT SPOUSE RELIEF

Congress encourages married couples to file joint tax returns by offering them reduced tax rates. Look what happens to the tax on $50,000 of taxable income computed at both the married filing jointly rates and the married filing separately rates. Under the married filing jointly rates, the tax on $50,000 is $7,303.[2] However, that same income incurs a tax of $10,405 under the married filing separately rates. Most couples do not stop to ask why Congress offers such a break. They simply take advantage of it.

The reason for the break has more to do with tax collection than it does with congressional beneficence. You see, most married couples hold their property jointly. By signing a joint tax return, they create a *joint* tax liability. A joint liability is collectible from all property and rights to property owned by the couple—whether owned separately or jointly.[3]

On the other hand, separate returns create separate liabilities.

The IRS can collect that tax only from the assets of the person who signed the return. In essence, Congress buys greatly expanded collection rights in exchange for a modest tax break. Congress thought ahead, but most joint filers do not.

This reality creates a substantial problem for many couples, married and divorced. In the case of a divorced couple (the more common example), if the IRS cannot collect the delinquent tax from the ex-husband, it pursues his former wife for payment, even if she did not earn the income or paid her taxes through wage withholding. This is also true even though a family court's dissolution order required the husband to pay all the taxes. The fact is that a family court's order cannot disturb the federal statutory scheme erected by Congress. The bottom line is that if both partners sign the return, they are both liable for all the tax—period. This is true whether or not the couple is divorced at the time the IRS undertakes collection.

In one case, the husband earned substantial income from a credit card fraud scam. He filed joint tax returns with his wife but reported none of the fraud income. Eventually he ended up in jail for his crimes. After a lengthy investigation, the IRS ascertained that he owed about $1.5 million in tax on his earnings. Because he and his wife had signed joint returns, the agency figured that she was equally responsible for the debt, though admittedly she had nothing to do with the illegal activity.

To make matters worse, there was no way the husband could pay, because he was in jail. That left the wife on the hook because she was gainfully employed, earning a whopping $24,000 per year as a receptionist. The IRS began enforcement action against her because her income was easy to reach. The IRS did not seem to care that she was unaware of the illegal scheme and did not profit from the income, or that she was taking care of three minor children—the IRS just wanted the money.

If your spouse has put you in such a position, the IRS Restructuring Act added a code section that offers relief from a joint tax debt in three ways. Let us address each of them.

1. Proving That You Are an Innocent Spouse

The law always allowed an "innocent spouse" to be relieved of a joint tax debt if she met certain conditions.[4] This is the so-called innocent spouse rule. The rule has now been expanded. It applies to couples that are currently married who signed a joint return. To take advantage of innocent spouse relief, use IRS Form 8857, *Request for Innocent Spouse Relief*. To prevail, you must prove four factual elements.

First is that the return contained an understatement of tax attributable to an erroneous item. An erroneous item is any tax return item that is not correct. This includes unreported income, invalid deductions (whether claimed in good faith or flatly bogus), and any other tax return item that when corrected increases your tax debt.

An understatement of tax exists when the tax return *does not* show the correct tax liability on its face. For example, if you file a return you believe to be accurate, but as the result of an audit the IRS assesses additional taxes, you may qualify as an innocent spouse. On the other hand, suppose you file a tax return with your spouse showing $5,000 of tax attributable to his business, but the tax is not paid. Because you knew or should have known about the debt when you signed the return (the debt is, after all, shown right on the return), you *are not* an innocent spouse under this rule. However, you may be entitled to relief under the rules I discuss later.

Second, you must prove that in signing the return, you did not know or have reason to know about the errors. If, at the time of filing, you were aware that the return either failed to report income or claimed incorrect deductions, you cannot obtain innocent spouse relief unless you were forced to sign the return under duress. To prove lack of knowledge, present a detailed affidavit to explain why you did not know about the specifics of the tax return. Document your claims to the fullest extent possible.

In the credit card fraud case, we proved that the wife was (1) completely disconnected from the business, a fact independently verified by an FBI investigation, (2) specifically kept unaware of what her husband was doing because of his acts of lying and deception, and (3) otherwise generally unfamiliar with his specific operations because of her own pursuits. She was a housewife immersed in the day-to-day tasks of caring for three small children.

Third, you must prove that based upon all the facts and circumstances, it is "inequitable" (read: unfair) to hold you liable for the tax. This is an intangible element that must be asserted in your argument in favor of innocent spouse relief. In our credit card case, we argued that the wife was as much a victim of the husband's criminal acts as the IRS. She was lied to, kept ignorant, and denied access to business records. When the couple split, she was left with nothing because creditors repossessed their house and cars. Moreover, by the time the IRS showed up, she was the sole support of their three children. To top it off, the former husband was in jail and there was no hope of his providing any support. These facts were enough to persuade the IRS that it would indeed be unfair to hold her responsible for the tax.

The fourth requirement is that you must file an election seeking innocent spouse treatment in a timely manner. The election is timely if submitted within two years after the IRS *first* begins collection action against you. The two-year rule is triggered when the innocent spouse becomes *aware* of the collection action, as through a wage levy, bank levy, notice of filing federal tax lien, or any other IRS communication.

Use Form 8857, *Request for Innocent Spouse Relief,* to submit an innocent spouse claim. An example of the form is shown in Exhibit 10–2. Submit the form to the IRS office shown in the instructions and provide such supplemental information, including affidavits, as is necessary to document your case.

EXHIBIT 10-2

Form **8857**
(Rev. May 2002)
Department of the Treasury
Internal Revenue Service

Request for Innocent Spouse Relief

(And Separation of Liability and Equitable Relief)

▶ Do not file with your tax return.   ▶ See instructions.

OMB No. 1545-1596

Do not file this form if:

• You did not file a joint return for the year(s) for which you are requesting relief. However, if you lived in a community property state, see instructions.

• All or part of your overpayment was (or is expected to be) applied against your spouse's past-due debt (such as child support). Instead, file **Form 8379**, Injured Spouse Claim and Allocation, to apply to have your share of the overpayment refunded to you.

TIP *To see if you may qualify for **Innocent Spouse Relief**, go to www.irs.gov, click on "Individuals," "Innocent Spouses," and "Explore if you are an Eligible Innocent Spouse"; or see **Pub. 971**, Innocent Spouse Relief.*

Part I	Your current name (see instructions)		Your social security number
See **Spousal Notification** in the instructions.	Your current home address (number and street). If a P.O. box, see instructions.		Apt. no.
	City, town or post office, state, and ZIP code. If a foreign address, see instructions.		Daytime phone number

If you have been a victim of domestic abuse and fear that filing a claim for innocent spouse relief will result in retaliation, check here . . . . ▶ ☐

Part II

1 Enter the year(s) for which you are requesting relief from liability of tax ▶ _____

2 Information about the person to whom you were married as of the end of the year(s) in line 1.

Name		Social security number
Current home address (number and street). If a P.O. box, see instructions.		Apt. no.
City, town or post office, state, and ZIP code. If a foreign address, see instructions.		Daytime phone number

3 Do you have an **Understatement of Tax** (that is, the IRS has determined there is a difference between the tax shown on your return and the tax that should have been shown)?

☐ **Yes.** Go to Part III.   ☐ **No.** Go to Part V.

Part III

4 Are you divorced from the person listed on line 2 or has that person died?

☐ **Yes.** Go to line 7.   ☐ **No.** Go to line 5.

5 Are you legally separated from the person listed on line 2?

☐ **Yes.** Go to line 7.   ☐ **No.** Go to line 6.

6 Have you lived apart from the person listed on line 2 at all times during the 12-month period prior to filing this form?

☐ **Yes.** Go to line 7.   ☐ **No.** Go to Part IV.

7 If line **4, 5,** or **6** is **Yes,** you may request **Separation of Liability** by **attaching a statement** (see instructions). Check here ▶ ☐ and go to Part IV.

Part IV

8 Is the understatement of tax due to the **Erroneous Items** of your spouse (see instructions)?

☐ **Yes.** You may request **Innocent Spouse Relief** by **attaching a statement** (see instructions). Go to Part V.   ☐ **No.** You may request **Equitable Relief** for the understatement of tax. Check **Yes** in Part V.

Part V

9 Do you have an **Underpayment of Tax** (that is, tax that is properly shown on your return but not paid) or another tax liability that qualifies for **Equitable Relief** (see instructions)?

☐ **Yes.** You may request **Equitable Relief** by **attaching a statement** (see instructions).   ☐ **No.** You cannot file this form unless line 3 is **Yes.**

Under penalties of perjury, I declare that I have examined this form and any accompanying schedules and statements, and to the best of my knowledge and belief, they are true, correct, and complete. Declaration of preparer (other than taxpayer) is based on all information of which preparer has any knowledge.

Sign Here Keep a copy for your records.	Your signature ▶		Date

Paid Preparer's Use Only	Preparer's signature ▶	Date	Check if self-employed ☐	Preparer's SSN or PTIN
	Firm's name (or yours if self-employed), address, and ZIP code ▶		EIN	
			Phone no.	

For Privacy Act and Paperwork Reduction Act Notice, see instructions.

Form **8857** (Rev. 5-2002)

ISA

2. What to Do If You Are Divorced or Separated

The second avenue of relief is available to spouses who become divorced or legally separated after filing a joint return that reports tax owed but that is not paid at the time of filing.[5] This is common in cases of divorce or separation, where one spouse (usually the husband) is ordered to pay the outstanding taxes, but after the divorce the husband bolts—dodging his tax and other obligations. That forces the innocent spouse to deal with the IRS despite the fact that she probably paid her rightful share of the taxes through wage withholding.

Under these facts, the innocent spouse relief explained in the above section is not available because the spouse knew about the tax debt when she signed the return. It is no defense that the debt is attributable to the other spouse's income. Nor is it a defense that a family court judge ordered the other spouse to pay the tax. A *joint* return creates a *joint* liability and each party is wholly responsible for its payment.

However, in this case, you can elect to be treated as a "separate taxpayer." That is to say, you have the right to terminate your joint filing status and separate yourself from your husband's unpaid tax debt, and you do not need his consent to make the election. The separate spouse election is made on Form 8857, *Request for Innocent Spouse Relief* (Exhibit 10–2). Use Part III of the form to make the election. You must prove the following three elements:

First, at the time of making the election, you must be divorced or legally separated, or you must not have been living with your spouse at any time during the one-year period preceding the date you file the election. To prove this, provide a copy (never original documents) of your divorce or separation agreement. If you are not divorced or separated, create an affidavit to establish the fact that you and your spouse have been living apart for the past year.

Second, to distinguish your tax obligation from your spouse's, you must prove your separate tax liability. This process is virtually identical to that of computing an injured spouse refund as set out earlier in this chapter. In short, show your separate income, your share of itemized deductions, if any, and your wage withholding or other payments as credits against the tax. Do this on a separate sheet attached to the innocent spouse election, Form 8857.

Third, there can be no fraudulent transfers of assets between the spouses prior to the divorce or separation. Suppose, for example, that the husband transfers all his assets to his wife and then quickly obtains a divorce. She then files a separate spouse election to zero-out her share of the tax liability. She now owns all the property but has no tax debt. The husband owes the tax but owns no property. Collection is defeated. But if the IRS can prove he transferred assets solely to defeat collection, the IRS can disregard the election. However, the IRS must prove that the transfer occurred to defeat collection.

This rule does not apply to assets transferred incident to a divorce or separate maintenance agreement. If questioned, submit an affidavit describing the background facts and justifying the transfers. This will help greatly to avoid a claim that the assets were transferred solely to avoid paying the tax.

This remedy does not relieve the innocent spouse of all tax debt. Even after making the separate spouse election, you are still responsible for your share of the tax debt. However, penalties and interest are recalculated to reflect the reduction in tax achieved by the separate spouse election. In most cases, this greatly reduces the tax burden.

3. What to Do When the First Two Remedies Do Not Apply

If for any reason you cannot obtain relief under either of the first two innocent spouse procedures, the IRS may nevertheless grant relief if, based on "all the facts and circumstances, it is inequitable" to hold you responsible for paying the tax.[6] This is a safety net available when the first two innocent spouse conditions do not apply.

This section grants the IRS broad discretion to look at each case on an individual basis to see whether a spouse should be relieved of a joint liability. The key factors that weigh in favor of the IRS granting equitable relief are:

- That you are currently divorced or living apart from your spouse.

- That you would suffer economic hardship if relief were not granted. The phrase "economic hardship" has the same meaning here as that applying to wage levies. Hardship exists when the IRS's actions render you "unable to pay reasonable basic living expenses." For more details, see p. 209.

- That you were abused by your spouse.

- That your spouse did not transfer property to you for the purposes of defrauding the IRS.

- That you did not file the tax return with the intent to defraud the IRS.

- That you neither knew nor had reason to know about the liability. In the case of a tax that is reported on a return but not paid, you must show that you did not know and had no reason to know that it would not be paid. You must show that you had every reason to believe that your spouse would pay the bill. In the case of a liability that arose from an audit, you must show that you did not know and had no reason to know about the unreported income or disallowed deductions giving rise to the debt. You must show that these items were attributable to your spouse's activities, not yours.

- That you did not significantly benefit (beyond normal support) from the unpaid liability. On the other hand, if you received lavish or extravagant gifts or lived such a lifestyle because your spouse did not pay the taxes, this weighs against obtaining relief.

- That your spouse has a legal obligation under your divorce decree or other agreement to pay the tax. However, this will *not* weigh in your favor if, at the time of the decree or agreement, you knew or had reason to know that your spouse would not pay.

- That the liability is solely attributable to your spouse. You cannot get relief under this provision for a tax that is attributable to your activities.[7]

Use Form 8857, *Request for Innocent Spouse Relief* (Exhibit 10–2), Part V, to apply for equitable relief from a joint liability. The form must be filed within two years of the IRS's first collection contact with you. To support your claim, submit a detailed affidavit that addresses the factors set forth above. You should address each of the above points, making a strong case that your spouse was responsible for the debt, that collection from you will cause a hardship, and that you did not have knowledge of the liability, as outlined above. Document your claims to the fullest extent possible.

EXTRA HELP IN COMMUNITY PROPERTY STATES

Community property states present special problems in innocent spouse cases. The reason is that community property laws give each spouse an ownership interest in the property of the other spouse, regardless of how that property is titled. This also applies to the wage or self-employment income of each spouse. This can create a problem if your spouse is a nonfiler.

Suppose, for example, that the wife files a tax return but her husband does not. She files a separate return reporting all her income and her share of the deductions and exemptions. She pays all the taxes she owes. Later, when the IRS tracks down the husband, it determines his income, but in the process of assessing the tax, the IRS assigns one-half the income to the wife because they were married during the period in question.

As a result, she ends up paying taxes on all her income *plus* she now owes additional taxes on half her husband's income. This is true despite the fact that the couple may currently be divorced. The IRS's response to the obvious inequity is to shrug, point to the community property laws, then demand that she pay the bill.

But if that is true, why cannot the wife reduce her own income by attributing one-half of it to the husband, thus balancing the scales? The answer is, she can, but only if she amends her return within three years of filing. Beyond that period, the IRS does not allow amended returns. Unfortunately, in most cases, by the time the IRS catches up to the nonfiling husband, three years have lapsed. This means the wife is stuck—or so it seems.

A little known code section still allows for innocent spouse relief in this case, however. Though buried deep in the tax code, the law allows the spouse who filed to be relieved of the tax attributable to the nonfiling spouse's separate community property income.[8]

To claim relief under this provision, use a detailed affidavit as a supplement to the innocent spouse claim, Form 8857. Document your claims to the fullest extent possible as outlined above.

To win relief under this provision, you must prove that:

- You did not file a joint return.

- The income in question was the separate income of your spouse.

- You did not know or have reason to know about the income.

- Taking into consideration all the facts and circumstances, it is inequitable to hold you liable for the tax. Review the list of criteria above for help with this question.

As you can see, these standards are not unlike those that apply to traditional innocent spouse relief as discussed at length above. But because this rule is obscure and few people know about it, it is very common for innocent spouses in community property states to be blindsided by assessments for which there appear to be no solution.

THE RIGHT TO APPEAL INNOCENT SPOUSE DECISIONS

An important procedural change brought about by the Restructuring Act provides that you may challenge an adverse innocent spouse decision in the United States Tax Court. If your request for relief is rejected, you have ninety days from the date of a final determination in which to file a petition with the Tax Court seeking review of the decision. The IRS's decision must be sent via certified or registered mail in order to fix the date of mailing.

Should the IRS fail to act on your claim in a timely manner, you may file a Tax Court petition even without a decision. However, you must wait six months from the date of submitting the original claim before acting.[9] The right to file in court even without a decision prevents the IRS from stonewalling your claim and pursuing collection despite your objection.

While the ninety-day grace period is pending, the IRS is foreclosed from taking any collection action.[10] If it does, the Tax Court has jurisdiction to stop the IRS. Not only does the collection limitation apply during the ninety-day grace period, but it applies during the entire time a Tax Court case is pending, assuming you file a timely petition. The prohibition is effective until the decision of the Tax Court becomes final.

AN OUNCE OF PREVENTION

If you are currently involved in a marriage with a spouse who owes taxes, you must consider a few steps to minimize your exposure to potential enforced collection. Here are just a few simple ideas.

Do not commingle funds. While most couples contribute both paychecks to a joint account, the IRS does not distinguish between the owners of those funds when seizing the account. It shoots first and lets you ask the questions later. Recovery of wrongfully levied property is a lengthy process. The better solution is to keep separate accounts.

Do not co-own assets acquired after marriage. This is especially helpful in non–community property states but might have limited impact in community property states. If you purchase a car, for example, do not place your spouse's name on that vehicle if he owes delinquent taxes. By keeping his name off the asset, you clearly establish your exclusive ownership right. Likewise, do not add your delinquent spouse's name to the title of any assets you bring into the marriage.

If you live in a community property state and are considering marriage to a person with tax debt, seriously consider a prenuptial agreement. This is a contract between the parties to protect their respective interests from the effects of community property laws. Consult counsel prior to entering into such an agreement.

In all events, be sure you correctly figure your wage withholding so you do not overpay your taxes. Not only does this protect you from an improper offset, but it also ensures that the IRS does not hold your money interest-free for long periods of time.

If you deal with perennial delinquencies during your marriage, very strongly consider filing your return as married filing separately. While the tax rates are higher when married filing separately, you do not bind yourself to the problems of your delinquent spouse. I am generally not in favor of paying more taxes than you owe. But in this situation, the cost of dealing with a delinquent joint liability almost always *far outweighs* the cost of paying the increased taxes. Plus, you get the peace of mind that comes with knowing that the IRS cannot chase you for your spouse's unpaid debt.

By following the steps discussed in this chapter, you can redress any adverse determination and ensure that if you are indeed an innocent spouse, you will not pay taxes you do not owe.

11

Insulating Yourself from the IRS

Simple Steps That Avoid Problems

I declared at the outset of this book that virtually every major IRS problem begins as a small one. If the small problem is handled properly in the first instance, the horrors of a worst-case scenario can be avoided in almost every case. By now I hope you understand that while the IRS makes considerable errors—inadvertent or otherwise—the outcome of your encounters is controlled largely by you, the results being dictated by the actions you take to address the situation.

It is also true that you can take steps well ahead of any IRS action to help insulate yourself from the ravages of tax collection. The audit-proofing strategies discussed in chapter 7 are one step, but protection goes far beyond that. In this chapter, I focus upon other steps that can keep you out of trouble with the IRS.

STAY ON THE IRS'S MAILING LIST

Most people dream of dropping *off* the IRS's mailing list so that they no longer have to cope with the agency. Unfortunately, simply dropping off the mailing list is no guarantee that you will never have to deal with tax enforcement. In fact, dropping off the mailing list might well make matters worse for you. This is why I strongly recommend you stay on the IRS's mailing list.

To do so, make sure you file a change of address form with the IRS anytime you move. Use IRS Form 8822, *Change of Address*, to accomplish this. File this simple form with the service center where you file your tax return. Be sure to file the form using certified mail and keep a copy of the form with your USPS postage receipts in a permanent file.

The IRS has an obligation to mail all its correspondence to your "last known address." This is the address on your most recently filed tax return or the address shown in the change of address form, whichever is filed later. Because Americans move so often, there is no comfort in resting on the most recently filed return as providing your last known address. Always file a change of address form if you move your residence or your business. This ensures that you are not blindsided by IRS correspondence.

A good example of this is the case of Susan. After spending years in a troubled marriage, Susan's divorce spelled for her the beginning of a new life. However, after just a few short years on her own, she woke up one day to find that the IRS had filed a tax lien against her for taxes associated with her former husband's business. The lien involved taxes for years she was married to her husband, but she had had no contact either with him or the IRS since her divorce. Now the IRS was trying to collect the tax from her.

Susan was blindsided by the IRS's tax lien because she never received notices from the agency while it was in the process of making the assessment (the IRS sent its notices to the wrong address). Most notably, the notice of deficiency, the administrative action requisite to an assessment, was not mailed to Susan. Rather, the IRS mailed it to her former husband. Because she never received the notice, she could not file a Tax Court petition. That allowed the IRS to assess the tax against her.

Eventually we proved that Susan was actually an innocent spouse (see chapter 10) and succeeded in getting the assessment dissolved. However, the stress and uncertainty Susan suffered in the process would have been avoided if the IRS's letter had been sent to her correct address.

GET MORE TIME TO FILE PERSONAL TAX RETURNS

Many penalties for late filing can be avoided by using the simple filing extension forms. And while it is true that filing extensions do not help you if you owe taxes, they do help when you need additional time to gather the records necessary to complete a correct tax return.

Most people are aware of the initial filing extension, Form 4868, *Application for Automatic Extension of Time to File US Individual Income Tax Return*. File this form on or before April 15 and you get up to four additional months to file your return—no questions asked. However, this is *not* an extension of time to pay. If you owe taxes, they must be paid with the filing extension when you submit it. A simple work sheet on the form allows you to estimate your tax liability.

Still, in many cases, four months are not enough time to get all the records necessary to ensure an accurate return. In that case, use the second filing extension, Form 2688, *Application for Additional Extension of Time to File US Individual Income Tax Return*. Filing this form before the extended due date can get you two more months—up to and including October 15, in which to file your tax return. However, the second extension is *not* automatic. To persuade the agency to grant the request, you must provide it with an adequate explanation as to why you need more time.

Do not provide vague or incomplete information. Be specific and detailed. Note that the IRS generally does not grant a second extension for the convenience of your return preparer. The extension is granted when you can show that due to circumstances beyond your control (or that of your preparer), you cannot file on time.

It is a good idea to file the request for an additional extension well before the August 15 deadline. That way, if it is denied, you will have time to file your return before the deadline. The IRS can also grant a ten-day grace period if it denies the request. If it does, you are notified in writing.

GET MORE TIME TO FILE BUSINESS TAX RETURNS AND PAY TAXES

Corporations routinely encounter problems that prevent them from filing tax returns on time. These might include:

- Delay in getting records from customers or vendors

- Difficulty in reconciling tax and bank records

- Delay in obtaining records from related companies, such as a parent or subsidiary

- Delay associated with documents related to pension or profit-sharing plans.

If your small business corporation needs more time to file its tax return, you can obtain filing extensions for both income tax returns and information returns. Form 7004, *Application for Automatic Extension of Time to File Corporation Income Tax Return*, gets you six additional months to file your corporation's income tax return. The filing extension is automatic but provides no payment extension. You must estimate your corporate income tax liability (if there is one) and send the payment at the time of seeking the extension.

Failure to file information returns (W-2s and 1099s) on time can be very costly because the penalties apply to *each* information return not filed. For this reason, companies must be aware of Form 8809, *Request for Extension of Time to File Information Returns*. You can use one Form 8809 to seek a filing extension for all information returns you must file.

The filing extension is not automatic. You must provide a compelling reason why you need the extension. If granted, the extension is good for thirty days. A second extension is possible but again, your reasons must be compelling. To seek a second extension, also use Form 8809 (there is no separate form for this process). As with all extensions, they must be filed before the due date of the return. If the filing extension is submitted late, you have no chance of winning the extension. Be sure to file your request using certified mail with return receipt requested and keep a copy of your submission and USPS receipts in your permanent file.

Corporations can also obtain an extension of time to pay taxes. First off, understand that the small business corporation, the so-called S corporation, does not pay taxes. Its tax return, Form 1120S, is an information return that reports the income and expenses of the corporation. The corporation's shareholders report the company's profit or loss on their own tax returns.

However, regular corporations do pay taxes, and these companies can obtain an extension of time to pay in one of two ways. First is by using Form 1127, *Application for Extension of Time to Pay*, a form that can be used for *any* tax liability. The extension is not automatic. To prevail, you must show that you exercised reasonable business care and prudence in providing for your tax, but due to unforeseen circumstances beyond your control, you are not able to pay on time.[1] This process can get you up to six additional months to pay, without penalties. For more details, see p. 199.

The second method applies to corporations that expect to realize an operating loss in the current year. Operating losses can be carried back to offset taxes due for a prior year. If your regular corporation is in this situation, use Form 1138, *Application for Extension of Time for Payment of Taxes by Corporation Expecting an Operating Loss Carryback*. The title of the form is a mouthful, but the process is very simple. You simply explain why you believe the corporation will incur a loss this year. You estimate the amount of the loss, then offset it against the debt the corporation owes for the prior year.[2] If granted, the extension is good until the due date of the return for the year in which the loss is expected, or until the IRS revokes it.

AVOID TAX SCAMS

As long as there have been taxes, there have been people considering ways around taxes. And as long as there have been people considering ways around taxes, there have been tax scams. The prevalence of tax scams in America seems to rise and fall with the tax burden. The higher the burden, the more desperate people become to escape it. The more desperate they become, the more willing they are to entertain a strategy that might otherwise seem marginal.

In my work as a tax litigation consultant for more than twenty-five years, I have seen every kind of tax scam you can imagine and a few you could not imagine. Some are more creative than others. Some have a ring of truth to them, and in fact, in some cases the presentation made by promoters is grounded in some modicum of truth and therefore the scam looks pretty darn good—at least to the *untrained* eye. However, the law books are filled with cases that shoot scams out of the water, leaving wrecked lives, families, and businesses in their wake.

These scams are marketed in a number of ways. Lately, much marketing is done on the Internet, where all manner of claims are made regarding the ability of a given program to reduce or eliminate taxes. Another common method is through newspaper, magazine, and newsletter advertising, especially in highly conservative publications. And direct mail is a favorite tool.

For years I have worked to identify tax scams in an effort to keep people out of trouble. To this end, I discuss here some of the more popular scams. Before delving into these ideas, let me say that I do not intend to write a legal memorandum debunking each scam. I have done that in the past, publishing my work in the form of Special Research Reports through my newsletter, *Dan Pilla's Confidential Tax Bulletin*.

Unfortunately, the forum of this book does not provide the means to explore the nuances of each scam. Doing so would end up being a book in itself. But I do provide some background to the scams so you can recognize them for what they are.

It is also important to point out that the IRS *very aggressively* attacks what it calls "abusive tax schemes," contending that they "represent a rapidly growing risk to the tax base."[3] For this reason, the IRS has in place and continues to develop systems to identify and deal with those employing abusive schemes.

Home-Based Businesses

Millions of citizens operate legitimate for-profit businesses out of their homes. When a legitimate business operation, engaged in for profit, is operated out of your home, you have the right to claim deductions you might not otherwise be entitled to claim. This reality provides the basis of the home-based business scam.

The home-based business scam suggests that merely *claiming* to establish a business in your home is sufficient to transform all your otherwise nondeductible personal expenses into deductible business expenses. For example, promoters claim that once you are in business for yourself, all your automobile travel is tax deductible on the theory that everywhere you go, you are conducting business. This fails because, for example, a trip to the grocery store to restock your refrigerator cannot be considered a business trip.

Promoters of this scheme have people convinced that they can claim deductions for all their clothing, food, vacations, and personal travel as well as all expenses associated with operating their homes. Some even suggest that paying your children to answer the home telephone or to wash the family car creates deductible business expenses.

In order for expenditures to be deductible businesses expenses, they must be incurred for the purposes of earning income. Businesses are entitled to deductions only when the business has a legitimate profit motive. That means the business must offer a bona fide product or service and the operation must be carried out in a businesslike manner. See chapter 8, under the heading "The Hobby Loss Rule."

If you are engaged in a home-based business, I recommend you seek experienced counsel to assist you in ascertaining what is and is not deductible in your case. The reality is, not all expenses are deductible for all businesses. A key rule of code section 165, which establishes the right to deduct business expenses, is that the expense must be "ordinary and necessary" to the success of that business.

What is ordinary and necessary in one business may not be in another. As such, the legitimacy of many deductions must be scrutinized on a case-by-case basis. Therefore, beware of any promoter trying to sell a "package" that puts you in business and gives you a host of deductions that purport to cut your tax liability.

Domestic Trusts

Domestic trusts are separate legal entities—like corporations—based in the United States. Trusts have been used for decades in the world of estate planning. Trusts allow assets to be held by an entity other than a natural person. The advantage is that trusts do not die and therefore assets can remain in a family estate and avoid the ravages of estate and gift taxes. This is the legitimate premise upon which the trust scam is built.

Unfortunately, for about thirty years, promoters have marketed domestic trusts as a means of eliminating income taxes. While there are a variety of different trust formulas, the basic plan suggests that by creating a trust and assigning one's income to the trust, you become an employee of the trust, that is, the "trust manager." It is argued that the trust, as employer, can provide all manner of nontaxable benefits to its employee—you—such as housing, clothing, food, medical care, etc. The theory is that these expenses of the trust are deductible as business expenses because they are paid to you as trust manager. At the same time, the value of the benefits is not taxed to you because they are employee benefits free of taxation.

The fact is, very few payments to employees are legally considered tax-free, even assuming you were considered a legitimate employee of your own trust. This latter idea strikes right at the core of the domestic trust scam. One of the oldest doctrines in tax law is the idea that you cannot "assign" your income to another person or entity and through that assignment substantially change how the income is taxed.

As early as 1930, the Supreme Court used a "tree and fruit" analogy to kill the idea of assigning income. The court said that you cannot attribute the fruit to a tree other than that on which it grew.[4] The tree is the income-producing asset—in this case your personal services. The fruit is the wage income produced by your labor. The income is taxed to you because you earned it. The fact that you assigned the income to a trust does not defeat that rule. Remember: he who earns the income pays the tax.

Offshore Trusts

A similar arrangement involves trusts that are domiciled in a foreign country, usually a tax haven nation such as the Bahamas, the Cayman Islands, or the Turks and Cacaos Islands. The offshore trust scam usually involves layers of trusts, starting with one or more domestic trusts and ending with one or more offshore trusts, accompanied by a bank account in the tax haven nation. The idea is to send the money through enough entities and into a foreign bank account so that the IRS eventually loses the trail and consequently the ability to tax the income. It helps if the country in which the bank is located has tough bank-privacy laws, thereby keeping the IRS away from the bank's records.

The real problem with the offshore scam is the fact that people who send their money offshore cannot spend it while it is there. That means they have to get it back somehow. This is usually accomplished by bogus loans from the offshore trust to the individual or, more commonly, through the use of a debit or credit card issued to the individual against an offshore bank account.

The individual uses the credit card for a plethora of personal expenses and pays the credit card bill with a check drawn on the offshore bank account. This way, the individual is able to effectively repatriate the money and use it to improve his standard of living. Of course, this is illegal, since the entire structure is built on a series of false premises, not the least of which is the underlying premise of moving money offshore solely for the purpose of evading taxes.

But even if you could make the case that the trust structure itself was legal (and assuming you can defeat the assignment-of-income problem), you must face the fact that money is repatriated and used for personal purposes. At the very least, there is a tax liability on the repatriated funds—a small detail promoters overlook in their sales presentations. By the way, these scams generally sell for many thousands of dollars.

In the three years 2000 to 2002, the IRS has aggressively investigated credit card companies that issue debit or credit cards through offshore banks. On October 30, 2000, a federal judge in Florida authorized the IRS to use a so-called John Doe summons against American Express and MasterCard International.[5] The summonses seek the names of individuals with charge, debit, or credit cards issued by or through or paid for with funds drawn on banks in Antigua and Barbuda, the Bahamas, or the Cayman Islands during 1998 and 1999.[6]

The investigation generates the names of American citizens who use such cards. With the information obtained from the card companies, the IRS then follows up with a full-scale audit of the people involved. On the basis of the data received from MasterCard alone, the IRS identified about 235,000 accounts issued through twenty-eight banks in three countries. Based upon these numbers, the IRS estimates that there are between one and two million U.S. citizens with credit or debit cards issued by offshore banks.[7] The IRS intends to go after each one of them.

The resulting audits lead to large tax assessments, interest, and, routinely, assessments of the fraud penalty. In more egregious cases, the IRS criminally prosecutes those involved. The IRS regularly prosecutes the promoters of trust schemes—both of the domestic and offshore variety. For example, in the three years 1999 to 2001, the IRS obtained convictions against thirty-five promoters of both domestic and offshore trust schemes and won convictions against one hundred participants. Even as I write, the IRS is turning up the heat in the form of more criminal prosecutions, this for the express purpose of "deterring individuals from engaging in abusive trusts."[8]

The problem is that every time one promoter is sent away to jail, it seems two more pop up to take his place. Apparently the money involved in promoting illegal tax schemes is just too good to pass up, even considering the risk of prison. Even now, the Internet is alive with these schemes.

Slavery Reparations

In 2001 alone, more than eighty thousand African-American citizens filed tax returns claiming a credit or refund of anywhere between $40,000 and $80,000 for slavery reparations. The problem is, there is no provision of law allowing anybody a credit or refund for slavery reparations. Unscrupulous promoters deceive people into paying money for advice on how to claim the nonexistent credit.

This scam is now being expanded to other groups. In 2001 the IRS saw about two hundred tax returns making claims for Native American reparations. Of course, there is no legal provision for that either.

In January 2002 the IRS announced that it is sending warning letters to anybody filing claims for reparations.[9] Those who do not abandon their claim face a penalty of up to $500 for filing a frivolous tax return.[10]

Tax-Sheltered Investments

A phenomenon of the 1980s was tax-sheltered investments. The idea was built upon certain provisions of the tax code that existed at the time, especially those allowing for accelerated depreciation and investment tax credits. The concept behind the laws was to encourage businesses to invest in research and development to spur the nation out of the deep recession of the late 1970s and early 1980s.

Limited partnerships were formed around the idea of investing in and developing a particular product or industry. Shares of the limited partnership were offered to investors. The deals were structured in such a way as to generate multiple dollars of tax deductions for every dollar of out-of-pocket investment.

For example, a person might invest $10,000 for a small share of a limited partnership. His $10,000 investment might generate $50,000 in current tax deductions because of the depreciation, investment tax, and other credits attributed to his ownership. If that person paid federal and state taxes at the combined rate of 45 percent, his $10,000 investment saved $22,500 in taxes, a net gain of $12,500. It does not require much savvy to realize that every dollar saved in taxes is worth about 2.3 dollars of income earned.

There were—and still are—two key problems with the limited partnerships. First, most were scams operated by promoters as a means of enriching themselves. In the usual scenario, the promoters bilked the partnerships for millions of dollars in consulting, legal, accounting, engineering, and other fees, expenses, and commissions contrived as a means of funneling money to businesses owned by the promoters but independent of the partnership itself. In many cases, so thorough was the job of skimming the partnership that there actually was very little or no investment at all in the product or industry from which the partnership was intended to profit. Unfortunately, where there is no legitimate business, there are no legitimate business deductions. Consequently, the IRS disallows all the deductions attributable to the business.

The second problem is that it is very difficult to identify which partnership is a scam and which is a legitimate business. This is because of the impressive marketing package used to sell the investment. The typical package consists of:

- A written report from a marketing or research team discussing the potential marketplace for the product and likelihood of sales success

- An engineer or scientist's report discussing the merits and viability of the intended product or industry

- A legal or accounting opinion addressing the merits and legality of the intended tax treatment of the investment

- Slick, full-color brochures describing the product or industry with pictures of the product itself together with the manufacturing or research facility and staff

- A large, three-ring presentation binder containing all of the above, plus a detailed business and marketing plan, complete with sales projections, revenue and profit projections, and a breakdown of the pro rata profit expected for each share of ownership in the partnership, with the projections carried out several years into the future

- A highly polished, know-it-all salesman with a fast answer to your every possible objection.

It is easy to see how even the most skeptical among us could be seduced by such a presentation. And while the IRS cracked down heavily on abusive tax shelters during the 1980s with aggressive enforcement, the problem remains—expressly because (1) there are tens of millions of dollars to be made by crooked promoters, and (2) the potential for high profits with tax breaks at the same time is very attractive to investors.

This is why the IRS is at this moment turning up the heat on tax shelter enforcement. As of July 2002, the IRS had issued 132 administrative summonses to eight accounting, law, and investment banking firms demanding customer lists, opinion letters, and other documents surrounding tax-sheltered investment offerings.[11]

Once the IRS identifies a tax-sheltered investment program, the audits run in two directions. First, the IRS attacks the limited partnership itself, examining every aspect of the business. Normally these audits take years to complete and often involve lengthy and costly Tax Court litigation. Next, the IRS goes after the individual investors with the information and legal precedents achieved through the first attack. By the time tax assessments filter down to the individual investor level, the tax has ballooned four to six times greater than it otherwise would be. The chief culprit is interest, which continues to accrue even while the case is being audited and litigated.

"Untax" Strategies

How would you like to "untax" yourself; that is, set yourself up in such a way that you never have to pay income taxes again? Does that concept sound too good to be true? Well, *it is*, and you should run— not walk—away from anybody offering to "untax" you using any of a number of arguments.

The untaxers are at the core of the so-called tax protester movement. This movement is a consortium of loosely knit groups of individuals who oppose the income tax and the IRS on moral, legal, or religious grounds and have made it their life's work to foster what amounts to a pattern of civil disobedience against the system. The problem is that in order to accomplish the level of disruption that leaders hope to achieve, they need pawns for their war. For this reason, untaxers promote schemes to the public that purport to be legal strategies for removing you from the tax system.

The schemes are based upon the general proposition that the IRS "tricks" people into filing tax returns and paying taxes; that filing and payment are not actual legal requirements. Promoters argue that you need only carry out their suggested rituals in order to break the spell of the income tax and be forever free of its grip. Among the most popular untax arguments advanced are:

- The income tax is voluntary and there is no law requiring you to file returns or pay taxes.

- Wages earned for performing personal services are not actually taxable income.

- The Sixteenth Amendment was never legally ratified, and therefore there is no valid income tax law in the first place.

- Filing returns is a violation of your Fifth Amendment right to be free of self-incrimination, and therefore you cannot be legally compelled to file.

- The income tax in general is unconstitutional and therefore not legally enforceable.

- The income tax laws do not apply to citizens who were born and live in one of the fifty states, but only to residents of Washington, D.C., the Virgin Islands, Puerto Rico, American Samoa, and other U.S. possessions.

- Income tax must be paid only on foreign income, and therefore wage or other income earned within the United States is not taxable.

- The Internal Revenue Service is actually a private company collecting taxes not for the federal government but for the privately owned Federal Reserve Bank.

The specific nature of these basic arguments mutates and the popularity of a given argument rises and falls depending upon a number of factors—chief among them whether or not the IRS is currently prosecuting promoters of a particular scam. Promoters of these scams generally prey upon those already suffering with tax problems. Face it—people facing crushing collection action are more likely to succumb to these arguments than those with no current enforcement problems.

Each promoter puts his own spin on exactly how to go about untaxing yourself. Generally the process involves submitting documents to the IRS that assert the legal argument necessary to "make the case" against the income tax. From there, the scam might also involve rescinding your social security number, closing bank accounts, and establishing one or more domestic or offshore trusts to hold assets and receive income.

Wage earners are counseled to file "exempt" W-4s with their

employers to stop withholding. Self-employed people are told they no longer have to make estimated tax payments. At tax return filing time, some promoters encourage their followers to file no return at all, while others encourage the filing of a "zero" tax return (a 1040 that reports zero income) or a 1040NR, *U.S. Non-Resident Alien Income Tax Return,* claiming to be a nonresident and free of all income tax.

There is a rich history of promoters of these arguments that dates to the mid-1960s—this topic alone could fill a book. One thing I have always found fascinating about untaxers is that while the personalities change—some being more charismatic while others are clear charlatans—the basic arguments do not. This is why I find it so amazing that otherwise reasonably intelligent people are duped by untaxers. As litigious as the tax laws are, there is no area of the tax law more litigious than that dealing with the claims of untaxers. Hundreds of these promoters have been prosecuted and convicted over the years, and many thousands of followers have likewise been prosecuted, convicted, and sent to prison.

And for every individual or promoter prosecuted and convicted of tax crimes associated with these claims, many thousands more find themselves on the business end of whopping tax assessments, interest, and penalties that lead to enforced collection. Of course, the law books contain thousands of reported cases—both civil and criminal—from every court in the land, rejecting the claims, subclaims, mutated claims, extended claims, and anticipatory claims of untaxers. In a word, *none* of these arguments has *ever* worked to "untax" anyone—and yet people are persuaded by verbal presentations, videotapes, extensive Web site productions, and written material to the effect that "it will work for you." What is even more amazing is that sometimes the arguments are made by promoters who themselves have *already* been convicted ("I did it wrong the first time," they say, "but my new plan is better." One can only hope so).

In the many radio shows I have been on throughout the nation, I am often confronted by a caller who is either an untax promoter or an avowed disciple of one. The caller quickly makes his untax case and asserts that all my defense strategies would be unnecessary if one would just untax himself. Of course, the caller "guarantees" that his method is successful.

In addition to reciting the above facts regarding the prosecution and conviction of those who adhere to these tenets, I respond by requesting that the caller cite *just one* court decision wherein a federal judge ruled favorably on his specific legal claims. As you might expect, in all my years of asking this question, I have never heard of such a single case, nor will I—because such a case *does not exist*.

What I said earlier bears restating: there has *never* been a single court decision that approves of the substantive tax claims made by the untaxers, regardless of the nature of the claim. Quite the opposite is true—these arguments are repeatedly rejected, and the people making them are *always* hit with a mountain of penalties and interest in addition to the tax, if not jail time.

In fact, the courts are so tired of being burdened with these cases that they refuse to even hear the arguments. For the past several years, courts have summarily dismissed the claims and routinely assessed court costs and fees against those making them. In addition, the Tax Court regularly assesses the penalty under code section 6673, which authorizes a damage assessment in favor of the IRS of up to $25,000 for filing cases solely for the purposes of delay or that are patently frivolous.

IF IT SOUNDS TOO GOOD TO BE TRUE . . .

. . . it probably is. This sage advice should not be overlooked when it comes to the claims of those selling tax reduction strategies. Always view with a jaundiced eye the claims of those who purport to have "uncovered" secret strategies to radically reduce or even eliminate your taxes.

If you are considering a tax reduction strategy, be sure to fully investigate the promoters' claims. I recommend researching the specific strategy to see whether the courts have already passed upon its legality. They probably have. Uncovering court cases that address the plan might save you untold thousands of dollars in fees, costs, interest, and penalties, not to mention the human cost of a protracted fight with the IRS.

If you are currently involved in such a plan, you must consider an exit strategy before the IRS gets hold of you. I strongly recommend you consult counsel experienced in dealing with the type of case you are involved with. Do not hire a lawyer or accountant off the street to assist with such a problem. There are so many nuances and pitfalls associated with these cases that only experienced counsel can safely navigate the waters. For help in finding counsel, my Web site offers a list of the members of my professional association, the Tax Freedom Institute. Many of these members have the kind of experience needed to extricate you from such a problem. To find that list, go to www. taxhelponline.com. Click on the Tax Freedom Institute button and you will find my list of recommended tax professionals.

12

The IRS in the Twenty-First Century

What's in Store for America?

With the IRS restructured, refinanced, and reinvigorated, we must now ask the question "What can we expect from the agency as it carries out its duties into the twenty-first century?" Many new challenges face America—both domestically and internationally—that will have a direct bearing on the political pressure levied upon the agency. Most notably, as America once again moves into a period of budgetary deficits, lawmakers will call upon the IRS more openly to employ the heavy hand of tax collection.

Understand that long before the tragic events of September 11, 2001, the attack on the Taliban in Afghanistan, the worldwide manhunt for Osama bin Laden, the war against al Qaeda, the war in Iraq, and the nuclear standoff on the Korean peninsula, the Internal Revenue Service was working hard to restore its enforcement capabilities to levels that existed prior to the 1998 Restructuring Act. The epic world events effectively shielded the agency's plans and intentions from the public eye.

I do not suggest at any level that these events were part of a *Wag the Dog* scenario carried out by any administration. Nevertheless, the IRS has been able to operate under the radar for some time as a result. It is now time to bring to light the agency's various plans and acts so that American citizens have fair warning of what the IRS has in store for them.

To do this, let us analyze in turn: (1) the IRS's new strategic plan, (2) the testimony of former IRS Commissioner Charles O. Rossotti before the congressional Joint Committee on Taxation just prior to his stepping down, (3) the IRS's audit dragnet initiatives, and (4) the IRS's legislative wish list.

THE IRS'S NEW STRATEGIC PLAN

In 1984 the IRS issued a strategic plan that called for, among other things, an increase in the number of computer-generated contacts and the installation of an audit program that would systematically audit every taxpayer. A primary purpose of the plan was to "create and maintain a sense of presence" in the lives of all Americans.

The adoption of that plan led to an explosion in computer letters, computer-generated assessments, penalty assessments, and audits. There was a corresponding explosion in the number of delinquent citizens. The IRS's accounts receivable ledger jumped dramatically beginning in about 1985 and has continued to grow ever since.

Now the IRS has a new plan, and though phrased less ominously than its predecessor, it is no less ominous in its likely impact on citizens. The new plan, approved and issued by the IRS in January 2000, sets forth three broad "strategic goals and objectives." Of concern to this discussion is the objective to provide "top quality service to all taxpayers through fair and uniform application of the law."[1]

In the 1984 plan, the IRS plainly declared that it would take steps to "create and maintain a sense of presence"—that is, a sense of ubiquity in America—in order that citizens would "voluntarily" comply with the tax code. In the 2000 plan, the IRS eschews the use of such Machiavellian phrases. Rather, it speaks in terms of "integrity" and "equity" as being essential components of the tax system. It argues (not unreasonably) that it must apply the law in such a manner as to "not allow those taxpayers who do not comply to place a burden on those who do." The IRS asserts that this stance is necessary to both "protect revenues flowing to the Treasury and as a matter of fundamental fairness."

But in reality, the plan speaks directly to the issue of tax law enforcement. The IRS states that "examinations, collection actions and criminal investigations will be essential components of our effort to ensure fairness and compliance." Stated simply, the IRS means to greatly intensify enforcement since it sees enforcement as an element of fairness.

The strategic plan places heavy emphasis on the need to "stabilize compliance activities." This call is in direct response to the fact that collection actions dropped so much during the three years from 1998 through 2000. Citing the same statistics I presented in the introduction, the IRS flatly concludes that "the current number of liens, levies and seizures is too low." Even beyond that, the IRS observes that the number of cases referred for criminal investigation and prosecution have likewise dropped to unacceptable levels. The IRS states, "we are losing enormous sums through failures to pay taxes owed and we have major problem areas of substantial non-compliance."

The IRS's goal, therefore, is to:

stabilize and improve our traditional compliance programs in the near term, while working through the business systems modernization program [the continued revamping of IRS computer systems] for longer term and more fundamental improvements.[2]

A number of more specific initiatives support this overall plan, many of which either have been or are in the process of being implemented. They include:

- Document matching. I discuss later in this chapter an IRS plan to match information returns to individual tax returns to uncover income underreporters.

- Targeting nonfilers. The IRS has intensified its search for nonfilers. Using the matching program discussed later and "augmenting the current information document program," the IRS has embarked upon an aggressive undertaking to "aid in the identification of non-filers."

- Targeting abusive trusts. Abusive trusts are those that purport to eliminate the income tax liability of their creators. The IRS estimates that there are as many as three to five million citizens involved in domestic and offshore trusts. The IRS promises to "increase the number of abusive trust cases undergoing examination and criminal investigation."

- Targeting corporate tax shelters. These are shelters that use "partnerships, trusts and offshore entities in their tax schemes to unlawfully reduce or eliminate taxes." They generally involve "large amounts of money and many complex transactions but with no real business purpose other than reducing taxes."

- Heightened employment tax enforcement. Employment taxes are taxes incurred by companies using employees as part of their business activities. Unpaid trust fund employment taxes often escalate very quickly, leading to substantial tax liabilities for the employer. The IRS has begun issuing "warning letters" informing employers of potential penalties for nonpayment of trust taxes. In "extreme cases" the IRS will place the employer "under special filing and deposit requirements and refer the taxpayer for civil or criminal legal action."

- Earned Income Tax Credit refund enforcement. The IRS instituted a three-phase program to address "fraudulent claims and schemes" involving the EITC. Phase one consists of "outreach and education visits" to tax preparers with high volumes of EITC returns. Phase two involves "compliance visits" to tax preparers to ensure that they are in "compliance with the due diligence requirements" of the EITC. The third phase entails "criminal investigations" of fraudulent claims and schemes, "resulting in indictment and conviction of directing or participating individuals."

The IRS has also implemented programs to increase audit coverage and collection action. In the area of audits, the IRS has developed a new audit selection unit, known as the Planning and Special Projects Unit. Its purpose is to manage the selection of audit cases at the national level. The IRS is now using its "existing compliance databases to stratify portions of taxpayer population to determine where possible areas of non-compliance exist." In this way, the IRS can "profile" citizens to better "target" those whose tax returns have a greater potential for increased tax liability.

The collection process has been further staffed, enhanced, and automated through three key modifications. First, more collection work is being assigned from field collection offices to "compliance service centers." In this way, collection work is handled over the phone and through the mail using more automated methods. Second, field examination and collection personnel are increasing. This is accomplished by using personnel in the taxpayer assistance functions to perform filing-season duties rather than transferring audit and collection personnel into filing-season duties. Third, the IRS has "completely reengineered" the Offer in Compromise program, a program available to delinquent citizens to negotiate settlements of their debts. The new design is intended to "streamline, centralize and specialize" the processing of offers. Offer processing is now centered in just two compliance service centers and is handled through those sites exclusively, unless a field examination is required. This move is intended to "free up substantial numbers of field collection officers for collection cases."

Finally, the IRS's Criminal Investigation unit is focusing its energies on "legal income cases." Consistent with the recommendations of the Webster Commission, the IRS is no longer expending resources on non–tax-related cases, such as organized crime, drug dealers, and money launderers.[3] Already we have seen an increase of 50 percent in the number of criminal charges brought by the IRS against Joe and Jane American citizens because of these moves.

The 2000 strategic plan evidences that the IRS has shaken off the chains that shackled its ability or willingness to enforce collection. This plan makes it quite evident that enforcement action is again a chief priority. Moreover, it is important to appreciate that the IRS does not propose merely to return to the levels of enforcement that existed prior to restructuring. In many ways, it intends to surpass those levels. In particular, the areas of criminal investigation and employment tax enforcement are new enforcement objectives for the agency.

ROSSOTTI'S CONGRESSIONAL TESTIMONY

In his May 8, 2001, testimony, former IRS Commissioner Rossotti restated the IRS's need and desire to increase audit coverage, saying, "One of my real concerns about the decline in audits is fairness to the majority of taxpayers whose income is reported and can be verified."[4]

Is Rossotti saying that because many people have sources of income that are verifiable through third-party records, those who do not have an unfair advantage? The presumption seems to be that those with unverifiable incomes cheat at the expense of those with verifiable incomes. The IRS is turning up the heat in the audit area. In fact, Rossotti stated in his testimony that "the number of returns audited is projected to rise by 28 percent" in the immediate future. This will be accomplished in two key ways. The first is to expand the IRS's computerized document matching program, and the second is the old-fashioned way—more face-to-face audits.

Computer matching programs are just what the name implies. IRS computers match the data shown on information returns, such as W-2s or 1099s, with the data shown on income tax returns. The computers flag income reported on information returns but not reported on tax returns, then mail a notice claiming the citizen underreported his income. Next, the IRS assesses the additional tax alleged, adds interest and penalties, and demands payment of the debt. Review chapter 2 for the details of this process.

The IRS intends to focus intensive attention on the so-called pass-through entities. These are businesses that themselves pay no taxes but whose profit or loss passes through to the owners or shareholders. The business files what amounts to an information return that reports income and expenses, and the owners report any profit on their individual tax returns. In turn, the entity files an information return, known as Form K-1, that reports to the IRS the profit distributed to the various owners.

Primary examples of these entities are partnerships, subchapter S corporations, and trusts. In 2000, 7.4 million entities of this nature filed tax returns and reported five trillion dollars in gross receipts. Just since 1995, there has been a 26.2 percent growth in the number of partnership returns alone. Based upon these numbers, it is easy to see why the IRS is interested in hiking the audit rates of these entities.

Historically the IRS has not used its computers to match Form K-1 information with individual tax returns. The IRS estimates that as much as 20 percent of all pass-through income is not reported on individual tax returns. That is why the IRS created a new matching program. Rossotti told Congress that "we do plan to begin a program to match income reported on K-1 forms from these [pass-through] entities to individual tax returns." The IRS hired 350 new employees to staff this matching program.

And the IRS does not intend to stop there. Rossotti points out that

> document matching is not useful for verifying business income, gain or loss on asset sales, or most itemized deductions. We estimate that the total personal income that cannot be verified by document matching represented about $1.2 trillion in FY 1998, or 19.7 percent of total reported personal income. An important role of audits is to verify these major categories of income and deductions.[5]

For this reason, a wide-scale audit program is now being constructed with the intention of ferreting out unreported income in general and, to a lesser extent, overstated deductions. This can only mean a return to highly invasive probes of a person's personal and private affairs at the same scale that caused so much consternation in past years.

The need to conduct these audits in a face-to-face environment rather than through any computer matching or other computerized audit program is also clearly explained by Rossotti. He states:

> The significance of verifying income and deduction items through audits is illustrated by the fact that the average in-person audit of an individual return results in an assessment of approximately $9,540, while the average assessment from a document matching case is $1,506. In FY 2000, the IRS closed 277,212 in-person audits of individual returns and assessed $2.4 billion from this program; in the document matching program in FY 2000, the IRS closed 1,353,545 cases and assessed $2.1 billion.[6]

As you can see, the amount assessed from face-to-face audits is more than six times higher than that of a document-matching audit.

THE AUDIT DRAGNET INITIATIVE

In his congressional testimony, Rossotti promised an immediate 28 percent increase in the IRS's audit coverage, with even greater coverage over a longer period of time. The institution of the National Research Program (NRP) announced in January 2002, is the first installment toward making good on that promise.

The National Research Program is the resurrected Taxpayer Compliance Measurement Program (TCMP) audit. The TCMP audit was the grueling line-by-line examination of randomly selected tax returns. The purpose of the TCMP audit was to compile statistical data used to build the IRS's Discriminate Function System (DIF) database. The DIF system is the computer audit selection program I explained in chapter 6, under the heading "How the IRS Selects Returns for Audit."

The IRS has not updated its DIF data in more than ten years. The agency claims the data is vastly out-of-date and that its use leads to many citizens being audited unnecessarily while those who need to be questioned go unchallenged. In introducing this program in January 2002, former Commissioner Rossotti stated, "Honest taxpayers shouldn't have to shoulder the burden for those who don't pay what they owe."[7]

Rossotti cast the National Research Program in such a light as to lead a casual observer to conclude that the program will only help the average citizen by equipping the IRS to better target those who deliberately cheat. Not only does the IRS say that honest taxpayers have nothing to fear and will only benefit from this new wave of audits, but it claims that these audits "will shift more of the burden onto itself—and away from taxpayers." This claim likewise leads one to believe that the National Research Project is in fact a welcome change to the way the IRS conducts audits. Let me bring this assertion into sharper focus.

Through the process of allegedly "shifting the burden" to the IRS, the agency claims the NRP audits will be "far less intrusive and burdensome than previous [TCMP] compliance studies." But to achieve this, the IRS intends to rely heavily upon preaudit work. This consists of compiling Census Bureau data, utilizing information the agency already has available, and engaging in the undefined process of "extensive case building."

Though the agency does not admit this, the obvious conclusion is that instead of confronting the citizen directly with demands for information, the IRS will move behind the scenes to ferret out data without the citizen's knowledge or consent. Moreover, the agency's capacity to gather information from third-party sources has grown impressively over the past ten years. Both in terms of legislative authority and technical resources, the agency has ready access to virtually every kind of personal, business, and financial data you can name.

And while one may argue that obtaining information from third-party sources is less burdensome to the citizen, the process is hardly "less intrusive." This is especially true considering the kind of information the agency either already has in its possession or has access to through other government agencies and other sources. As I document in my research study entitled "A Monument of Deficient Wisdom,"[8] published by the Institute for Policy Innovation, there are thirty-seven federal and 215 state and local government agencies with which the IRS regularly shares data. In addition, the IRS routinely seeks information from such sources as court records, trade associations, property records, banks and other financial institutions, Dunn and Bradstreet, insurance providers, even newspaper articles.

After such "extensive case building," it is no wonder the IRS expects to collect less data directly from citizens. In fact, with the kind of approach outlined by the IRS, the process of conducting audits assumes a much more "investigative" posture, rather than the typical "verification" process of past audits. In other words, expect the IRS to become more confrontational in audits and far less willing to accept citizen-provided proof at face value.

That the IRS has this in mind is clearly reflected in the agency's description of the four levels of research audits to be conducted under the NRP. The four levels of audit are, first, internal review without taxpayer notification or participation—about eight thousand returns will be checked using this process; second, contact by mail with limited questions—the agency expects that some nine thousand returns will be checked in this manner; and third, thirty thousand face-to-face examinations with in-depth questions and data requests.

That brings us to the fourth type of audit. In a statement that is classically contradictory, the IRS first *denies* that it will conduct lengthy line-by-line audits, then declares that it will in fact conduct two thousand of what it calls "calibration audits," the fourth category. According to the IRS, a calibration audit is one that "will check each line of the return." We are not to worry about these line-by-line examinations, however, because the IRS flatly claims—without explanation—that these line-by-line examinations "will not be as burdensome" as the TCMP audits of old. As far as I can tell, the only differences between the TCMP audit of yesteryear and the NRP "calibration" audit of today is the name and the fact that the IRS is aided in its new audits by substantial information garnered beforehand from outside sources.

In light of this, one must question whether the process is indeed less burdensome to the citizen. (It certainly is *not* less intrusive.) At present, the IRS annually mails millions of computer notices. These notices cover collection demands as well as a host of other audit-related contacts. Usually the notices communicate to the citizen action the IRS has *already executed* to change an alleged error in a tax return. In essence, the notice says, "You made an error. We fixed it. You owe X dollars."

As evidenced by the Taxpayer Advocate's annual report to Congress, errant computer notices are perennially listed among the top twenty most common problems citizens experience when dealing with the IRS. Citizens experience great frustration when trying to correct errant notices. The process involves—at a minimum—phone calls and letters to the IRS that often leave one believing he is dealing with people who neither know nor care about how to correct the problem.

But even if the IRS is able to remove the burden and invasiveness of a tax audit, it seems wholly unable to eliminate the one aspect of a tax audit that people are most concerned about—an *erroneous* tax bill. As I have thoroughly documented in past writings and testimony to congressional committees, the IRS's error rate for tax audits ranges from 60 to 90 percent, depending upon the issue under examination. In fact, it was my explanation of this error rate to the IRS Oversight subcommittee of the House of Representatives in July 1995 that was chiefly responsible for killing the last TCMP audit survey the IRS proposed.[9]

But that was then; this is now. Congress's propensity to slap the hand of the IRS has greatly subsided. Congress is more willing to see the IRS "get the money" than to pay further lip service to the notion of taxpayers' rights, especially since the IRS is using more refined language to describe this wave of research audits. Apparently it is comforting to merely state that these audits are "not burdensome or invasive."

What is overlooked, however, is the fact that the chief reason for the error rates is worse today than when I testified to Congress in

1995. The reason is the confusing tax code and the IRS's inability to keep tax auditors educated on the changes. During the three years from 1996 to 1998, six major tax reform laws changed more than three thousand code sections and subsections. To make matters worse, of the changes made during that period, eighty were made to apply retroactively, and of those, twenty-seven were applied retroactively by more than one year.[10]

According to the Taxpayer Advocate's FY 2000 report to Congress:

> Complexity remains the number one problem facing taxpayers and is the root-cause of many of the other problems on the Top 20 list. Despite IRS restructuring to target services to taxpayer needs, the fact remains that the Internal Revenue code is riddled with complexities that often defy explanation.[11]

And while the river of complexity swamps the average citizen, the IRS is also buffeted by its current. Former Commissioner Rossotti addressed this very issue when answering the question of why the IRS was unable to keep its workforce adequately trained to administer the law. In May 2000, Rossotti wrote:

> Fundamentally, we are attempting the impossible. We are expecting employees and our managers to be trained in areas of the law that are much too broad to ever succeed, and our manuals and training courses are, therefore, unmanageable in scope and complexity.[12]

Rossotti's own words could be the most stinging indictment of the accuracy of the IRS ever uttered by a sitting commissioner. And to further amplify the magnitude of this admission, consider that it was made *after* the IRS spent 6.5 million *hours* during 1999 retraining its workforce.

Consequently, the NRP cannot eliminate unnecessary audits. The fact is, with the agency's error rate as high as it is and in light of the stunning admission by Rossotti that the IRS has no hope of getting it right, the only reasonable conclusion is that *no* audit can be expected to achieve accurate results. This being the case, to conduct audits, the purpose of which is to build a database from which countless citizens will be selected for even more extensive audits, is not only irrational, but meets the classic definition of unreasonable and invasive.

In September 2002, the IRS began the process of targeting fifty thousand citizens for one of the four new NRP audits. In one final attempt to assuage fears, the agency claimed that these audits will comprise "only about 1.1 percent of the total audit-related contacts planned for the year." If that is true, expect the IRS to audit more than 4.5 million citizens in 2003, a staggering jump in IRS audit coverage. According to former Commissioner Rossotti, "This approach symbolizes how we will do business in the new IRS."

That is exactly what I am afraid of.

THE IRS'S LEGISLATIVE WISH LIST

In his May 8, 2001, testimony, Rossotti announced that he wished to "begin a dialogue with Congress about certain changes" to the Restructuring Act that will remove important legal restrictions on the agency. If this is successful, it could sound the death knell for the concept of taxpayers' rights in general and a kinder and gentler IRS in particular.

The IRS alleges that three areas in particular hamper the agency's efforts at summary collection and, admittedly, impose upon it substantial staffing and funding burdens. They are:

- Act section 1203—the so-called ten deadly sins—which requires that IRS agents be "terminated" if they violate certain taxpayer rights or otherwise intentionally disregard IRS laws, rules, and regulations in the enforcement process. This provision, according to Rossotti, caused a great deal of "uncertainty" among IRS employees and led to a substantial reduction in "productivity" together with an increase in the time it takes to work enforcement cases.

- The collection due process remedies, which allow citizens to challenge any IRS collection action prior to its taking effect. These remedies prevent the IRS from filing liens or carrying out levies or seizures if the citizen challenges the collection action in time. Under the governing statutes—code sections 6320 and 6330—the citizen may challenge the collection action on any appropriate ground and pose alternatives—which must be considered—to the intended enforcement action. The IRS is in the process of requesting amendments to "simplify procedures" associated with these appeals.

- The innocent spouse and Offer in Compromise programs, which allow unjustly assessed citizens to be free of tax collection entirely and allow those who cannot pay to negotiate settlements for less than is owed. Since the Restructuring Act substantially amended and broadened these remedies, there has been an understandable increase in the number of cases filed under both provisions. In fact, the IRS grossly underestimated the response to the innocent spouse program and as a result found itself awash in a backlog of tens of thousands of cases. The IRS seeks measures to "reduce the impact of the frivolous use" of the procedures available in these areas.

CONCLUSION

In every sense of the word, the IRS has been reborn. This is true from an organizational standpoint and from a mission standpoint. And while the IRS is now practiced at mouthing words necessary to impart the belief that it is sensitive to taxpayers' rights, the fact of the matter is that the agency is well on its way toward reducing or eliminating the restrictions on its powers that were imposed by the Restructuring Act. Over time, as the agency is successful in its efforts to erode these protections, we will wake up one day to find that it is once again the unmanageable monster that led to its restructuring in the first place.

about the author

D aniel J. Pilla is a tax litigation consultant and author of eleven IRS self-help defense books, hundreds of articles on taxes and the IRS, and dozens of scholarly research reports on tax law and procedure. His writings have been featured in numerous financial and political magazines and newspapers across the nation. He is the founder and executive director of the Tax Freedom Institute, a national association of attorneys, accountants, and enrolled agents. For the past twenty-six years, his products and services have provided people with practical solutions to all kinds of IRS enforcement problems. Through the Tax Freedom Institute, he provides continuing education to tax professionals working in the areas of taxpayers' rights defense, problem resolution, and IRS abuse prevention and cure.

Pilla was a consultant to the National Commission on Restructuring the IRS, presented testimony to Congress on a number of tax policy and administrative issues, and presently works with numerous public policy research organizations. In 2001 he was named to the editorial board of the Institute for Policy Innovation's Road Map to Tax Reform project.

The Associated Press once wrote, "Pilla probably knows more about the IRS than the commissioner."

Pilla's 1995 policy analysis entitled "Why You Can't Trust the

IRS," published by the Cato Institute, combined with his 1996 book, *IRS, Taxes and the Beast,* provided the intellectual foundation for the 1997 congressional hearings into IRS abuse.

DAN PILLA'S PRODUCTS AND SERVICES

Dan Pilla's books and research reports have changed the face of tax collection, permanently etching into the law the idea that citizens have rights and that the IRS does not have a free hand when collecting taxes. Dan's book *How to Get Tax Amnesty* speaks to those who owe taxes they cannot pay. Current IRS programs allow you to be forgiven of all or part of that debt. There are several programs available and the book provides step-by-step guidance for utilizing each of them.

In *How to Double Your Tax Refund,* Dan's smart-tax techniques help you find an extra $1,000 in tax deductions. Manage your taxes by putting this simple step-by-step plan to work for you now. Learn how to claim more deductions legally without the risk of audit.

The book *IRS, Taxes and the Beast* is the most comprehensive audit defense guide ever written. With painstaking detail, Dan walks you step-by-step through every aspect of a tax audit, including how to recognize and defend against the IRS's highly intrusive "lifestyle" audit.

Through his newsletter, *Dan Pilla's Confidential Tax Bulletin,* Dan keeps you up to speed on all the tax law changes that affect you. In each issue, you get news on the latest tax strategies to cut your taxes, developments in taxpayers' rights that help you with any IRS battle, and Dan's unique insight into future IRS and tax collection developments. The information you get makes this publication a national treasure.

Dan's personal consultation and evaluation services put you in direct contact with the nation's leading IRS problem solver. Dan can personally evaluate your specific situation and put you on the road to solving your problem. Whether you are dealing with an audit, tax collection, penalties and interest, or any other IRS problem, Dan can give you the sound help you need without wasting time, energy, or money.

For more information on any of Dan's publications and services,

contact:

The Tax Freedom Institute, Inc.

2372 Leibel Street

White Bear Lake, MN 55110

1-800-346-6829

www.taxhelponline.com

notes

Introduction

1. United States Senate, Opening Statement of Senator William Roth, Hearings before the Committee on Finance, Senate Hearing 105-190, September 24, 1997, p. 2.
2. Code section 7491(A)(2)(A).
3. An excellent analysis of the real-world impact of code section 7491 is provided by the Tax Court in *Higbee v. Commissioner*, 116 T.C. No. 28, June 6, 2001.
4. Code section 7802(d)(5).
5. Code section 7802(c)(2); emphasis added.
6. Department of the Treasury, "Management Advisory Report: Analysis of the Trends in Compliance Activities through Fiscal Year 2001," Treasury Inspector General for Tax Administration, Reference No. 2002-30-184, September 2002, pp. 19–20.
7. Ibid., p. 3.

1. Basic Things You Need to Know

1. Internal Revenue Service, *2001 Data Book*, Publication 55B, March 2002, Table 18—Criminal Investigation Program, p. 22.
2. *Morissette v. United States*, 342 U.S. 246 (1952).
3. Department of the Treasury, "Management Advisory Report: Analysis of the Trends in Compliance Activities through Fiscal Year 2001," Treasury

Inspector General for Tax Administration, Reference No. 2002-30-184, September 2002, p. 17.

4. For all the details on the IRS's current structure, see Internal Revenue Service, "Modernizing America's Tax Agency," IRS Publication 3349, January 2000.

2. End the Fear of Going to the Mailbox

1. These procedures are named after the "notice of deficiency" provided for in sections 6212 and 6213 of the Internal Revenue code.
2. General Accounting Office, "Tax Administration: IRS' Service Centers Need to Improve Handling of Taxpayer Correspondence," GAO/GGD-88-101, July 1988, p. 14.
3. General Accounting Office, "Tax Administration: IRS Efforts to Improve Taxpayer Correspondence," GAO/IMTEC-90-26, March 1990, p. 1.
4. General Accounting Office, "Tax Administration: IRS Notices Can Be Improved," GAO/GGD-95-6, December 1994.
5. Internal Revenue Service, "National Taxpayer Advocate's FY 1996 Annual Report to Congress," December 1996, p. 26.
6. Internal Revenue Service, "National Taxpayer Advocate's FY 2002 Annual Report to Congress," December 31, 2002, p. 30.
7. Internal Revenue Service, "National Taxpayer Advocate's FY 2001 Annual Report to Congress," December 31, 2001, p. 33.
8. All data from IRS *Data Books* for the periods stated; amounts shown are in millions.
9. Internal Revenue Service, Office of Chief Counsel, Service Center Advice Memorandum 1998-040, April 2, 1998; emphasis added.
10. Code section 6213(g).
11. Ibid., note 7.
12. A large percentage of correction notices are so-called low-dollar notices. However, the amount claimed is a *net amount*, after adjustment. For example, a citizen may be expecting a $600 refund. However, after adjustment for an alleged error, he may receive a bill for $65. The bill itself is not significant but represents a total loss to the citizen of $665.
13. Treasury Inspector General for Tax Administration, "Audit Reconsideration Cases Create Unnecessary Burden on Taxpayers and the Internal Revenue Service," Report No. 2001-40-053, March 2001, p. ii.

3. End the "My Word Against Yours" Stalemate

1. This record is usually IRS Form 4340, *Certificate of Assessment, Payments and Other Specified Matters,* and is accompanied by a Certificate of Official Record, a document signed by a service center employee declaring that these are "official records" of the service center.

2. General Accounting Office, "Financial Audit: IRS's Fiscal 1998 Financial Statements," GAO-GGD/AIMD-99-75, March 1999, p. 16.
3. General Accounting Office, "Tax Administration: IRS Continues to Face Management Challenges in its Business Practices and Modernization Efforts," GAO-02-619T, Testimony of Michael Brostek, GAO director of Tax Issues, to House Committee on Government Reform, April 15, 2002, pp. 6–7.
4. Internal Revenue Service, "National Taxpayer Advocate's FY 2001 Annual Report to Congress," December 31, 2001, p. 6.
5. Ibid., p. 202.
6. Internal Revenue Service, "National Taxpayer Advocate's FY 2002 Annual Report to Congress," December 31, 2002, p. 148.
7. Internal Revenue Service, "Progress Report from the Commissioner of IRS," Publication 3970, December 2001, p. 31.

4. Coping with Tax Penalties

1. Source of all data is the IRS Data Books for the years stated. The chart shows penalty assessments in millions and revenue assessments in billions of dollars.
2. Internal Revenue Manual section 20.1.1.2.1, hereinafter referred to as the Penalty Handbook or handbook.
3. Ibid., section 20.1.1.3.1.2.1, "Ignorance of the Law."
4. Ibid., section 20.1.1.3.2.4.3, "Advice from a Tax Advisor."
5. *United States v. Boyle,* 469 U.S. 421 (1985).
6. Handbook, section 20.1.1.3.2.4.2, "Oral Advice from the Service."
7. Ibid., section 20.1.1.3.1.2.2, "Mistake Was Made."
8. Code section 6651(a)(1).
9. Revenue Regulation section 301.6651-1.
10. Code section 6651(a)(3).
11. Revenue Regulation section 301.6651-l(c).
12. Revenue Regulation section 301.6343(b)(4).
13. Code section 6654(d)(1).
14. Code section 6654(e)(3).
15. Code section 6682.
16. Code section 3402(m).
17. Code section 3402(n).

5. Stop Compounding the Problem

1. Internal Revenue Service, "National Taxpayer Advocate's FY 1999 Annual Report to Congress," December 31, 1999, p. I-2.
2. Department of the Treasury, Office of Tax Policy, "Report to Congress on the Penalty and Interest Provisions of the Internal Revenue Code," October 1999, p. 133.

3. Revenue Regulation section 301.6404-2(b).

4. Senate Report 99-313, 1986-3 C.B. (vol. 3), p. 209.

5. The IRS has three years from the date a return is filed in which to audit that return. Carol's return was filed late. If no return is filed, there is no statute of limitations on the IRS's right to audit. It can be done at any time.

6. Revenue Regulation section 301.6404-2(b).

7. For example, see the case of *Berger v. United States*, Civil Docket No. 98-5835 (S.D.N.Y. 1999), 1999 WL 596270.

8. Senate Report 99-313, p. 208.

9. Internal Revenue Service, Service Center Advice, 2002-23001, June 7, 2002.

6. Handling the Tax Audit

1. Tax protesters are those who attempt to avoid paying taxes using various arguments suggesting that the tax laws are unconstitutional, that filing tax returns is somehow voluntary, or that the tax laws do not apply to U.S. citizens.

2. Code section 7521.

3. G. M. *Leasing Corp. v. United States*, 429 U.S. 338 (1977).

4. Internal Revenue Service, *2001 Data Book*, Table 10, p. 15.

5. Code section 6501. There are some exceptions to the general three-year rule that can extend the statute of limitations. That is why I recommend keeping records for six years from the filing date of your return. For more details on these exceptions, see my book *IRS, Taxes and the Beast*, pp. 111–115.

6. Internal Revenue Service, *2001 Data Book*, Table 10, p. 15.

7. The Million-Dollar Precaution

1. Revenue Regulation section 1.6662-4(b)(1).

2. This case was actually resolved in the Tax Court. The case citation is *Stein v. Commissioner*, T.C. Memo. 1992-651 (November 5, 1992).

3. Ibid.

4. Ibid.

5. Code section 7206.

8. Common Problems Businesses Face

1. General Accounting Office, "Small Business: Taxpayers Face Many Requirements," Statement of Margaret T. Wrightson, associate director, Tax Policy and Administration Issues, General Government Division, GAO/T-GGD-99-76, April 12, 1999, p. 4.

2. Code section 6656(b)(1).

3. Code section 6656(a).

4. *East Wind Industries, Inc. v. United States*, 196 F.3rd 499 (3rd Cir. 1999); *Fran Corp. v. United States*, 164 F.3rd 814 (2nd Cir. 1999); and *Van Camp & Bennion v. United States*, 241 F.3rd 862 (9th Cir. 2001).

5. See also Revenue Regulation section 301.6651-1(c).

6. Code sections 6721 and 6722.

7. Code section 6721(d).

8. Code section 6721(e).

9. Code section 6011(e).

10. Code section 6724(c).

11. Code section 6011(e).

12. Revenue Regulation section 301.6011-2(c)(1).

13. Code section 6672.

14. Revenue Ruling 87-41, 1987-1 CB 296. You can get a copy of this ruling by writing to the IRS Disclosure Officer at any service center. See chapter 1, under the heading "IRS Service Center Addresses."

15. Revenue Act of 1978, section 530(a)(1). Note: section 530 has never been codified into the Internal Revenue Code. Therefore act section 530 is not code section 530.

16. *Déjà Vu Entertainment Enterprises of Minnesota v. United States*, 1 F.Supp.2d 964 (D. Minn. 1998).

17. *Scheidt v. Commissioner*, T.C. Memo. 1992-9 (January 6, 1992). The taxpayer lost money from 1980 to 1987 and losses were allowed as business expenses.

18. Revenue Regulation section 1.183-2(b).

19. Ibid., section 1.183-2(b)(6).

20. Code section 183(b)(1).

21. Code section 183(b)(2).

9. Paying Taxes on Your Terms–Not Theirs

1. Code section 6331(d)(4).

2. Code section 6161.

3. Code section 6159(c).

4. Code section 6331(k)(2)(A).

5. Often, service centers seek financial information on Form 433-F. It is merely a shortened version of Form 433-A, *Collection Information Statement for Wage Earners and Self-Employed Individuals*.

6. Code section 7811.

7. Code section 6332(c).

8. Code section 6343.

9. Revenue Regulation section 301.6343-1(b)(4).

10. Ibid., section 301.6343-1(b)(4)(ii)(A)-(F).

11. Ibid., section 301.6343-1(b)(4)(iii).
12. Code section 6323(j).
13. IRS Publication 784, *Application for Subordination of Federal Tax Lien*, provides help in drafting the application.
14. Code section 6323(j)(2).
15. Code section 6325(d).
16. Revenue Regulation section 301.6325-1(d)(1).
17. Ibid., section 301.6325-1(a).
18. Code sections 6320 and 6330.
19. Code section 6320(a)(1)-(3).
20. Code section 6330(a)(1)-(3).
21. Code section 6015.
22. Code section 6330(c)(2)(A) and (B).

10. Divorcing Yourself from Tax Problems

1. For a more detailed explanation, see Revenue Ruling 85-70, 1985-1 C.B. 361 and the instructions for Form 8379.
2. Based upon the 2002 income tax rates as published by the IRS in the tax table.
3. Code section 6013(d)(3) and *Butler v. Commissioner*, 114 T.C. 276, 282 (2000).
4. Code section 6015(b).
5. Code section 6015(c).
6. Code section 6015(f).
7. Revenue Procedure 2000-15, sections 4.01 and 4.02.
8. Code section 66(c).
9. Code section 6015(e)(1).
10. Code section 6015(e)(1)(B).

11. Insulating Yourself from the IRS

1. Code section 6161.
2. Code section 6164.
3. General Accounting Office, "Internal Revenue Service: Efforts to Identify and Combat Abusive Tax Schemes Have Increased, but Challenges Remain," GAO-02-733, May 2002, p. 7.
4. *Lucas v. Earl*, 281 U.S. 111 (1930).
5. A John Doe summons is an investigative technique employed when the IRS does not know the names of those involved in potential wrongdoing. Code section 7609(f).

6. *In the Matter of the Tax Liabilities Of: John Does, United States Taxpayers Who, During the Years Ending December 31, 1998 and 1999, had Signatory Authority Over American Express or Mastercard Credit, Charge, or Debit Cards Issued by or through, or for Which Payment Was Received from, Banks in Antigua and Barbuda, The Bahamas, or The Cayman Islands, or Issued to Persons or Entities in Antigua and Barbuda, The Bahamas, or The Cayman Islands,* Docket No. 00-3919-CIV-JORDAN, 86 AFTR2d Par. 2000-5465 (So. Dist. Florida, October 2000).

7. Ibid., note 3, p. 8.

8. Ibid., note 3, p. 17.

9. Internal Revenue Service, New Release No. IR-2002-08, January 24, 2002.

10. This penalty is used liberally by the IRS. Authorized under code section 6702, the penalty is assessed in almost every tax scam case that utilizes claims on tax returns.

11. Tax Analysts, "The Service's Tough Shelter Talk Turns to Action," *Tax Practice,* vol. 35, no. 3, July 19, 2002.

12. The IRS in the Twenty-First Century

1. Internal Revenue Service, "IRS Strategic Plan, Fiscal Years 2000–2005," January 2000, p. 4.

2. Ibid., p. 58.

3. Internal Revenue Service, "Review of the Internal Revenue Service's Criminal Investigation Division," Hon. William Webster, Publication 3388, April 1999.

4. Internal Revenue Service, "Statement of Charles O. Rossotti before Annual RRA'98 Joint Hearing on IRS Progress," Joint Committee on Taxation, May 8, 2001, p. 6.

5. Ibid., p. 5–6.

6. Ibid., p. 6.

7. IRS News Release No. 2002-05, January 16, 2002, p. 1.

8. Daniel J. Pilla, "A Monument of Deficient Wisdom," Policy Report No. 165, Institute for Policy Innovation, Center for Tax Analysis, December 2001.

9. Daniel J. Pilla, Statement to House Ways and Means Subcommittee on Oversight, "Taxpayer Compliance Measurement Program," Serial 104-30, July 18, 1995, p. 145.

10. Internal Revenue Service, "Annual Report from the Commissioner on Tax Law Complexity," June 5, 2000.

11. Internal Revenue Service, "National Taxpayer Advocate's FY 2000 Annual Report to Congress," December 2000, p. 6.

12. Charles O. Rossotti, "Comments on Customer Service Employee Feedback Report," Internal Revenue Service, May 25, 2000.

index